CARDBOARD CHRISTIANS

Mara Reuben Faulkner

To Jeanne

Thank you so much for your valuable contributions to the completion of Cardboard Christians. The Lord willing I'll be in touch with you again when I have completed "The Widow's Might"

In Christ, Our Life

Marilyn Felton

ISBN: 1974519783
ISBN 13: 9781974519781

To my beloved husband, Pastor James Faulkner

ACKNOWLEDGMENTS

Thank you to my husband, Pastor James Faulkner. Jim was ushered into the presence of our Heavenly Father, after a brief illness, by his ministering angel on April 16, 2007.

Because of his unparalleled encouragement in persuading me to complete *Cardboard Christians* after his death, I can now say, ten years later, "I did it Jim, thanks to you. Though you are not here physically to share in the victory of the completed work, I feel confident in my spirit that you have been watching my slow but steady progress as *Cardboard Christians* has taken substantive form. I can see that familiar boyish grin on your face, that grin that always let me know that you had placed your stamp of approval on a job that you would have considered well done."

Thank you, Deidre Assenza, a special friend and professional proofreader, for taking on the mammoth task of proofing the final draft of *Cardboard Christians* prior to submitting it to the publisher for publication. In spite of overseeing a busy household and caring for a husband and brand-new baby girl, your desire to be a part of this ministry by your very important contribution to it is so greatly appreciated.

Thank you, Linda Smith, author and instructor of the creative writing class at the senior center in La Mesa, California. You and the members of your class encouraged me to press on with the writing of *Cardboard Christians* and complete it as you felt that it had sufficient merit to become a successful publication. I appreciate the faith that you had in my writing ability, which gave me the boost that I needed to carry on.

Last, but by no means least—thank you, Ros Oserin, my oldest of three children, for you and your wonderful husband, Dan, who welcomed me into your home in sunny Southern California to spend some time with you after the death of my beloved Jim. The change of climate and scenery, but more importantly, being with caring family members during such a dark time in my life will forever be appreciated. It was during those eight critical months of living in California that I made my decision to begin yet another chapter of my life. It was during this time that *Cardboard Christians* became more than a lifetime dream but the beginning of a reality.

CONTENTS

PREFACE

Cardboard Christians is the story of my life—both before and after Christ's redemptive work in me. It tells of a child who lost her way as the result of the unfortunate circumstances of her formative years. Though she became a casualty during her teens and progressed in this lifestyle through her early adulthood, someone yet unknown to her was praying that she would have a life-changing encounter with the Giver of Life, Jesus Christ. This wonderful salvation occurred at the age of thirty-three. It forever transformed a woman chained by sin and shame, by the enemy of her soul, to a child of God destined to spend eternity with Him in heaven.

Fast on the heels of this glorious experience came a second blessing from heaven which we Pentecostals refer to as the baptism of the Holy Spirit. With this experience came gifts of the Holy Spirit. Scripturally, those of us receiving this baptism also receive spiritual gifts at this time. The gift of which I became immediately aware was the gift of discernment. God had sovereignly ordained that this particular gift begin to operate in my life almost immediately upon reception. Our Heavenly Father certainly has a sense of humor. It is also evident to me that "His ways are not our ways." I say this because, by nature, I had been a very naive person from my earliest childhood. I accepted without question that whatever I was told was true.

From the onset of having received the fullness of the Spirit, I began to know that all that I had been led to believe as truth was not necessarily so. Many battles with the Lord ensued as I balked against what I had been told and what the Lord was attempting to show me as He began to instruct me in the gift of discernment.

It is my prayerful hope that those reading *Cardboard Christians* will realize the absolute necessity of receiving this little understood gift in today's ungodly world. We are fast approaching the return of Jesus Christ; and for this reason, our enemy, the prince of darkness, and his minions are working more diligently than ever before to capture unsuspecting souls to send to the multitude of those already awaiting the eternal judgment of hell.

INTRODUCTION

I was almost finished gathering the eggs when my attention was suddenly diverted by a scratching sound behind me. My aunt had assigned me my chores for the time that I would be spending with her and my uncle while I was on my summer break. Taking charge of the chicken coop was one of them.

Mom had put me on the train yesterday, assuring me that she would be joining me in a few weeks. She had accumulated several weeks' vacation at work and would be staying at the farm until after the fourth of July. I was a little apprehensive about traveling alone as this was my first time ever not to be accompanied by an adult. On the other hand, as the conductor escorted me to a window seat and punched the ticket that I handed him, I felt a swell of pride that my mom felt I was mature enough to handle this situation alone. As I got comfortable in my seat and peered out of the window, I heard the loud blast of the train, announcing to all concerned that it was about to leave the station. As we headed toward the Aliquippa Station some thirty miles away, my thoughts moved ahead to the great time I was anticipating.

The time flew by as quickly as the landscape that I observed as we moved along the tracks through the countryside, sometimes speeding through a small town along the way. There were only two stops before I reached my destination. It seemed like only a few moments had elapsed when I heard the conductor announce loudly, "We are approaching Aliquippa, folks. Prepare to disembark." I didn't know what it meant to *disembark* but guessed it had something to do with getting off the train. The brakes of the train began to screech furiously at this moment, and the train began to slow to a stop. I took one last look out of my window as I gathered up my few belongings, to see my aunt and uncle waving furiously, attempting to locate me in one of the windows. When our eyes met, I saw a look of relief come over my aunt's face. Evidently, she had less confidence in my making the trip alone than my mom did.

"I'll show them how grown up I've gotten since I last saw them at Christmastime. After all, I'll be going into the fourth grade after summer vacation is over. They'll see."

After a warm welcome from both of them, they hustled me into my uncle's car, which was parked in the nearby train parking lot. After inquiring about the folks that I had just left at home, their general health, and any other information that proved newsworthy, the conversation turned to future plans that were being made for my extended stay with them.

"We have lots of things planned for the summer because you're spending it with us, Mara. You don't know how happy it makes both of us to know that you want to be here at the farm during your vacation this summer," my uncle informed me. "Of course, Mara, you know that you'll have to make a contribution to the workload in order for your Aunt Harriet and me to be able to get away for these special events. There's always lots of work to do when you live on a farm."

I assured them that I was prepared for whatever they had for me to do, reminding them that I had my own little garden at home in which I planted and took care of all by myself. I also helped Gram in the kitchen. She had taught me to make her famous snickerdoodles and peanut butter cookies. The part I didn't like very much was cleaning up the pots and pans after the cookies were made. But I assured them I knew that this was a necessary part of cookie making, and I always helped with the cleanup even though it wasn't one of my favorite chores.

Arriving at the farm I loved to visit, I was treated to one of my favorite dinners, chicken and big puffy dumplings swimming in a pool of thick chicken gravy. My aunt was a great cook, like my gram. They both cooked Pennsylvania Dutch like the people in the central part of the state near Harrisburg cooked. Of course, there was always a crunchy salad and vegetable accompanying the main part of the meal. I had to endure these items so I could get to the dessert—which, for my first dinner with my aunt and uncle, was homemade shortcake with gobs of fresh strawberries right out of my aunt's strawberry patch and topped with real whipped cream.

After dinner, I helped clear the table and clean up the kitchen. Then came the part of the conversation that I had been anticipating. My uncle presented me with a list of chores that they had chosen for me to do during my stay. After hurriedly skimming through it, I assured him that I would be able to handle each of the items on the list. Bath and bed were next on the agenda. After that huge meal and a hot bath, I gladly jumped into my huge four-poster bed in my very own bedroom, which was mine to use whenever I visited the farm.

I must have been very tired after all the activities of the previous day because I went to sleep immediately, and I slept so hard that my aunt had a difficult time waking me.

"Mara, sweetheart, wake up. Come on, sleepyhead. Did you forget how early we get up at the farm? Your hungry animals are waiting to be fed. All the chicken feed and mash for the chicks are in the storage shed. Don't forget their water. When you finish with the goats, come in for breakfast. I'm sure that you will have worked up quite an appetite by then."

In a much more serious vein, she reminded me about our conversation of the previous evening regarding Satan.

"Make certain that you follow the instructions that your uncle gave you and everything will be fine. Oh yes, the basket to gather the eggs is with the chicken feed in the shed. Don't run with a full basket of eggs. If you should trip, you will end up with a skinned knee, and our kitchen will end up without any eggs for the next few days. Be careful, honey."

Hurriedly jumping into my jean shorts and a T-shirt, I stopped in the hall long enough to put on my sneakers, reminding myself to tie them when I had a free minute. This was going to be great fun. I loved feeding all the animals. This would be my first stop. The eggs had to be gathered first, I recalled, so the hens could begin their production for another day.

The hens remembered me from Christmastime and were very cooperative when, occasionally, it was necessary for me to reach under a laying hen and remove her egg from the day before. Then, as I was about to check out the new baby chicks in their incubator in the corner, my attention was once again diverted by that strange, unfamiliar sound coming from the other side of the room; only now it was closer.

As I turned, I looked directly into the angry, beady black eyes of Satan, the huge white leghorn rooster. Satan was in charge of the chicken coop and the many hens who called this place their home. This menacing rooster was fiercely protective of his harem and became very confrontational when anyone attempted to infringe on his domain. For this reason, my uncle had come up with a method to keep anyone entering the henhouse from becoming a victim of Satan's ire. He had cut a small flat board just a little larger than the opening between the henhouse and the fenced yard, where the chickens scratched for food and got their exercise. He had attached a long piece of clothesline to the board and drawn the line across the ceiling of the coop on hooks that acted as a pulley for the line. He allowed extra line, which he looped onto another hook at the entrance to the henhouse.

When anyone entered, all that was needed to keep Satan at bay was to unwind the extra line and drop the wood over the opening, keeping the rooster out in the yard. When leaving the coop, all that one needed to do was reverse the process. This would give the chickens freedom to enter or leave the coop at will. If Satan happened to be inside the henhouse, it was a simple matter to draw him out into the yard with extra corn. He had a ferocious appetite and was a sucker for extra corn.

This was a relatively simple procedure, even for an eight-year-old. The problem was that, in my excitement to enter the henhouse and begin my morning chores, I had forgotten to lower the board even though I could see Satan in the yard in the early morning light.

To my horror, I realized my mistake too late. Satan was slowly but deliberately heading straight for me. I became frozen in time. Though my body was in a state of total immobility, my mind began to race. What was near enough to me to grab and use as a buffer to ward off an attack by this predator? My eyes darted wildly around the room in desperate search of something—anything that I could grab in an effort to keep this bird from attacking me. I spied a long-handled push broom leaning against the wall about a foot away from the entrance. I estimated that it would take me three giant steps to reach it. Could I pull it off? It all depended on Satan and his plan of attack. The one thing I knew for certain was that the broom was my only hope. I somehow had to reach it before this monster reached me and pecked my eyes out.

I don't remember what happened next; only that there was some kind of a skirmish. I remember hearing the sound of wings beating against the side of the shed. The hens were in an uproar and were squawking loudly. I had the broom handle in both hands and unbelievably was backing Satan toward the opening to the yard. He was determined not to give up the fight, nonetheless, and would lunge toward me whenever he could see that he might have the advantage. The door of the henhouse flew open, and I fleetingly glanced in that direction to see my uncle, his shotgun aimed directly at Satan's body. The feisty rooster evidently sensed at that point that he was in danger of becoming Sunday dinner. He hurriedly retreated to the yard, throwing an evil glance in our direction as he left the henhouse. Uncle Clyde hurriedly released some line and closed the opening with the board.

The aftershock had set in, and I was shaking uncontrollably as my uncle came to determine if the old rooster had done any damage to me. Satisfied that I was all right, he unloaded his shells into his pocket, and with a combination of relief and amusement on his face, he looked down at my pitiful fifty-pound frame.

"I'm afraid you're no match for that bird, Mara. He's a lot bigger and meaner than you are. On the other hand, I'll say this for you. You used your head in a crisis. You thought fast and found a way to arm yourself against your adversary. At least you were able to hold him off until help came."

I thought that I was really going to catch it for not following their instructions. I was mistaken. I guess he must have figured that the experience I had endured was worth a thousand words of correction. We did make a pact that morning, though. I was sworn to secrecy about the entire incident. We both agreed that my aunt would never know what happened in the henhouse the first morning after my arrival at the farm.

Although my Aunt Harriet and Uncle Clyde were professional people employed at a nearby steel plant, they had an undeniable love for the land and devoted many of their evenings and weekends to vegetable gardening and raising small animals and poultry for food. They were a childless couple, and consequently, it was a treat to have a small child invade their lifestyle. They treated me like a princess, but in the times spent with them, I learned some valuable principles, which I later took with me into my Christian experience.

Needless to say, this was an environment tailor-made for a lively, free-spirited eight-year-old who loved the great outdoors and the constant companionship of several small downy-haired kittens and a friendly large dog of dubious origin named Jake. When no one was around, I would tie tin cans to the goats' tails and watch them scamper frantically in order to rid themselves of these unwelcome and noisy objects.

My happy, carefree summers, this first one and the summer that followed, were two high points of my elementary school years. I loved country living, and I told my folks many times that when I grew up, I wanted to own a farm and adopt all the animals I had room to keep that were abused or didn't have a home of their own.

Because I associated summer vacations with the farm, it was most unusual that, in the winter that I was to turn ten, my mom informed me that I would be with my aunt and uncle during Christmas vacation. Why would I be spending time with them this particular holiday? Sometime later, I found, much to my chagrin, that Mom and Dad were in the process of a divorce, and they felt it would be best for me to be absent during this traumatic time.

It turned out that winter at the farm was a far less desirable time to spend in the country. The warm, sun-soaked mornings of early dawn were now replaced by bitterly cold and completely dark surroundings as I set out to perform my first task of the day. Yes, you guessed it. I was still chief overseer of the henhouse, after Satan, of course.

My aunt, a devout Catholic lady, would literally drag me from my warm, cozy bed to perform my early morning tasks before shuffling me off to St. Catherine's where we attended daily mass. We walked to the church, which was a seemingly endless and bitterly cold ordeal for me. As I heard the packed snow crunching under my feet, my aunt, sensing my dismay, would daily lecture me on the marvelous health benefits of a brisk two-mile walk on a cold, wintry morning. Somehow, I was not impressed with this tidbit of information. Though, as a nurse, she ought to know what she was talking about. I thought that I would develop pneumonia and die in the local hospital, never to see my parents again. I was wrong. I went home that winter healthier than I had ever been. I had to concede—my aunt was right.

One such morning, as we approached the church about a week before Christmas, I saw—to my pleasant surprise—a myriad of twinkling colored lights illuminated by a soft floodlight, revealing a group of people clad in various types of garb. Animals of diverse color and size were in the midst of all these figures. As we drew nearer to this scene, I noticed a small straw-filled corncrib containing a tiny baby who was surrounded by these people and animals. All were within what appeared to be a portion of a rocky hillside, out of which had been carved an opening to accommodate this group and a few of the smaller animals.

Evidently, the men of St. Catherine's parish had been busy the previous weekend placing the images of Mary, Joseph, and the baby Jesus, the shepherds, wise men, and the animals in strategic places.

I was filled with awe in anticipation of very soon being able to run my mitten-clad hand over the blond curls on the baby's head and touch the soft fleece of the little lambs that had been placed close to the crib.

As my aunt and I drew near to the crib scene, I realized, to my dismay, that these figures that had appeared so lifelike from a distance were nothing more than heavy cardboard figures supported from behind by sturdy wooden stands. The disappointment that I experienced that day remained with me into my adult Christian life. Over the years, I have discovered that in the Christian community, there are many look-alikes. From a distance, these people appear to be the genuine articles. Upon closer inspection, however, one can discern artificiality.

The Bible states clearly in chapter 13 of the book of Matthew the parable of the wheat and the tare. Although the sower sowed good seed in his field, an enemy came at night and sowed weeds in the same field alongside the wheat. One of the laborers was discerning enough to see that though the wheat and the tare appeared to be the same when they were immature seedlings, when they both grew to maturity, there was a noticeable difference in them. Although the husbandman ordered the laborers to allow the two to grow together, it is quite possible that the weeds had a tendency to choke the life from some of the weaker wheat stalks. The husbandman's primary concern was that, in attempting to separate the wheat from the tare, the wheat would be damaged.

Certainly, the writer cannot argue with the husbandman's good advice. After all, the husbandman is Jesus Christ. I wonder sometimes, though, if some of the weaker stalks of wheat had been separated from the tare early in their growth, could they have been protected from the choking effect of the tare surrounding them and gone on to maturity rather than die? Or is it possible that the husbandman had foreknowledge that the weaker stalks were going to die regardless of how they were handled? Read my story and decide for yourself.

CHAPTER 1

DARK CLOUDS GATHER

The desolate country road unfolded before us like an unending roll of white satin ribbon. A fresh covering of snow, which had fallen sometime during the night, had left a myriad of fairylike tiny glistening images skipping frivolously across the landscape.

Unfortunately, the mood in our car did not reflect the quiet, pristine countryside surrounding us. We were the third vehicle in a seemingly endless funeral procession. Having started from the funeral home, which seemed like hours ago, we were slowly and painstakingly making our way to my aunt's final destination. The journey would take us to a small country cemetery many miles from Cleveland. The town, having no particular significance except for the space it occupied on an Ohio map, was called Chardon. It was on Lake Erie.

What in the world possessed Uncle Pete to choose a location like this as the final resting place for Aunt Millie? I mused. *This is a tough-enough situation without dragging it on endlessly. Besides, my flask is in the glove compartment of my car. Now I won't be able to get to it for hours.*

Oh, well, I concluded to myself with a distressed sigh. *I guess that Uncle Pete can bury his wife wherever he damn well pleases.*

As the hearse rounded a bend in the road, I was able to get a panoramic view of much of the procession. Behind our car was a long line of vehicles which appeared to stretch for miles. In front of us, the shiny long black hearse carried the remains of one of my mother's younger sisters, my Aunt Millicent—Aunt Millie, or simply Aunt Mo-Mo, as her nieces and nephews affectionately called her. Directly behind the hearse was the funeral director's limo carrying the immediate family.

I could clearly observe the passengers and took particular notice of my eleven-year -old cousin Matthew sitting in the rear seat. From time to time, he would gaze aimlessly out of the window, revealing a tearstained cheek and a left eye swollen almost shut as the result of his endless stream of tears.

My thoughts returned to the scene at St Patrick's Church a few hours earlier. I had arrived late and just in time to see the pallbearers laboriously carrying the coffin up the two steep flights of steps toward the double-door main entrance. They stopped briefly on the landing before entering the vestibule. Perhaps they needed to catch a breath after such a steep ascent, or perhaps they were instructed to do this as some type of protocol governing funerals.

In any event, it was at this particular moment that my Aunt Harriet spotted me parking my car on the street below. It had been my good fortune to slide into a parking spot across the street from the church just as someone was vacating it. As I had approached the church, I observed that the street was lined solid on either side with vehicles as far as the eye could see. The overnight snowfall had been cleared from the street, but the plow had banked a portion of it at the curbs on both sides making both driving and parking a difficult situation. My immediate thought upon my arrival had been that I would have to park blocks away from the church and walk back. This, I had estimated, would take several minutes. It was evident that most of these vehicles belonged to friends, relatives, and business associates of the family who had come to pay their final respects to the family, and perhaps many would join the procession to the cemetery.

How lucky can one person get? I thought, breathing a sigh of relief as I engaged the parking brake of my Pontiac. My glance was immediately drawn to the activity at the top of the church steps. Several people were gathered around the pallbearers, who had momentarily placed the coffin at the door's entrance and were evidently awaiting word from the funeral director to resume their task of proceeding with the coffin into the church.

As I made my ascent to the top of the steps, I saw my aunt coming toward me with an expression of extreme irritation. Her voice was rasping as it so often did when she was excited or upset that her plans were being disrupted. "Mara, you're late. Did you run into a traffic problem?" The accusing tone of her voice gave clear indication that she was greatly disturbed over my late arrival.

By this time, I was standing beside the coffin, directly confronting her as the immediate crowd waiting to enter the church looked on. She knew only too well that I had no intention of viewing my Aunt Millie's remains. Why did she persist in this nonsense when I had made it perfectly clear that I would be attending the funeral only?

"Aunt Hon, I thought I made it clear on the phone last night that I would be here for the funeral but would probably not make it to the funeral home for the final prayer with the family before they closed the coffin. Here I am. What more can I say?"

What I didn't say was that I purposely delayed leaving Pittsburgh four hours earlier because I didn't want to see Millie lying lifeless in the coffin. I wanted to remember her as I had always known her to be—vibrant, full of enthusiasm for life, and connecting positively with everyone she met. This gracious lady had an amazing zest for life, and that life had been quickly and cruelly snuffed out. She had been like a flaming torch lighting the way for her husband and children and for all who knew her well. The torch had been extinguished by an ominous wind that had suddenly blown into her life.

As I tearfully embraced my Uncle Pete and my cousins, I heard my Aunt Harriet's authoritative voice directing the head pallbearer to open the coffin so that her niece could view the remains. I flew into an immediate rage. I found this to be in the poorest of taste.

"Don't do that. What in the world is wrong with you, Aunt Hon? Don't you have any feeling for the family? Why in God's name would you put them through that again? They closed the casket at the funeral home. Let that be the end of it."

She appeared to be caught off guard at my sudden outburst. Evidently, the tone of my voice must have given her the impression that perhaps she had better leave well enough alone, even though she was not accustomed to having commands challenged. Without another word, she turned away from me and made her way through the open door of the church. There, an usher escorted her and my uncle to the front of the sanctuary, where the immediate family was already seated.

As I entered the church vestibule, I noticed the small frame of my Aunt Millie's youngest child, Matthew. He appeared to be waiting for me.

"What's up, Matt?" I whispered to him softly as he came quickly to my side and took my hand.

"I don't want to go to the front of the church where my mom is lying in that box. Can I stay back here with you until this is over?"

His red-rimmed eyes and swollen face touched me so deeply that I just wanted to take him in my arms and comfort him. I thought better of it, though, knowing that he would prefer to face this terrible situation like the little man that he was becoming rather than the small vulnerable boy that I sensed he was leaving behind this day.

"Sure, Matt, just as long as it's okay with your dad. He knows you're back here, doesn't he?"

"Yes," he responded instantly. "He knows that I was waiting for you to get here, and he said that it would be okay to stay with you. He will meet me back here after church is over. He said that I had to ride with him and Patrick and Elaine to the cemetery. He said that you would be in another car."

The church was filling up rapidly. I marveled at the many people who came out on this cold, blustery January morning to bid their farewells to a gracious lady who had touched many of their lives in some special way.

Matt and I stood in the aisle, which was now lined on either side with well-wishers. I placed my hand on his small thin shoulder during the service. He didn't seem to mind this at all. Actually, I believe that he welcomed the familiar touch of his older cousin from the Pittsburgh area. From time to time, I would feel a tremor seize his frail body as the tears would begin to fall silently. Throughout the entire mass, he maintained his composure as he had been taught to do. This young boy would always remember this day as the day a child became a young man in spite of his meager eleven years.

Once again, as I had done so many times since hearing of Aunt Millie's terminal condition, my thoughts turned to the Giver of Life, who this day had taken away Matt's precious mommy.

I questioned the justice of this situation, and my heart seemed to cry out to God for an answer. *Why, God? Why would you take this young boy's mother away from him? He needs a mom so much at this time in his life. How will he be able to overcome such a profound loss?*

The service was over fairly quickly for a requiem high mass. The eulogy had been quite touching. It was evident that the priest who delivered it was quite close to my aunt. His voice broke several times as he expounded her many virtues. He ended his comments by saying that not only would Aunt Millie be sorely missed by her family and the many parishioners who knew her well but by him personally, along with the entire staff of St. Patrick's Church. She was a woman who had worked tirelessly to promote with integrity the ministries in which she was involved.

All of this was more than Matt could handle emotionally. I felt his thin body shake violently as he began to lose control of the emotions that he had so valiantly controlled to this point. Yes, the quicker we got through all this, the better it would be for all of us. My wish was realized at this point as the priest, having completed his thoughts, blessed the congregation and dismissed them. The usher in the front of the church stood at the first pew where the immediate family had been seated and indicated that they should vacate their seats first.

As Uncle Pete moved down the aisle, followed by Patrick and Elaine, he spotted Matt and me at the entrance of the vestibule. He motioned for Matt to follow him to the parking area, where the limo stood waiting for its occupants

"Thanks for staying in the back of the church with me, Mar. I didn't want to go up front where people would be looking at me. I'll see you at the cemetery, okay?"

"Yeah, Matt, I'll see you in a little while," I assured him as I watched him move in the direction of his family. Once again, I could feel hot tears stinging my eyes as the reality of this situation hit me. I quickly regained my composure as I saw my Uncle Clyde moving toward me.

"Mara, the funeral director jus assigned my car to the third spot in the procession. You, your mom, and Henry will be riding with Harriet and me. I'll see you at the car in a few minutes."

"Oh, nuts," I muttered under my breath. I had been hoping that I would be able to drive alone in my own car. I thought about the flask of bourbon stashed away in the glove compartment and regretfully realized that it would be sometime before I could get my hands on it.

I'd give anything for a good long pull on that flask right now. I need something to stabilize me and get me through these next few hours. This

is brutal. No sense attempting to sneak over to where I'm parked, though. Someone would surely smell the booze on my breath. I had better leave well enough alone and try to hold myself together.

As my thoughts once again returned to the present, the long procession was making its way slowly and somberly through the flat snow-covered terrain to the cemetery. Uncle Clyde's car was directly behind the family who was riding in the limousine.

Aunt Hon was sitting sullenly beside him, still sulking over the verbal lashing so recently received from her favorite niece. Her hair, I noticed, always a warm honey brown, was beginning to show definite signs of age as random streaks of gray were evident. Uncle Clyde, in contrast, displayed a thick, nearly black crop of wavy hair.

These two had remained childless throughout their marriage. I often wondered why they didn't adopt children if they couldn't have any of their own. They appeared to have so much to offer a family. My uncle, a metallurgical engineer, commanded a huge salary where he was employed by a large steel company near Pittsburgh. My aunt, an industrial nurse at the same plant, also contributed substantially to their financial situation. Perhaps the summers that I had spent with them as a child fulfilled their parenting needs and still allowed my aunt to work whenever she desired.

I cast a sideways glance at my mother sitting to my right. To her right side was my Uncle Henry, her older brother, who had never married. These two had come to Cleveland yesterday with my aunt and uncle. I was relieved that this arrangement had been made in advance. Getting both of them ready for a four-hour trip so early in the morning would have been next to impossible.

What a waste of humanity, I thought. Henry—my grandparents' older son and, at one time, the darling of the family—was said to have displayed a marked resemblance to Rudolph Valentino, a popular movie star of the Roaring Twenties. Valentino was reputedly the most handsome man in the world at that time and was swooned over by tens of thousands of females—young and old alike.

As I caught a fleeting glance of his profile, it was painfully obvious that time and the unfortunate circumstances of his lifestyle had left their indelible mark on his once-striking good looks. His sallow, jaundiced cheeks created the background for a nose that had been regally straight and finely chiseled. In its place was a bulbous monstrosity, the product of years of immoral activity with the wrong women. A venereal disease had left its cruel stigma for the world to see. Unable to cope with the tragedy that life had dealt him, Henry was being cared for by my grandparents in their home. He was under psychiatric care and heavily sedated much of the time because of his schizophrenic condition.

I cast a fleeting glance at my mother's face as I sat back in my seat. It was difficult to determine how badly she had been affected by this recent loss and the events leading up to this moment.

Certainly the previous two months, since the news came of Aunt Millie's diagnosis, was a time of extreme stress and unbelief for our entire family. My concern was for my mother during this crisis. If little things were enough to set her off, how would she react to losing one of her favorite sisters?

My gaze returned once again to her expressionless face, this time resting there briefly in an effort to determine the amount of emotional stress she might be experiencing. Like her older brother Henry, whom she had adored when the two were growing up, my mother was the victim of a life too overwhelming for her to endure. In my early teen years, she had decided to give up on this thing called life. As a result, she withdrew into the dark, sinister world of the manic depressive. She sat expressionless, her eyes fastened on the black limo in front of us. She gave no clue as to what she might be feeling, if anything. Infrequently, she would make a visit to the outside world only to retreat to that secret place once again where no one could hurt her. Today's trauma was yet to reveal how well or, perhaps, how poorly Mom would be able to handle this adversity.

Unlike my Uncle Henry, Mom's lifestyle had not been the determining factor that resulted in the broken life beside me this morning. On the contrary, Mom had been a devout Catholic in her younger years, living out her faith the best way she knew how. She was the third of eight children and reputedly one of the prettiest of the six sisters. Without question, I was told, she was the most intelligent of the eight offspring born to my grandparents. From what I had been led to believe, Mom had been a ravishing beauty who loved life. She loved to dance and was a *swinger* during the Charleston dance era of the Roaring Twenties. In her late teens, she met and, a year later, married a handsome young Minor League baseball player from the neighboring state of Ohio who had literally swept her off her feet.

Looking at her now, I could see very little resemblance to the carefree, vivacious young woman whose pictures I had in my album.

I nudged her gently. "How we doin', Mom?" I asked, breaking the long silence in my uncle's vehicle.

"Oh, all right, I guess. As well as can be expected under the circumstances," she said, patting my hand affectionately.

Relieved that she was cognizant of the events unfolding around her, I put my arm around her shoulder and squeezed gently. "We should be at the cemetery very soon now. I just caught a glimpse of the frozen lake when we turned that last bend in the road."

Removing my arm from her shoulder and stretching my legs in the limited area allotted me, I found myself once again reliving the events of the past few months.

The news had come the week before Thanksgiving. Aunt Millie had gotten her test results from the Cleveland Clinic. The results were alarming—inoperable carcinoma. The cancer had already metastasized. It had originated in the stomach and spread rapidly into other vital organs of her body. The time remaining, according to her doctor, was very brief—perhaps a month, two at best.

The news devastated us. We were a large, close-knit family. Most of us lived in the Pittsburgh suburbs and saw one another on an almost daily basis. Aunt Darlene, my mother's youngest living sister, her husband, Len, and their daughter, Carol, born unexpectedly after fourteen years of marriage, had settled in the small agricultural town of Poland, Ohio. Len had secured a lucrative position as Cost Accountant with the nearby US Steel plant.

Darlene, Dar as we called her, had been the head psychiatric nurse at St. Joseph's Hospital in Pittsburgh. When my uncle accepted the position with US Steel, they sold their home in Pittsburgh and relocated. They had found the home of their dreams in a country setting within a mile of the new interstate highway that ran between metropolitan Pittsburgh and westward into the Cleveland area. This enabled them to make frequent trips to both locations for family visits.

Pete and Millie had been longtime residents in the upscale section of Cleveland Heights. Pete, a retired army colonel, had been pushing a pencil behind the desk of a government agency. He had taken on this venture on a part-time basis. Evidently, his employer had found him to be a valuable asset and had persuaded him to take a lucrative consulting position with the agency on a full-time basis.

Millie, always the extrovert, had discovered an outlet for her abundant energy in club work, volunteering her spare time in activities beneficial to her church and to the community. Now that the two older children were in college, she had only Matt at home. During school hours she occupied herself with her varied activities. She was always a wife and mom first, and in spite of the energetic schedule she had established for herself, Matt always knew that his mom would be home to greet him at the door after school with milk and freshly baked cookies.

This had been the model family—parents totally devoted to each other with three secure, well-adjusted kids, all eager to move on in their educational pursuits with the determination to accomplish the high goals that they had set for themselves. Elaine, the oldest, would be graduating this coming June from a local university. She didn't know what her degree in business would enable her to pursue in the way of employment. Like her parents, she was anxiously awaiting graduation so that she could test the waters with her newfound knowledge.

Patrick, in pursuit of a medical career, would soon be completing his second year of college with an eye toward premed in a couple of years, hopefully at the University of Michigan. Matt—the carefree, personable eleven-year old—was the apple of his parents' eye. This child, conceived during menopause and completely unplanned for, was now the focal point of his mom and dad's world. Much of Aunt Millie's time was spent transporting Matt to and from his many and varied activities and supporting him by her presence at Little League games and academic events.

Pete had accompanied her as often as he could work these special times into his busy schedule. The glint in his eye had been miraculously transformed into this energetic, loving eleven-year-old whom they both laughingly referred to as their surprise package from heaven.

Just as unexpectedly as Matthew had made his appearance on life's stage eleven years earlier, his beloved mother had taken her final curtain call just a few days ago. What was to become of this family now? How would they cope with the terrible void that would now overwhelm each of them?

Once again, I cast a fleeting glance at Mom who was beginning to show definite signs of agitation. Riding in a car for extended periods of time seemed to create an ever-heightening anxiety for her. Perhaps she needed to use the restroom. No sense asking her if this was the problem; she wouldn't admit to it anyway. I could never get her to admit to anything when she felt that she was inconveniencing someone. She would just remain stoic and withdraw further into the safe black hole that had become her secure haven when she felt threatened by the outside world.

My God, I mused, checking my watch for what seemed to be the fiftieth time in the last half hour, *how much longer before we get to the cemetery? How in the hell did Uncle Pete find this place anyway, and why choose a cemetery so far from Cleveland Heights? It will take the family an entire day of driving when they visit the grave site.*

I gazed through the car window at a seemingly endless blur of snow-covered fields, interrupted by the frozen lake, when it would occasionally come into view. The monotony of the landscape caused my mind to return once again to the events leading up to this day.

CHAPTER 2

WRESTLING WITH GOD

New Year's Eve had been one like I had never remembered, and I hoped that an event similar to this would never be repeated. Normally, a party at the Reuben home was the place to be on New Year's Eve. This had been a tradition for several years and, over time, had gained notoriety as "the most fun place in town to bring in the New Year." In actuality, it began as a neighborhood gathering that eventually evolved into a drunken debacle. It was one of the few occasions that I had to get absolutely smashed out of my mind and not have to make an excuse for my behavior. After all, it was a time to celebrate the coming of the New Year, and our guests were like-minded in their practice of observing this holiday. Each "morning after" would be one of attempting to remember the events of the previous evening and an even greater attempt to remedy the horrendous hangovers most of us were experiencing.

No, certainly, this last New Year's Eve was anything but a celebration. Several of us had gathered around the dining-room table attempting to enjoy a friendly game of penny ante. We were on edge, waiting for a telephone call from Aunt Dar that we knew was imminent. That call came about 11:35 p.m. Millie never made it into the New Year. Thank God for Aunt Dar. With her many years of nursing, she had been a bulwark of strength over the last two weeks as Millie's caretaker and constant companion. She was with her at the end, as was each member of her immediate family.

Thank God, I said to myself. *Thank God*, I repeated, as though I were expressing verbally something foreign to my nature. *Okay, I'll give you that much, God. I suppose it was because of you that Millie had a comfortable ending. Dar said that she suffered very little and the family was at her bedside to say good-bye. I guess I just don't understand why you do the things that you do. You are supposed to be in charge of human affairs, as the nuns endlessly drummed into our sponge like young minds. But as far as this whole lousy situation is concerned, I think you really screwed up on this one. I am so angry with you for taking Matt's beloved mother from him. He needs a mom so much in his formative years. It was your decision to take Millie, a vibrant, vitally important person in this little boy's world. Why couldn't you have taken Henry or my own mother? They're both vegetables. They serve no earthly purpose but to be burdens to those of us who are forced to be caretakers for them.*

Why not Randall? Sure, I know, I reasoned within myself. *We all make choices, and we're stuck with those choices—right or wrong. I'm stuck with this one, that's for certain. He's a lousy husband and an even worse father. I'd be more than willing to end this farce called a marriage tomorrow if the opportunity presented itself and I had the financial resources to care for my children's needs without his contribution. Every time I bring up the subject of divorce, he agrees to leave but, in the same breath, warns me that I'm on my own financially if he does. At that point, he washes his hands of all responsibility. The prospect of this becoming a reality stops me short of carrying out my plan. Once again, I face the reality that I am stuck in a relationship that is intolerable.*

I just have to be honest with you, God. The way I see it, you don't play fair. You seem to get some sort of sadistic pleasure in destroying your creation—one miserable person at a time. I guess the nuns were right. They said that you are a great big grandfather-like spirit wielding a huge stick and ready to whop anyone who gets out of line. If that is the case, then why

Millie? Why that innocent little kid? Why that loving husband and those two well- adjusted older siblings? They were the model family with no skeletons in their family closet, at least none that any of our family is aware of. Everyone who knows them and those who know them well love them and hold them in high respect. Did they get out of line? I don't think so. They have lived exemplary and productive lives, all of them. And so what did you do? You decided to rob that loving husband and devoted children of their most precious possession.

My mind was racing now with thoughts of contempt and disgust for this so-called loving God whom we were taught to worship. I was angry, angrier than I had ever remembered being, at what I saw as the epitome of a grave injustice.

Whoa, hold on there, Mara, an almost imperceptible voice seemed to echo within the depths of my being. *There's much more to this story than what you see right now.*

Where did that thought come from?

Who do you think you are anyway, giving the Almighty advice as to how his universe should be run?

Once again, I found myself having what I perceived to be a one-way conversation with him. Strangely, this was a practice I was repeating all too frequently in recent weeks. This was so out of character for me. I knew that God exists, at least this is what I had been taught to believe. Was all of this really true? Had my family and the nuns and priests been somehow conveying the wrong information all this time? Had they passed down wrong doctrine to the next generation and to their flocks? How did they know what was right anyhow? Who told them?

Oh, come on, Mara, I reasoned within myself. *Of course, God exists. Who else could have created such a beautiful world, fully functional and complete in every way? Who else could have devised such an intricate mechanism like the human body? Who but God could pull off the wonderful work of bringing a tiny baby into the world merely by the joint actions of a man and woman caught in the ecstasy of the passionate experience of lovemaking? You, lady, are just angry because God has chosen to take one of your favorite aunts, and you can't understand why he would do such a thing.*

God or his dealings with the human race were not subjects I felt comfortable discussing with my friends or family members. Religion was a very personal thing and meant to be kept to one-self, I was told. True, my entire family was of the Roman Catholic faith. Though I had attended Catholic schools for all my elementary years and most of my high school years, I knew very little about this great ethereal Being somewhere up there in the great heavenly expanse, manipulating the strings of his marionettes down here on the earth.

During my formative years I was required to study the Catholic faith and its many intricate doctrines. Even as a small child, I just couldn't swallow a lot of this gobble-dee-goop. It didn't make sense to me. I could never get a satisfactory answer to the many questions that I would ask about God and Jesus Christ and how I could get to heaven and escape the eternal fires of hell. The only answer I ever got, in one form or another, was that I needed to confess my sins to a priest often, take the Holy Eucharist after I did, and attend the sacrifice of the mass regularly every Sunday and the holy days. Of course, it went without saying that I needed to live as good a life as I could and keep the Ten Commandments to the best of my ability. When I was old enough to marry, I was to choose a God-fearing Catholic man and have lots and lots of babies who, within two or three weeks after birth, were required to be baptized into the Catholic faith. They, in turn, would repeat the cycle all over again when they reached maturity.

When all these things were faithfully accomplished, my hope was that I would have done everything to God's satisfaction. Just to be on the safe side, I was also instructed of the necessity of giving sufficient money to my local church so that the pastor and the nuns would receive their proper compensation and that all the expenses necessary to maintain the grounds, the rectory, and nuns' quarters would be covered. Of course, I needed to be aware that the diocese to which I belonged also required a great amount of financial support. It was through the diocese that the bishop assigned to this particular geographical area would be well compensated for his many and varied duties.

To be absolutely certain that I wouldn't end up in hell in spite of everything "good" that I had done, lighting sufficient votive candles to make reparation for the sins that I may have forgotten to confess was something of importance that I could add to the mix. Of course, when seeking contrition by doing this, I was required to contribute a nominal sum of money for this opportunity afforded me. There was a small metal box affixed to the ornately decorated metal candleholder that held the multitude of tiny votive candles. These candles were housed in red glass containers. They were placed at the foot of the altar where I was encouraged to visit when petitioning God for someone or something special that I needed to pray for at that particular time.

Kneeling there, I would ask God for His forgiveness for the sin that was burdening my heart. In every location where these candles were placed, directly behind the stand, was a statue of the Blessed Virgin Mary or perhaps one of my favorite saints. St. Anthony was usually my favorite when I had lost something and wanted to retrieve it. St. Jude was the one I went to when I had a seemingly impossible situation in my life that I needed to have fixed. I did take my petitions to the Blessed Mother on occasion because she was the intercessor and would take my prayers to her Son, who—being the dutiful Son that he was—would probably answer my prayer without delay. It never occurred to me to go directly to Jesus when I had a need. It is possible that we were taught not to bother someone as important as the Son of God. He had more significant matters to deal with than spend time being concerned with my puny, little problems.

Having completed the requirements expected of me, when my number was up, whether I died accidentally or by a terminal disease, I would be judged accordingly. If I happened to be fortunate enough to live a long life and die a natural death, as so often occurred in my family, I would hopefully be in the "state of grace" when my number was called.

In the event that I had minor sins on my soul at the time of my death, I would most likely be assigned to purgatory (another name for the halfway house to heaven), where my less-significant sins would be burned away to prepare me for heaven. If I happened to be one of the very fortunate few who had lived an exemplary life and God was pleased with me, I wouldn't be required to stop off at the scary halfway house but would be taken by God's angels immediately into heaven.

I had no aspiration for such a happy ending. I knew I could never meet the qualifications. None of this made sense to me. I just knew that, out there somewhere where I had not yet ventured, there was another story to be told that would make more sense and be more palatable to me. I had great faith that someday I would find someone who would be able to satisfy my unquenchable desire to know the truth.

I had a great amount of curiosity about this book called the Bible, much to the dismay of the nuns. During some of our religious classes, this mystery book would be mentioned in passing. But during these infrequent times, the nuns would never fail to warn us that the Bible was not for the laity to read. This was an absolute no-no. Only the clergy had the religious education and the divine inspiration that enabled them to interpret it accurately. They, in turn, would break it down into small doses and spoon-feed it to us from the pulpit during mass each Sunday. By the time this part of the mass occurred, I was desperately struggling to keep my eyes open and look like I was interested in what was going on.

As so often happened, my mother, or whichever relative happened to be sitting on the right of me, would give me an elbow in my side to bring me back to reality. Even as a small child, it wasn't the sacrifice of the mass that held my attention; it was that mysterious black book that captured my curiosity. My natural instinct was such that when something was forbidden to me, my desire to investigate it fully could not be assuaged. Unfortunately, my folks were of the same mind as the nuns. Although I asked repeatedly to receive a Bible for Christmas or for my birthday, my request was always denied.

The Bible remained a mystery like the subject of sex. As I reached puberty, I began to experience major changes occurring in my body. Playing in the woods and beating up the boys just for the fun of it were being replaced by spending time in front of the full-length mirror that had previously stood unnoticed in the corner of my bedroom. The mirror had been in the same spot for several years, completely ignored by a little girl who had absolutely no interest in how she looked. Gradually this changed—especially when a new boy a year or two older than me moved into the neighborhood. That old mirror really got a workout during those times. I would find myself taking more frequent baths, which to my way of thinking had been a total waste of time. Now it appeared that I was having a change of heart. I would search the medicine cabinet until I came upon some sweet-smelling bath salts belonging to my aunt or my mom. I would dump a large amount into the bathwater so I could smell good when being tackled by one of these new neighbor kids when we were playing football or while being engaged in some other close-contact sports activity.

It was during this period of my growing-up years that I would be warned repeatedly by my mother, my aunts, my grandmother (whom I adored), and the nuns at school about the dangers ahead for me as I associated with boys and then later with men. There were severe consequences for any young girl who made the wrong choices in dealing with them, I was told. Like a broken record, my mother would continually repeat this warning, "Mara, remember this and remember it well: beauty can be a blessing, but it can also be a curse."

Here again, I could not be dissuaded. None of this made any sense to me. After all, didn't my mom's sisters grow up and got married to nice men? They seemed happy enough. What mistakes did they make? They all had nice families. They appeared to be relatively satisfied with their lives. Such was not the case with my parents. I realized that mystery shrouded my mom and dad's relationship. As I grew older I often wondered what had happened to their marriage, why my daddy left us to fend for ourselves. I had loved him so much, but he left us when I was three, returning for a brief period a few years later. He deserted us once again after a brief attempt at reconciliation. I did not see him again for a few more years. My mom became embittered over the separations and blamed my dad entirely for what was happening to their marriage. I was never told what the problem was but I continued to love him anyhow. He had been a good daddy to me and I missed him. I often wondered if I had anything to do with their separating. Could it have been my fault somehow?

Suddenly my thoughts were brought to a halt as the vehicle in front of us carrying Aunt Millie's family had come to a sudden stop. Peering through the windshield of our car I quickly appraised the situation and realized that the hearse had evidently hit some black ice and had begun to spin the rear wheels. Fortunately, because we were all traveling at a slow rate of speed, the funeral director was able to get control of the vehicle before it slid off the road and into a drain ditch, averting a multivehicle pileup.

Looking around, I observed that we had finally arrived at our destination. A small white clapboard church with a huge bell tower stood forlornly in front of us. It was the only structure in the middle of a large field dotted with various snow-covered pine trees. Behind the church, I could see the tops of several grave markers barely visible in the otherwise barren landscape. The fresh snowfall had all but covered the small ones so that only their tops were visible. Back in the far right-hand corner of the grave-yard I observed a huge mound of fresh soil that had recently been removed from the frozen ground to accommodate a new casket.

A large canvas tent had been placed close to the open grave site. Under the tent, several folding chairs had been arranged in neat rows. This evidently was to be Millie's final resting place. I could feel unwelcome emotions welling up inside me as I faced the prospect of never seeing Aunt Millie again during our frequent visits to Cleveland or when their family felt the desire to travel to the Pittsburgh area for a weekend visit. I struggled to hold back the hot tears that had begun to sting my eyes. The luxury of displaying emotion at the loss of my beloved aunt had to be postponed for now. I was responsible for keeping things as normal as possible for my mom and my Uncle Henry. They were both totally unpredict-able when confronted with traumatic situations, so it was impor-tant that I not display any outward show of grief at this time. There would be plenty of time to grieve later.

One of the gentlemen assisting the funeral director had left the hearse and headed in the direction of our car with some last-minute instructions for us before we began our brief hike to the grave site. We were instructed to stay in our cars for a few minutes longer until some final preparations were completed.

"Oh damn, another delay!" I was becoming increasingly impa-tient with the amount of time it was taking to get my aunt buried. I threw a headlong glance toward my mother and uncle to see what responses this latest announcement might evoke from them. To my relieved surprise, they both had their eyes closed and appeared to be comfortable. Perhaps they had dropped off to sleep during the lengthy ride to this remote little town in North Central Ohio.

I sullenly acknowledged the gentleman's request and quickly returned to my interrupted thoughts.

CHAPTER 3

CAREFREE CHILDHOOD MEMORIES

There had been that one final attempt to reconcile the marriage. This had occurred when I was getting ready to enter the second grade. Dad evidently persuaded Mom to join him in the small town of Girard, a suburb of Youngstown, Ohio. This was where my dad was born and had grown up with his five brothers and four sisters. Everyone lived in white clapboard two-story houses that all looked alike. My first impression of these look-alike houses was that they resembled a row of big white teeth with small spaces between them that served as tiny side yards between the structures.

What a stark contrast from where I had spent the last four years of my life in suburban Pittsburgh. There, the houses were mostly red brick or stone. Many of these structures sat on large parcels of lush-green terrain. There were small farms interspersed with the houses in this area. Although we didn't live on a farm, our stone Dutch-Tudor home sat at the top of a hill overlooking the rolling hills of Southwestern Pennsylvania, with homes and farmhouses dotting the landscape as far as the eye could see.

We had a huge garden behind the backyard, where one could often find my grandmother laboriously tending her vegetables. Beside her garden was a miniature version shaped in the form of a V, which I proudly claimed as my own since I planted and maintained it. I didn't fully understand the significance of this V. I understood that it signified victory and that our country was at war with Germany and Japan. Somehow the correlation between these two facts did not register in my young mind.

How could growing a victory garden in a Pittsburgh suburb put an end to a war that was being fought by our servicemen in faraway countries? I needed a clearer explanation, which unfortunately I never received. The one thing that left an indelible mark on my memory was the front doors of a few homes in our neighborhood on which hung banners with a single gold star in the center of each of them. When I questioned my granny about these banners, her response was brief and to the point: "Mara, these are here to remind all of us that these stars represent young men and women who gave their lives so that we could be free. Pray that our family won't ever have to hang one of these banners on any of our front doors."

I wanted to question her further about this, but it was obvious that she didn't want to discuss the matter. Try as I would to reason this out, I always came to the same conclusion. War was stupid, and if people would just get along with one another, young people wouldn't have to go to a faraway land and kill other young people they didn't even know. More importantly to my young mind, they wouldn't have to get killed either. I did notice that any time the subject of war or the death of our servicemen and women came up, my granny became strangely quiet. I dared not pursue the subject. Since I loved my granny, I didn't want to be the cause of sadness or trouble to her.

This move to Ohio, as exciting as the prospect was, would be quite an adjustment for me as we prepared to make our home with my dad in this tight-knit little community of Girard. I knew that I would miss playing with (and sometimes tormenting) the many kittens that my grandmother kept around our home. These were the offspring of the large female ratter Whiskers, which was my granny's pride and joy. This feline had a notorious reputation for trapping and doing away with the multitude of rodents that frequently invaded her henhouse in search of plump, tasty chickens to share with their ever-famished offspring.

Granny had a goat as well as her many chickens, dogs, and cats. This goat was used to keep the weeds from getting too high around the henhouse and the garden area. Gracie was her name, and she was my special target of torment when no one was around to catch me in the act. I loved to tie tin cans to her tail while she was on her chain and then turn her loose. She would become hysterical with the clattering noise of the cans banging together and would butt like a bronco until someone would come to her rescue. Needless to say, Gracie attempted to keep her distance from me when she spied me coming anywhere near her. I knew that this type of amusement would not be available to me when I lived with my daddy, much to my regret.

The pride of having my own little victory garden every summer would be greatly missed as well. I had been told that when we joined my dad, we would be living in a relative's second-story apartment until we found a house to buy. Any thought of having a garden would have to be put on hold for the time being. This announcement came as a great disappointment to me. As much as I enjoyed spending time with my friends, some of my best times were spent with my granny, who never seemed to grow weary of teaching me the fine art of organic gardening. It was such fun preparing the soil and sowing a variety of herb and vegetable seeds. The sense of pride and accomplishment would come the first time I saw the tiny seedlings forcing their way upward in search of sunlight and fresh air.

Just before I started back to school, the fruit of our labor over the spring and summer months would be realized. Harvest time would have come for many of the crops. Our large family would meet after church on Sundays to enjoy the luscious tomatoes, beans and corn on the cob fresh picked early that morning. Accompanying the vegetables would be the predictable beef chuck roast braised to tender perfection by Granny, mounds of creamy white mashed potatoes, and Granny's delicious gravy. The meal would be topped off with fresh apple, blackberry, or peach pie, whichever fruit happened to be available that weekend.

On very special occasions, when out-of-town relatives or friends of the family would join us for Sunday dinner, all of us kids would be commissioned to take turns churning fresh cream from the nearby dairy into creamy, delicious ice cream to accompany the pie. This was always a fun event. We took turns with the churning, but there was a good amount of horseplay in the process.

During these waning days of summer, there would be a flutter of activity in our large cellar. I remember, with a sense of pleasure, that no matter how hot and humid the late August days might be, our basement was always cool and inviting. In spite of the fact that the enormous pots used for canning the vegetables were there from the canning kitchen, it was a relief to come indoors after playing tag or baseball much of the day with the neighborhood gang. Here, my cousins and I could enjoy the cool comfort of the basement surrounded by the busy canners. We knew that by joining the family for this activity, we would be asked to give a helping hand with some of the minor tasks. We didn't mind helping out. We were a close-knit family who enjoyed being together, so we were glad for the opportunity to be with one another for this annual event and for the change of pace.

Although none of us kids would admit it, we were anxious to return to the more-structured environment of the classroom in these waning weeks of summer. There we could meet our new teachers and potential friends. As always, new faces began to pop up everywhere on the school grounds and in the halls. These were kids who were transferring from other schools or possibly relocating with their families from other areas. Though none of us would readily admit that we were anxious to begin a new school year, many of my neighborhood buddies and I were looking forward to September and all the new experiences that the coming year would provide us.

Indeed, I was torn by the prospect of leaving all these memories behind and moving on to an unfamiliar environment. Although I had so longed to be with my daddy once again, I knew that the transition was going to be a difficult one.

Recalling with pleasure the dense woods behind our home where I could frequently be found, I sensed that my present lifestyle fulfilled a deep inner need in me. Being able to explore every nook and cranny of this mysterious but beautiful place was always a welcome change from the time I spent with my friends or even those precious summer mornings with Granny as we worked in our gardens. I preferred to be alone in the woods where I could listen to the many melodic sounds of the various kinds of birds that made their homes in the branches of the taller trees.

When I expressed interest in knowing more about this subject, I received a book one Christmas providing all the information I needed to identify each bird I saw. The book, which I eventually wore out, had beautiful illustrations of each of these little creatures. Accompanying this book, which I dearly loved, was something even more wonderful. It was a small 45-rpm record with each birdcall given. The narrator identified the bird and provided many interesting facts about that particular species. I also wore out the record eventually, but not before I was able to identify each bird that I encountered by the song it sang.

I loved the woods with its many and varied-shaped trees, many of which I would climb to the very top as a challenge to my agility and strength. On hot July days when even the deeply shaded, wooded areas offered little relief from the heat, I would pull off my sneakers and wade in one of the inviting streams that ran through the property. I would check my balance by stepping or sometimes jumping from one rock to another. Occasionally, because of a miscalculation, I would end up missing a rock and land in the cool, refreshing water, soaked from head to foot. If it happened to be an extraordinarily hot day, I would just sit there for a while, watching the minnows darting through the clear, crisp water in schools. On occasion, I might have the good fortune of spotting a large green frog perched on a rock a few feet from where I had landed, peering curiously at me with his big black bulging eyes.

In the spring of the year, as I headed for home after my adventures in this wooded wonderland, I would pick violets and various other early-blooming wildflowers that grew by the well-worn paths my friends and I had carved out during our many times together. Sometimes I would take a bunch of violets down to our basement where I had made a small alter to the Blessed Mother and place them in front of her statue. Other days when I knew that Granny would be baking, I would present her with my labor of love. My ulterior motive, of course, was to extract an extra snickerdoodle or perhaps one of her delicious peanut butter cookies from the large platter on the kitchen table, which was laden with a variety of delicious snacks.

Yes, to be sure, it would be with great difficulty that I would leave this home with my mom to join my dad in a strange town, a town that was so different from which I had been accustomed. I was sad when I thought about leaving the granny whom I loved so much. I would miss my cousins and all of my aunts and uncles, my grandpa, and my neighborhood friends. I would miss my garden and my woods. I would miss so many things about this place. But then, I told myself, once again I would be reunited with my daddy whom I adored. We would be a real family again. I would no longer have to listen to the taunts of the kids at school who constantly reminded me that I was the only first grader who didn't have a daddy.

Yes, I reminded myself that it would be good. Mom said that I needed to take a piece of paper and make a Benjamin Franklin list. On this list I was to enumerate all the good things and all the not-so-good things about each place. She felt confident that I would choose the place where my daddy was. I wasn't quite as certain about that as my mom was. After all, I knew what I had here, but I had yet to find out what kind of a life I would have in Ohio. One thing I did know for certain; I would be with my dad again, and for the moment, that was a very exciting and comforting thought.

My dad and my uncles were all quite active in various sports activities. I sensed that Daddy would be in his glory teaching me the proper way to field and throw any ball that I retrieved order to make a necessary out for our team. He would teach me to run the base pads speedily and effectively enabling me to get home safely and thereby score a run for our team. In perfecting these skills he pointed out to me the absolute importance of team effort. I wasn't in the game to make a name for myself but to play the game to the best of my ability with the final result being a win for our team. His sense of pride in me exploded the first time I cleared the bases with a home run. This had occurred the previous summer when Mom and I had visited him for a long weekend. This gave me an unusual sense of achievement and the admiration of my dad, my uncles, and my many cousins. They were amazed at my strength and dexterity. After all, I was just a little skinny seven-year-old kid playing against some of my boy cousins who were two and three years my senior.

I continually weighed one lifestyle against the other those few weeks of August when Mom and I were preparing for this big change in our lives. This upheaval was disturbing to me, but the expectancy of a brand-new life with both a father and a mother was something that I had secretly longed for since I realized that this was what a normal family was all about.

The next two years in Ohio were all that I had hoped they would be. My dad was the greatest dad in the world to my way of thinking. He spent quality time with me when he was not at work. Not only was he a skilled athlete, but he was an accomplished artist and writer as well.

It appeared that his greatest challenge in life, as well as his greatest joy, was to pass his talents on to his only child. Unfortunately, this wonderful segment of my childhood was abruptly ended after two years in this new environment.

One morning, a few weeks before the end of the school year, my mother announced to me that we would be returning to our home in the Pittsburgh area and my dad would not be accompanying us. Needless to say, I was crushed beyond words. I begged my daddy to return to Pittsburgh with us to no avail. He was kind and gentle in his response to my many pleas, but he was also very firm.

"I'm sorry, Mara. You know that I love you and I'd give you the world if I could, but, honey, this is beyond my control. I just can't go back to Pittsburgh with you and your mom at this time. You know that I'll miss you, don't you?"

Mom and I did leave our home in Ohio a few weeks after school dismissed for summer vacation. I recalled, for many months after that horrible day, the agony I had experienced as I tearfully clutched my daddy's hand at the train station, hoping against hope that he would have a last-minute change of heart and board the train with us.

For the present time, I tried to console myself over the loss of my dad with the fact that I would once again be back with my granny and the rest of my family in Pittsburgh. I had been assured that my garden, the wooded areas that I frequented, and all my old friends would be waiting there for me. Daddy told me to "bite my lip and handle it like a little soldier." I promised him through a myriad of tears that I would try, even though I knew in my heart that it would take a long time to rid myself of the horrendous pain of separation that I was experiencing at this moment. I was remembering with dismay how I had felt that day two years ago when I had to say good-bye to Granny and the rest of the family. The very thought that this same scenario was being repeated devastated me.

We moved into the stone house that belonged to my Uncle Clyde and Aunt Harriet once again. This had been our home before leaving for Ohio. My old bedroom was just as I had left it and perhaps should have served as a source of comfort to me. For whatever reason, it failed to accomplish this purpose. I felt alone and confused. The adults in my life appeared to be oblivious of the effect this constant upheaval was having on me. I tried to talk to Granny about my feelings, to no avail. For some reason unbeknown to me, Grandma, Grandpa, and Uncle Henry had moved out of the big house and were living in the small bungalow adjacent to us. Grandpa had originally owned several acres of ground where our houses presently stood, and this house was on the property when we had moved from the city. Everything else appeared to be the same on the surface, but to me, it was very different from what it had been when I left for Girard with Mom two years before.

It appeared, much to my dismay, that nothing stays the same. All things are subject to change. This was very unnerving to a nine-year-old child who longed for some sense of permanency.

CHAPTER 4
DISASTER STRIKES

Shortly after returning to the Pittsburgh area I began to notice definite changes in my mother. Even though I had spent much more time with my grandma in previous years than I did with Mom, my mom had always been there for me when I needed her to fix a skinned knee or tuck me securely into my bed each night. She had always treated me with love and understanding when I was with her, though she seemed to be preoccupied with secret thoughts much of the time which she never expressed openly.

She had taken a job in downtown Pittsburgh as a bookkeeper to support us, both before and after we lived with Dad, so it went without saying that she was tired most evenings after the dinner dishes had been put away. More often than not, she would retire to her room and insisted that I do the same so that I wouldn't disturb my aunt and uncle who enjoyed quiet evenings at home when they had completed the demands of their challenging careers each day.

Indeed, my mother had a reputation for having a quick and nasty temper and would sometimes fly off the handle for no obvious reason. Because of this, I made every effort to distance myself from her on the occasions that this would occur.

Now that my grandparents were living in another house, I naturally interacted more with Mom than I had done before going to Ohio. I began to notice that she was becoming very impatient with my childish antics. I had always tormented my younger cousin Janice. I called her Neecie, which infuriated her. She would insist that her name was Janice and she didn't want to be called Neecie. I countered with the fact that she called me Mame.

I reminded her that my name was not Mame but Mara. If she wanted to be called by her real name, I had the right to be called by my given name as well. This argument would invariably result in tears of indignation on Janice's part. The end result was that I would be sent to my room for the remainder of the day. With the punishment would be an admonishment from my mother that, because I was five years older than Janice, I should know better than to argue over insignificant things.

Relationship with my cousin was becoming intolerable as far as I was concerned. The more I attempted to eliminate her from my life, the more she pursued me. I would chase her home when she followed me into the woods where I planned to meet with my friends. She followed me when the neighborhood gang would get together to play baseball or kick the can. She always wanted to be part of the activities but, being five years younger than I, she was not capable of doing the things that my friends and I did. I considered her a thorn in my side, a real nuisance.

Nevertheless, each time I chased her home and Mom was not at work, I would hear, within five or ten minutes of her tearful departure, my mother's enraged voice demanding that I return home immediately. Her voice was loud and appeared to reverberate throughout the neighborhood. Having chased Janice home, I anticipated such a reaction from my mother and was programmed to respond immediately. This did not endear my little cousin to me one bit. It became a source of extreme embarrassment because my friends were aware of what was happening and tormented me for not being smart enough to lose Janice in the woods on my way to meeting them.

In the beginning, it would be punishment by sending me to my room. This was bad enough. But when this type of correction didn't seem to have the desired effect, I would be met by an irate mother wielding a yardstick or a cat-o'-nine-tails, which she used effectively on the appropriate area of my anatomy.

More and more frequently, I would retreat to my grandparents' home so that I could experience once again the love and understanding that I had always known with my beloved granny. But again, I became painfully aware that her attitude toward me appeared to be changing as well. Instead of being sympathetic to my situation, she seemed always to side with my mother. She would remind me that it was my duty to be obedient to my mother even if her requirements seemed to be too strict and her discipline too extreme. Granny advised me not to cause my mom any grief because she was not well.

I didn't understand any of this. Certainly, I couldn't see anything physically wrong with my mom. She looked the same as she had always looked. I did notice that she had begun to spend much more time in her bedroom than she had previously done. There were afternoons when I would return home from school and find her still in bed. The door would be closed, which was a signal to me not to disturb her. She had quit her bookkeeping position with the large steel company in the city where she had been employed since our return to the Pittsburgh area.

She explained that the workload was getting increasingly larger as the company continued to grow, adding more and more accounts for her to handle. The company had offered her a substantial increase in pay to compensate for this, but she turned in her resignation in spite of the fact that her department head had urged her not to leave. Evidently, her bookkeeping skills had been outstanding and they didn't want to lose a good employee. It was much later when I learned what really happened. Mom had been fired from her position due to incompetence and her inability to get along with many of the people she worked with.

She must have sensed my concern that she had left such a good-paying position and that the money we needed to live comfortably would no longer be available. She assured me that when her health improved, she would seek employment once again. In the meantime, it would be necessary for both of us to "pull our belts a little tighter" until this crisis passed.

My dad was sending me checks twice a month to cover school expenses with a little extra for those "things that girls my age liked to buy." Other than that, we were living on Mom's savings which she had accrued since we returned home.

Life for me was changing rapidly and I didn't like any of it. Why could things never remain the same? We were so happy in Girard living with Daddy, or at least I thought so. I was beginning to realize that kids think differently than grown-ups. A kid's life is simple and mostly fun. If we have people around us whom we love and they love us in return, friends whom we like to spend time with doing things we all like to do-- life is good.

Not so with adults. It seemed to me that their lives were filled with anxiety about so many unimportant things. Would there be enough money to take that much-desired vacation? Why was it so important that Mom wanted to buy a house when Dad didn't? What caused Mom to fly into a tantrum if Dad stayed out late with his friends some nights?

During the last several months of our brief stay in Ohio, I had become increasingly aware that Mom and Dad were not as happy together as they had been when we first moved there. We had a nice apartment on the second floor of my cousin's big older home. Dad had a job as a bartender at the local Eagles club and worked part-time in Youngstown doing artistic design and window dressing in the two major department stores located there.

Mom had made a few new friends with ladies who needed a fourth player for their bridge club. I made many new friends at school, some of whom lived in my neighborhood. Of course, we had Daddy's enormous family who all lived in the area. We visited all of them often, and my cousins and I, along with our dads, would invariably get together to play baseball. On the surface everything appeared to be going well—but was it? Deep down inside, there had been a new and unfamiliar feeling of uneasiness gnawing at me. Though I couldn't identify the reason for this, I sensed that things were going to change once again. My observations and unexplained feelings of impending doom soon became a reality, for change they did.

Mom and I, without my precious daddy, moved into my Aunt Harriet and Uncle Clyde's home once again. This is where Mom and I had lived before moving to Ohio.

For the duration of the summer, I was able to console myself with the thought of being separated from Daddy. I missed him terribly but was happy to be reunited with my family and neighborhood friends. The empty plot of ground where my garden had been was now overgrown with weeds. No one had touched it—not even Gracie. Grandma must have known that I would return one day and have another garden beside hers. My precious woods remained unchanged, and the thought of returning to the enchantment that I found there gave me the assurance that this was my real home. I didn't have Grandma or the garden or the woods in Ohio. I assured myself that everything would work out well. Daddy would be joining us as soon as he could, I told myself.

I reentered the parochial school that I had left two years before. Being reunited with some of the school friends to whom I had to say good-bye was a happy event in my life. The sister who taught fourth grade was kind and patient with her students. Her teaching ability was extraordinary. She had a way that made everything she taught us so interesting that we kids thoroughly enjoyed our year with her. We had learned much from Sister Andrew Marie.

With the Christmas holiday over we moved swiftly into spring and the warm May weather. The fragrant smell of wildflowers blooming in the woods and the many birds busy building new nests to house their babies caused us to yearn for the great outdoors. We had mixed emotions about leaving our fourth-grade experience behind us. We looked forward to the coming summer vacation, of course, but were saddened by the thought of leaving this wonderful nun whom we had all come to love.

One Friday afternoon, shortly before school was scheduled to end for summer vacation, I was called into the principal's office. Sister Thomasine, usually stern and unsmiling in her mannerism, was strangely gentle as she looked up from her desk when I opened the door to her office.

"Mara, your mother has been taken to the hospital. I believe that your Aunt Darlene and your Uncle Len were called early this morning after you left for school. They have come to Pittsburgh to handle this situation. Your uncle is waiting for you outside, and I am giving you permission to be dismissed a little early. Get your things together, dear. You have my permission to go with your uncle."

That was all. Nothing more was said. This ominous feeling that had been gripping my entire being for some time now was becoming a reality. My worst fears were being realized. I hurried back to my homeroom, my heart pounding wildly in my chest.

What in the world was wrong? What could have happened to my mother? Was she still alive? Had she had an accident in our house while she was alone there with no one around to help her? Why was it necessary for Aunt Dar and Uncle Len to come here right now? They were expected to make their regular semi-monthly visit to Pittsburgh next week. Why were they here a week early?

I retrieved my book bag and lunch bucket from the coatroom which was adjacent to the fourth-grade homeroom. I literally bolted the length of the long corridor that led to the parking lot where I knew I would find my Uncle Len waiting for me. My Uncle Lenny was a great guy. I really loved him and Aunt Dar. Uncle Len treated me as though I were an intelligent grown-up person, capable of understanding that life was full of challenging situations that each of us must face sooner or later.

He made me feel important because he treated me like an adult when everyone else in the family never seemed to allow me to forget that I was the first grandchild born into our large family. He made it very clear to me that it was the way we handled these situations that made the difference. Many people, he said, were weak. They wanted everything to be just perfect all the time. When a situation developed that brought their world crashing down, they couldn't face it. They fell apart. If they had been taught to use that situation as a means to grow stronger, before long they would be capable of facing any adversity that came their way.

Uncle Lenny saw me as I rounded the bend of the walk leading to where he had parked. Our eyes met at exactly the same time. I could see the concern on his kind but now somber face as he jumped out of his side of the car and made his way around the front to open the door for me. I literally fell into his outstretched arms as his long lanky frame bent down low to give me a loving embrace.

"Mar, honey, I guess it's your turn to begin the growing-up process that we've talked about. You're kind of young to have to face what's ahead for you, but I think that you're going to be okay. This is one of those things in life that can either make or break a person, no matter what age he or she may be."

"Where's my mom, Uncle Len, and how come you and Aunt Dar came to Pittsburgh this week? What's going on? Is she all right, and where's Aunt Dar?"

As Uncle Len straightened his long slender frame, he took a deep breath and grabbed my free hand. "Mara, Aunt Darlene is over at St. Joe's Hospital with your mom. Your mom had a nervous breakdown, honey. From what I understand, one of your neighbors saw her on the roof of your house threatening to jump. I guess the neighbor was able to talk her out of it long enough for her dad, who was in the house, to get the police and the fire truck. By the time both vehicles arrived, your mom had settled down somewhat. The firemen extended their ladder and gently and safely brought her down off the roof to the yard below after a period of coaxing."

I was horrified. Evidently, Uncle Lenny realized that I needed more of an explanation than he had given me so far.

"Look, honey, your mom isn't well. It's not her body that is sick. It's her mind. She's been thinking wrong thoughts for a long time, and her thoughts have gotten out of control. You know how people explain it? They call it stinkin' thinkin'. Aunt Dar and I discussed the situation driving here this morning. My aunt, Sister Mary Francis, is the Administrator of St. Joseph's Hospital. We decided that we would take her over there for observation. She will get good care with the people at the hospital, and they will assign her to a doctor who will be able to get to the root of the problem.

"Now, Mar, I'm going to give it to you straight because I think that you need to know what is going on here," he continued. A look of extreme concern overshadowed his usually easygoing, carefree facial expression. "It generally takes about two weeks for the doctors to make a true evaluation as to what the problem is. During that time your mom will be in the hospital where they can keep an eye on her at all times."

I was hanging on every word as he attempted to let me know what I would have to face over the next weeks, perhaps months. At one point, I shut him off. I didn't want to hear any more of this nightmare I was now living. I just wanted to wake up one sunny morning and find that it had all been a bad dream. I thought about the recurring dream I had had over the past several months about a large pack of wild dogs chasing me.

In my dreams, I managed to keep just one step ahead of the lead dog. Then I woke up, bathed in perspiration, to find myself alone in my comfortable bed. It had just been a bad dream. I was so relieved that it was just a dream. But now, as I became aware of my uncle's voice, I realized that this was real. My mom was sick, so sick that my aunt and uncle had to come to Pittsburgh in a hurry and take her to the hospital. I suddenly felt sick to my stomach. I thought that I was going to throw up right there on the parking lot. I held it back, and the wave of nausea passed as quickly as it had come on me. I was so relieved. I didn't want to be sick with Uncle Lenny watching me.

Once again, that old familiar feeling of total hopelessness grasped my entire being. What was I to do? My whole world was turning inside out and upside down.

I'm just a kid, I thought to myself, *but I can't run away from this. Mom needs me to be brave now while she is sick. I have to stand strong like Daddy and Uncle Len said.*

The words of my Uncle Lenny became so real to me now as I realized that I had become the imaginary person he had been describing. This is the kind of trouble that people have to go through sometime in life. When they do, they must make a decision at that time. Can they face it directly and allow time and circumstances to work it out, or do they fall under the heavy weight of the problem too weak to deal with it? This one incident becomes a turning point that can change a person's life forever. Somehow, even at my young age, I realized that this was a strategic crossroad that I had come to. It was critical that I make the correct choice. Evidently, my mother had come to a crossroad in her life a short time ago and had made the wrong choice. I must not repeat this in my own life.

At that moment, I wanted my daddy to be with me, or Granny. They loved me. They would know what to do to make this bad dream go away. But it was the sound of Uncle Lenny's voice that broke into my deep, dark thoughts.

"Listen to me, honey," he said. "Everything is going to work out for you and your mom. This is what Aunt Dar and I have decided to do. She will stay here with you until school lets out in two weeks. Then I will come and get you two and take you back to our house for the summer. We can all come to Pittsburgh together to visit your mom while she is in the hospital. We're only allowed to visit her once every two weeks while she is under observation anyhow, so this plan should work out just fine.

"In the meantime, I'm going to get in touch with your dad. He will have to make a few decisions of his own. Maybe he will decide to return to this area and find work in the city so he can be close to you. Let's just take one step at a time, okay, Mar?" he concluded briskly, adding that some changes were about to occur in my life, and he felt confident that I would be strong enough to handle them—one hurdle at a time.

I spent the entire summer with Aunt Dar and Uncle Len at their home in the country in a pretty little town called Poland. It was only an hour's drive from where my dad lived in Girard, so things worked out better than we had expected. I got to see Daddy much more often than I did when I lived in the Pittsburgh area.

Aunt Dar and Uncle Len had a nice home with a built-in swimming pool in their huge backyard. They had a cute little dog named Pity that took an immediate liking to me. We became fast friends for the time I spent with my aunt and uncle that summer. I felt love and concern from these two wonderful people. They filled a huge gap in my life created by the temporary loss of my mom and my grandmother, whom I had to say good-bye to once again. This time, however, I knew that I would be returning to the Pittsburgh area when school resumed in the fall.

It was a good summer, except for the times that I had to visit Mom at the hospital. The first time we visited, I didn't recognize my mother. She had lost a lot of weight, and the simple blue hospital garb that she was required to wear hung in folds around her thin body. She was not permitted to have a belt of any type to fasten around her waist. Her hair, though recently washed and brushed, was not the style that I was accustomed to seeing on my mom. It had grown to shoulder-length by the time I was finally permitted a visit and it hung limply around her face.

What I dreaded most about these visits was the expression on her face. Her once-piercing blue eyes had become dull and lifeless. The only time her facial expression changed was when I walked into the visitors' room with members of my family. When she saw me, she would burst into tears and then quickly turn away in an effort to hide the emotional turmoil that was erupting inside of her. The initial visit had been a shock to all of us because the change in her was so extreme. Other than that one outburst of emotion, she sat silently in her chair, staring straight ahead until the visit was ended. The nurses and those other aides attending her made every effort to bring her out of her shell, to no avail.

After a few visits, my aunt and uncle decided that this experience was traumatizing me and made the decision that I would not be put through the agony of future visits to the hospital for the present time. Should there be a marked improvement in her condition after the shock therapy was completed, I would accompany them to the hospital.

To my extreme relief, I was permitted to stay at a neighbor's home on the days that they travelled to Pittsburgh to see my mother. The girl who lived there and I had become fast friends during the summer. She came to swim with me in my aunt and uncle's pool on hot days, and we would ride our bikes together on days when the weather was cooler.

I did not see my mother again for several weeks. When I returned home in late August to prepare for fifth grade, I was taken to the state hospital a few miles from where our home was located to visit her. She had been transferred there after her treatments were completed. The prognosis was not good. Mom had not improved appreciably as her doctors had hoped. As bad as the experience had been of visiting her at St. Joseph's Hospital, the state hospital was intolerable. I dreaded each subsequent visit, which I made twice a month with various members of my family.

The large sparsely furnished room where the attendants brought the patients to meet their visitors was drab and void of any cheerfulness. The wooden floors were bare, except for a few oval-shaped cotton throw rugs that had been placed under small tables or in front overstuffed couches. On visitation day, several straight-backed chairs were brought into the room and placed around each couch for the benefit of those visiting the patients. This arrangement afforded a small amount of privacy for the families to visit their loved ones without too much interruption from the other patients.

There were no lamps in the room, no pictures on the walls, nothing anywhere that could be picked up and thrown at an attendant or another patient. The only lighting came from the several barred windows located on the outside wall. On sunny days the sunrays would filter through these windows into the room creating a small amount of cheer. On dull days, however, the room was almost dark and so very depressing.

All the patients were women. The male patients had their own building and were kept segregated from the women. Many times during visiting hour one or more of the patients would become agitated about some imaginary thing going on in their heads and would pick a fight with one of the other patients. When this happened two or three of the attendants on duty would be alerted to take these disturbed women out of the visiting area. There were times when they were literally dragged out by the attendants, kicking and screaming.

It was difficult for me as a child not to shrink from these experiences, but over time, I had become somewhat immune to them. What I could not fathom was the drastic change in my mother's appearance in such a short period of time. It was so painful to see how much she was changing. From what I had been told, mom had been the prettiest of the six sisters born to my grandparents. She had loved to dance in her early years and, as a result, she had had a marvelous figure.

Often as a child, I would look at her in total admiration, hoping that when I grew up I would look just like her. I know that Daddy thought that she was very pretty too. The two years that we all lived together in Ohio he would tell me so. Jokingly he would comment that it was too bad that I looked like him instead of Mom.

"Daddy, don't be silly," I would counter. "You're very handsome, like the movie star who played your favorite baseball player in that movie you took me to see. I don't mind looking like you now. But when I grow up to be a lady, I want to look like Mommy."

As I watched my mother deteriorate right before my eyes, month after month, I came to the realization that when someone gets sick like Mommy did, everything changes for the worse. The one who gets sick doesn't look the same and doesn't act the same anymore.

I remember asking God not to let this happen to me when I grew up. Somehow, even as a child, God was in my life during this difficult time. He answered that prayer many years later.

CHAPTER 5
THE DOWNWARD SPIRAL

Over the next few years Mom began to show signs of improvement. The head psychiatrist and his team had assessed her progress and made the decision to release her into the custody of my Aunt Harriet and Uncle Clyde. This was a rather simple matter since Mom and I lived with my aunt and uncle. Although they were both gone during the day, my grandparents and other close relatives were nearby to assist in case anything unforeseen occurred to necessitate returning her to the institution. I was at school during the day but I would be home with her during the late afternoon and evening hours and on weekends.

My dad who had been called at the request of my Uncle Lenny when Mom had her initial breakdown relocated to Pittsburgh. He and Uncle Clyde had never gotten along with each other. That issue, coupled with the fact that he would be in the same house with Mom, would have undoubtedly complicated the situation since they were now legally separated.

My grandparents offered him the use of the empty dormitory rooms on the second floor of their little bungalow. He readily accepted their invitation and, in short order, he converted the empty rooms into a comfortable apartment. He evidently felt that this would be a good move for him at this particular time. My life was in a state of uncertain change and, evidently, he felt that it was his duty as my father to be near me where he could support me emotionally as well as financially. He took a job with a large popular downtown department store, where he quickly became the head window dresser.

Although Dad was elated that his talent had been recognized in a city the size of Pittsburgh, I sensed his discontent at having to leave his hometown and family in Ohio. He would assure me that he was putting my welfare first because I was the most important person in his life, and he wanted to do what was right for me. Somehow, I wasn't convinced that my father was being totally sincere. As a matter of fact, his discontent made me feel guilty. It was because of me that he had agreed to relocate to an area that uprooted him from his family and familiar environment. His carefree, jovial manner had changed. He had become much more serious-minded and just wasn't as much fun to be with as I had remembered him to be a few years before. It was obvious that he was burdened by thoughts of having to leave his hometown.

His mom, my Grandmother Carothers, had been diagnosed with incurable stomach cancer several years before Mom and I had joined Daddy in Ohio. Although her type of cancer was slow-moving, it continued to linger and would not allow her to die. She languished year after year in my Uncle Bernie's home where his wife, my Aunt May, cared for her. Dad was very close to my Grandma Carothers, and I knew that watching her die a slow, torturous death was tearing him apart. It had to be very difficult for him to leave his dying mother in order to be with me during this tumultuous time in both of our lives. Dad had never liked the Pittsburgh area, and I could see that if circumstances had been different, he would not have returned.

Mom's release from the mental institution appeared to have a positive effect on her condition. Over the next several months, her health, both mental and physical, improved appreciably. Gradually she began to take on the responsibility of assuming some household chores once again. She had always been an excellent cook; and to my Aunt Harriet's great relief, both she and my Uncle Clyde, upon their return home from work each evening, would find a well-prepared meal waiting for them. Mom also began to do the routine housework and enlisted my assistance on Fridays after school in completing it for the weekend. She felt that I was old enough now to help out on a regular basis around the house. I happily did whatever needed to be done, grateful that I had my mom back and signs of her returning to normalcy were becoming more evident each day.

I visited my dad on a regular basis at his apartment in my grandparents' home. I was old enough now to realize that Dad was entertaining female company with some frequency. The signs were everywhere—lipstick smudges on cigarette butts in unemptied ashtrays, earrings, and other female apparel left on end tables or draped over chairs—the smell of stale perfume permeating the small apartment. He made no attempt to hide the evidence.

It had been my hope that, now that Mom was recuperating so rapidly, she and Dad would give it one more try, if not for their sakes, perhaps for mine. I couldn't have been more wrong. Evidently, Dad had had enough of the ups and downs of marriage with a wife who, for reasons of her own, couldn't live up to his expectations of what a wife should be.

As far as my mother was concerned, she seemed oblivious to what my father was doing. Her primary concern was that she would be able to return to complete normalcy as quickly as possible. This would enable her to become gainfully employed once again and have the ability to provide me with the things that were so important to a young teenager who would soon be preparing to enter high school and, later on, college.

Observing both of them and their apparent lack of interest in each other made me very sad.

What's wrong with these two people whom I so dearly loved? I wondered to myself. *If they loved each other when they decided to get married, why don't they love each other now? Didn't they take a vow when they got married that they would remain faithful to each other in sickness and in health, until death do us part? How could two people who were so in love at one time abandon that love so easily? What really happened?*

From the time I was old enough to know what it meant to be a part of a family, that's all I ever wanted, just to have a mom and dad who loved each other, who loved me, and for me to return that love. It didn't take me long to realize that this was never to be.

This fact became a reality. Within six months of my mother's discharge from the state hospital, Dad called me on the phone one Friday after school inviting me to spend the evening with him. He suggested a movie that I might like to see. Before the movie, he wanted to take me to a great new restaurant that he had found by accident in a nearby community. We had done this often when he first returned to Pittsburgh, and I had loved being with him. He had always treated me like his little princess.

He had set up an easel and a small table where I could keep my palate, brushes, oil paints, and other items required to do my artwork. This was my special place, a small corner of his living room that he dubbed Mara's happy corner. I was not permitted to go anywhere on weeknights because of homework. On weekends, however, I could often be found in Daddy's apartment, painting in my little happy corner while he attended to paperwork that he had brought home. We never said too much to each other during these quiet times together. Just being with him gave me a warm feeling of intimacy. It was almost like the two years when I had been with him in Ohio.

There was only one important element missing. Mom was not with us. Before leaving him in the evening he would put his work aside and carefully critique what I had accomplished with my painting. I was always eager to have him give me some constructive criticism where he saw fit to do so. I knew that I was learning new techniques that would enable me to improve my growing skill, and I was learning from a master.

But slowly over time, the strong father-daughter bond that we shared began to fade somewhat. The presence of other women in Daddy's apartment made me resentful. My mom's place was with my dad, and these other women were usurping her rightful position, I thought. Our times together were becoming less and less frequent. I had become interested in going roller-skating with my friends on Friday evenings. These were my very favorite friends, sisters who were a year and two years older than I.

Their dad never seemed to mind picking me up and taking me home after the session was finished. I'm sure Daddy would have offered to share the driving but, at this particular time, he did not have an automobile. He travelled to and from work by trolley and never seemed to mind not having local transportation. My grandmother did his cooking, so the few items he would require through the week he would pick up in the city before returning from work.

I was both pleasantly surprised and also apprehensive at the same time when he invited me to dinner and a movie on this particular Friday evening. We hadn't done this for some time, so I was especially anxious to share the evening with him. I was also a little suspicious as to his motive for this "special night out." I sensed that he had something important on his mind that he wanted to discuss with me. I felt a swell of pride that he would confide something to me that appeared to be of such importance. Perhaps he had observed that I was fast approaching adulthood and would be mature enough to share ideas with him on an adult level.

The feeling of apprehension proved to be quite accurate. What a bombshell he dropped! After the movie we came home and he invited me to go up to his apartment with him. He had something important come up that he wanted to talk to me about. We said hello to my grandparents and headed upstairs. He wasted little time getting right to the point.

"Mara, I got a call from Aunt May this morning. Your Grandmother Carothers has taken a turn for the worse. Dr. Gordon paid her a house visit last evening. He told Aunt May and Uncle Bernie that they had better think about getting the family together for quite possibly a last visit."

I drew in my breath and waited for him to continue. The thought of losing a member of my family was something I instinctively shrank from. I had not experienced losing a loved one as yet. True, I had had my share of grief to deal with over the past few years. But the death of a family member was not yet something I had experienced. Trouble could eventually work itself out, but death was something else. When a loved one died it was so final. That person whom you had loved was gone from your life, never to return. I had a friend in school who had lost her mom to cancer the previous year. It had to be the worst possible thing that could happen to anyone.

I looked intently at my father as he appeared to be having a struggle continuing the conversation. His eyes were filled with tears. I had never seen my dad cry before, and this depth of emotion in him nearly brought me to tears as well.

"Mara, honey," he managed to choke out his next words. "I'm…a…going to have to leave you for a while. We don't know how much time your grandmother has left to live. Aunt May said that she's been calling for me. I have to go to her. You understand, don't you?"

"Of course, I do, Dad. She's your mom, and you need to be with her. I can't go with you because of Mom and school and all that. Maybe I could come up on the train next weekend if someone will take me to the station."

"No, honey. You have enough to cope with right now. You stay here and take care of your mother. She needs you to be with her. I'll be back soon."

Strangely, his announcement didn't have the impact that I expected. I had been aware of the change taking place in him since his return to this area. This change was becoming especially apparent in recent weeks. The close relationship that we had was slowly dissipating. Something very important was missing, and I couldn't put my finger on it. There was change in me as well. I was beginning to put an invisible wall of protection around my emotions. There had been so much chaos and grief in my life over the past few years, I had programmed myself to accept adversity without reacting emotionally to it. It wasn't that I was hiding my true feelings. I had actually come to a place where those feelings no longer appeared to exist. I had successfully found a way to guard myself against future disappointment.

Daddy left for Ohio very early the next morning. We had said our good-byes the night before with his promise to return as soon as circumstances enabled him to do so. He had taken a six-week emergency leave of absence from work putting his apprentice in charge of his department until he returned.

I did not see my father again for many years. We got a phone call from Girard a few weeks after Daddy returned to his home state. The call was not from him. It was from Aunt May. Grandma Carothers had passed away peacefully the previous evening, with all members of her immediate family at her bedside. Daddy, she said, being the oldest son, had been appointed executor of her will. It would be necessary for him to remain in Ohio until the will was read. We waited for a letter or a phone call from him for several weeks which never came. It was as though he had fallen off the face of the earth--disappeared. It seemed that he ceased to exist. I wasn't surprised or disappointed. Something in my emotional makeup had prepared me for this.

My mother, on the other hand, did not handle this turn of events well. Although she had given the impression that she no longer had any interest in my father, she was unable to cope with his sudden disappearance, under what she considered the guise of having to be with his mother during her final days of life. When it became evident that he was not coming back to the Pittsburgh area, she exploded with rage and disbelief.

"How could he do this to you, Mara? How could he sneak away like he did, knowing full well that he wouldn't be back? How could he be so deceptive with your grandparents, leaving them to clean up the apartment that he left behind with all his belongings?"

Her accusations turned to ranting over the next few months. She became so disruptive in the presence of my aunt and uncle that, regretfully, my aunt was forced to tell us that we were no longer welcome to live in their home. My uncle, she said, absolutely would not tolerate this kind of uproar day in and day out. He needed peace and quiet when he returned from a stressful day at the plant.

Evidently, Aunt Harriet, because of the nursing background that she had, could foresee trouble brewing once again with Mom. Although my mother was not yet at the point of having another complete breakdown, the danger signs were in view. She had become embittered over Dad's actions and was taking her anger out on everyone with whom she came in contact.

My Aunt Marcie and Uncle Jack who lived nearby evidently had talked with Aunt Harriet regarding this unwelcome turn of events. Although they lived in a small three-bedroom Cape Cod just a stone's throw from my aunt and uncle's home, they had agreed to allow Mom and me to stay with them until more suitable arrangements could be made. They realized that we were in dire straits. Mom wasn't emotionally or financially able to make it on her own under the circumstances. Uncle Jack and Aunt Marcie knew that they would be strapped for bedroom space having my two other cousins, Jackie and Julie, as well as Janice, their older sister; but because we had nowhere to go, they decided to take us in. It was the right thing to do, they concluded.

It may have been the right thing to do, but the move created havoc for everyone involved. The two girls were forced out of their bedroom to accommodate my mother and me. Jackie ended up in the game room on a foldout daybed. He was forced to give up his bedroom to his two sisters. Once again, that uncomfortable feeling of guilt overtook me. In some strange way, I felt that this was my fault. Mom and I were being forced to be uprooted once again and we were the cause of putting another family in the state of chaotic change.

They felt that I was the one who was being affected the most by all this upheaval, and they were sympathetic to my many problems. I was now in my teen years and had no home of my own, no place to bring friends, nowhere to keep my personal belongings. They were doing the best that they knew how to do. But their best was not enough. I was miserably unhappy. I just wanted to die. Why did I have a "crazy" mother? How could my father, whom I had once adored, a daddy who could do no harm, suddenly walk out of my life without a word of explanation? Why couldn't I have a normal life like other kids? These questions plagued me day and night.

The desire to take my own life intensified over the next few weeks, until I began to secretly examine the various methods that might be available to me to accomplish this. I knew that Uncle Jack had a gun cabinet where he kept several different rifles. He was an avid deer hunter and went to Northern Pennsylvania each deer season to get his limit. But what could I do with a rifle? I couldn't shoot myself with a rifle. He had handguns too. But they were locked up and out of sight somewhere in the house. I considered other possibilities.

I would sneak down to the kitchen after everyone was in bed for the night and examine the knives in Aunt Marcie's knife drawer. I noticed that there was a certain knife among the others that would probably do the job. It was extremely sharp and pointed. I would remove it from its place in the drawer and hold it in my hand just to see how it felt. Could I slit my wrist? It would have to be a deliberate and deep thrust into my veins so that the job would be done correctly.

Did I have the nerve to do this, I wondered? There would be a lot of blood. I would be the cause of much anguish among my relatives. They had been kind enough to give us a place to live. Could I do something like this to them when they were good enough to allow Mom and me to move into their home when we were in such desperate need? How would Mom react to this? Would it cause her to have another emotional setback? No doubt it would.

Uncle Lenny's words continued to haunt me. He had said that when difficult times came into a person's life, that person would be required to make a choice. He or she could give up and check out or continue to fight the battle, knowing that, having stood firm, victory would come eventually, and the person would be stronger as a result. What choice would I make? This was one of those critical crossroads in my life.

These many questions remained unanswered because of immediate and unforeseen circumstances that occurred in rapid succession over the next few weeks.

One morning while I was preparing for school I noticed that the bathroom door was closed. Mom had not been in bed when I got up to turn off the alarm clock. I supposed that she had gotten out of bed to use the bathroom. I waited for several minutes and when there was no response, I knocked gently on the bathroom door. The response I heard coming from the other side of the door was unnerving.

"I can't come out, Mara. I locked myself in here, and I can't find my way out. Besides that, I've been trying to get these dark spots off my hands, and they won't come off. No matter how hard I scrub my hands, I can't get rid of them."

I finished dressing and then ran downstairs where Aunt Marcie was just getting up to call the kids for school. I told her what was going on in the upstairs bathroom. She immediately awakened Uncle Jack, who bolted up to the second floor and, unable to open the door, picked the lock with a wire clothes hanger. By this time, Aunt Marcie and I were by his side.

The open door revealed my mother kneeling by the tub frantically attempting to scrub away imaginary spots on her hands, which she found impossible to remove. The hot water was running in the tub and she had evidently burned her hands holding them under the spigot. They were red from the temperature of the water and the irritation that the toothbrush created in her attempt to remove the spots. She was very disturbed with the situation in which she found herself.

"Marcie, call an ambulance and tell them to get here as quickly as possible, will you? I'll get the kids up and ready for school. I can take them this morning because it looks like they're going to miss their buses with all this confusion. You and Mara get Liz dressed and ready to go. If she gives you a hard time tell her that you found a way to get rid of her spots. I think that she'll cooperate with you if she hears that."

Uncle Jack was great in dealing with emergencies. His own life was one of surviving many obstacles. I thought about this all the way to the hospital. I was so relieved that he had still been home. It's very likely that Aunt Marcie would have become frantic having to face a situation like this.

Nonetheless, Aunt Marcie and I were successful in convincing Mom that everything would be all right. The people in the ambulance would be able to take her to a place where the spots would be removed. It might take some time, we assured her, but they would take care of those spots. Throughout the entire ordeal of admitting Mom once again to St. Joseph's psychiatric division, I thought about Uncle Jack and the masterful way he handled the situation with Mom earlier this morning. Why couldn't I be like him and Uncle Lenny? They both had their acts together. These two men were winners—both of them. Both of my uncles had been through some of the rough bumps that life had them travel over, and both had come through like champions.

A small, almost imperceptible voice seemed to be speaking to me from deep down inside of me. *Mara, you can do this too. You can make the right choices and come out on the victory side. You just need some help, that's all. You don't have your mom and dad to help you and you can't do it alone. They made the wrong choices. That doesn't mean that you have to do the same. There is help for you. All you have to do is to look for it.*

Where did that thought come from? I wondered. How could I possibly have all these lofty thoughts about making right choices and overcoming obstacles when a few days ago I was considering the possibility of ending it all by slashing my wrists?

On our way home from the hospital, both my aunt and I were strangely silent. It was as though both of us had been drained of all energy during the events of the morning. Aunt Marcie broke the silence as she pulled her car into the driveway.

"Mara, I know how difficult life has been for you in recent years. But, honey, I know you, and you are a survivor. I know that you can make it through these rough times. Just hold on, sweetie cakes, and one day you will find that pot of gold at the end of the rainbow and I'm not talking about wealth or the tangible things that most people chase after. I'm talking about the real pot of gold at the end of the rainbow."

CHAPTER 6

A RAY OF SUNSHINE

We got the bad news from Dr. Sheridan a few days later. Mom's mental condition had become so unstable that he feared it would be several months before she would be well enough to return home. Our living conditions also played a large part in his decision to keep her at the hospital at this time. We really had no permanent place to live right now. The insecurity that such a situation created was, in itself, reason not to expose her to this type of environment.

Once again, Uncle Lenny's aunt, Sister Mary Francis, came to our rescue. She felt that our situation constituted a real hardship case. Coupled with the fact that we were close relatives of her nephew and that Aunt Dar had been supervisor of the psychiatric department of the hospital before giving up her position to relocate, Sister Mary Francis made the decision to keep Mom at St. Joe's for whatever length of time it would require to get her back on her feet.

Besides, the doctor had ordered another round of electric shock treatments for Mom. These treatments were very difficult to endure from what I could observe. Each time that we visited with her immediately following shock therapy, Mom would be frantic to be released from the horror being forced upon her. Although she did appear somewhat improved after each of these treatments, she pleaded with us to take her home. She felt that the doctors and hospital staff were attempting to kill her and, with each treatment, would very soon accomplish their purpose.

I stayed with Aunt Marcie and Uncle Jack for the duration of the year. Janice and I had remained mortal enemies because of the way I had treated her in previous years. Though she no longer tagged along with her older cousin, she was still feeling the pricks of rejection that I had inflicted upon her as a little girl. Our relationship created a significant amount of stress in the home. Though Uncle Jack advised Janice repeatedly to treat me with a little kindness, the past hurts that had been deeply rooted within her would not permit her to do so. As far as I was concerned, I had too many weighty problems on my mind to concern myself with my younger cousin's petty grievances. For the most part, I ignored her efforts to start an argument. Occasionally though my thinning patience would come to an end and we would end up in a proverbial sparring match.

My aunt and uncle put up with this nonsense for as long as they could. Weighing all of the circumstances, they had attempted to keep some semblance of order in the home. My relationship with Janice was causing problems between Jackie and Julie. When they became aware that their parents had relaxed some of the rules of the household governing sibling behavior, they began to squabble with each other as well.

I was smart enough to realize that my presence was the primary cause of all this discord in what had once been a peaceful, happy family unit. At this point, I began to entertain thoughts of suicide once again. Why was this stigma on my life? What did I do to deserve all this? Was I really an evil person receiving the wrath of God for my sinful life?

I really didn't expect an answer to my emotional plea. Nonetheless, this self-examination was enough to make me realize that somehow, some way, I had to hold on. Mom's condition hadn't improved for months, but still there was a possibility that one day she would begin to stabilize once again as she had done in the past.

Should this happen, where would we go? We're running out of family members who would take us into their homes, I conjectured.

Mara, you must live one day at a time. Didn't I tell you that the answer to your dilemma is right before your eyes? All you have to do is look for it and wait for it to become a reality.

There it was again. That inner awareness that things were going to work out no matter how impossible life seemed. Where did that come from?

I did not have to wait long to find out what that inner voice seemed to be telling me.

Aunt Marcie and Uncle Jack had evidently called Uncle Lenny and Aunt Dar and explained the dilemma they were in because I was living in their home. Aunt Dar suggested that perhaps I could stay with their youngest sister, Tammy, and her husband, Hank, for a while.

Aunt Tammy had always been my role model. She was pretty, energetic, and popular in high school, and I idolized her. Since she was only eleven years older than I, she was like a big sister to me, the sister I never had. She had married her childhood sweetheart four years earlier, and they recently had their first child, a baby girl whom they named Rene. Aunt Tammy had come down with some kind of a mysterious illness shortly after the baby was born. Although she had been seen by several specialists in the Pittsburgh area, no one was able to diagnose her condition.

My Uncle Hank, anxious to get to the root of the problem so that Aunt Tammy could be properly treated and able to regain her health quickly, took her to the Mayo Clinic in Minnesota. They spent two weeks there and she underwent numerous tests to uncover this mysterious illness she had fallen prey to.

Unfortunately, the prognosis was not good. The specialists assigned to her case were of one mind regarding her illness. They diagnosed her with a rare disease known as myasthenia gravis, which causes deterioration of the muscles. At the onset of the illness, the facial area and the throat are affected. In the event the patient survived beyond that point, the muscular system in general would be affected throughout the body. There was no known cure for this disease.

This was a devastating blow to the family. We were a close-knit group who cared very much for one another. Everyone in the family was overwhelmed at my mother's situation. But severe as it was, there was hope for her. Aunt Tammy did not have that in her favor; plus, she had a young husband and a two-year-old child. Her life and that of her family was just beginning.

As her health deteriorated, it became increasingly difficult for her to carry on with her daily chores. They had already placed Rene in the care of a sitter for most of the day until Uncle Hank got home from work to take over.

Uncle Lenny and Aunt Dar had come from Ohio over the weekend to visit Mom at the hospital and to spend some time with Aunt Tammy, Uncle Hank, and Rene.

Both my aunt and uncle were appalled at the rapid deterioration of Tammy's health. It must have been at this point that the suggestion was made to have me move in with them and help with Rene and some of the housework and cooking. This would help them out considerably, and it would lighten Aunt Marcie and Uncle Jack's burden at the same time.

When I was told about my next move, I was both relieved and resentful: relieved that I would be leaving my present situation and resentful because, once again, I was being moved around like a checker piece on a giant play board. I tried to look at the bright side of this new development. I would have a bedroom of my own once again and no one would be messing with my things while I was at school. I truly loved my Aunt Marcie and Uncle Jack, but the kids got on my nerves. Janice was always spoiling for a fight in an effort to put the blame on me for having initiated it. Jackie and Julie were okay but very noisy. I guess being an only child and being left alone when I wanted to be alone was an established way of life for me for as long as I could remember. The constant noise was very annoying.

On the other hand, it would be difficult living with Aunt Tammy, whom I absolutely idolized. It made me sad to realize that she was so desperately ill. She had lost a lot of weight because the muscles in her throat had deteriorated to the point that she could not swallow anything solid. Her entire menu consisted of soups, puddings, and Cream of Wheat. After being in their home for a few months, I noticed that she had to hold her mouth in place, and sometimes it was necessary for her to use her index finger to hold her left eyelid open. It seemed as though each week she was losing ground. She prayed a lot and carried rosary beads around with her as she slowly and painfully made her way through the house.

What good was a rosary bead now? The Blessed Mother appears to be busy with more important matters. I was becoming very cynical about religion at an early age.

What have we done, God, to deserve all the misery we're experiencing in this family of ours? First, my mother has a mental breakdown. Then Dad leaves early one morning, never to be heard from again. Now this—my favorite aunt, with a two-year-old child, dying of some strange disease at an early age. It seemed so unfair, so unjust.

What would happen to my little Rene if her mom died? What about Uncle Hank? They had been married such a short time. They were so in love and had so many plans for their future together.

My time spent with Aunt Tammy and Uncle Hank turned out to be of brief duration. I had enjoyed taking care of Rene. She helped me forget about the mess my life had become. Rene was a sweet little toddler and very easy to care for. Because her mom hadn't been able to provide her with the time and attention a two-year-old requires, the transition from Aunt Tammy to me as her caretaker was easy. Rene took a liking to me immediately because I was able to spend a lot of time with her after school and on weekends. She would be at the living-room window each weekday when I returned from school. As I entered the house, she would run to me, emitting a squeal of delight as I scooped her up in my arms and held her tiny frame close to me.

I didn't do quite so well with the cooking as with the childcare, but Uncle Hank and I worked together with the dinners. Breakfast and lunch were easy—cereal for breakfast and a sandwich and soup for lunch and jarred junior food for Rene. Of course, Tammy was limited to soft foods only, so planning her meals was quite simple.

The situation that caused yet another upheaval in my life was due to the fact that Aunt Tammy's condition was worsening so rapidly. Uncle Hank knew that I was not equipped to handle the required nursing care to keep Aunt Tammy comfortable through her remaining weeks or months of life. At this point, he felt the necessity of securing the assistance of a registered nurse who would be qualified to assume this responsibility twenty-four hours a day. This meant that the bedroom I now occupied would have to be given up to provide the nurse with overnight accommodations.

Once again I would be without a bedroom and a place to keep my things. Uncle Hank assured me that he would attempt to make a place for me in their home. Hank was a carpenter and had begun to convert their open basement into a finished game room when Tammy became ill. He didn't know how long it would take him to complete this project, but he was determined to keep me with them for as long as I was willing to stay. Rene loved me and would miss me if it became necessary for me to leave her.

Leave her? How could I leave her? I wondered. *I have nowhere to go. The only family members I have left are my grandparents, who I feel would be happy to have me move in with them. But what if Mom gets a discharge from the hospital sometime in the future? She couldn't live in my grandparents' house because Uncle Henry lives there. Grandma has her hands full just taking care of Grandpa and Uncle Henry. Now that my dad is gone their income isn't sufficient to feed all of us.*

That old familiar feeling of panic gripped me as I struggled with this latest development. *Is this my lot in life, to search endlessly for somewhere to live, a place where I can call home and be comfortable in knowing that I'm secure in that place?*

Once again, through a sudden turn of events that occurred a few weeks later, I wondered if, out there somewhere, unbeknown to me, there was something or someone in the vast universe responding to my concerns and taking care of my immediate needs. It certainly seemed that way. But after what I had been through, I doubted it. Because of my religious upbringing, I knew that there had to be a God or a higher power. I just couldn't figure out what role he played in my life. He certainly didn't appear to be interested in me and my miserable existence. Though I attended a parochial school and would be expected to continue my high school education next year in a Catholic high school, I really didn't believe much of their hogwash anymore. God couldn't possibly be interested in his creation. Look what He had allowed to happen to my family and me.

Nonetheless, I was having a difficult time believing what I had just learned. Evidently, Aunt Dar and Uncle Lenny had spoken with Sister Mary Francis during their most recent visit with my mother. The news was good for a change. Mom was responding beautifully to the newest medication she was receiving for her condition. She had been diagnosed as being manic depressive. The series of electric shock treatments was complete, and this new miracle drug was being given to her. The hospital was ready to release her for a period of three months as a trial to determine if she could adapt to living on the outside once again. The only problem was that she had no place to live at this time.

Later, when I had the opportunity to speak with Uncle Lenny and Aunt Dar privately, Aunt Dar revealed to me that Aunt Harriet had made a decision to turn the stone house over to me permanently. She and Uncle Clyde had experienced a turn of unexpected events in their lives as well. Although Uncle Clyde was a brilliant metallurgist and an asset to the company that had hired him several years before, he had received a pink slip, terminating his employment.

He had reached the company's "magic number." This was a calculated move on the part of this company at which time employees were evaluated on the basis of their continued usefulness. At age fifty-five they knew that, looking ahead to the time of retirement, they may not want to pay out this additional money plus more than adequate retirement benefits the company was under contract to pay, unless the employee who was being evaluated would be useful to them between age fifty-five and that date.

There was no question regarding Uncle Clyde's ability. The problem that existed was due to the fact that he had developed a new and inexpensive method of tempering steel. Before he had an opportunity to patent this process, the company took all the rights away from him to do so. They maintained that, because he was their employee, any invention of his that would be useful to the company belonged to them.

He was bitter about this decision because he had done all this work on his own time and at his own expense. He felt that he had been robbed by a company in which he had invested many years of his life, serving them faithfully.

The result of the decision he made regarding this unfortunate incident played a major part in my receiving this home, which I loved and had grown up in before the tragic turn of events involving my mother and her illness.

Aunt Harriet confided in Aunt Dar, confessing that she had regretted asking Mom and me to leave the only home I had ever known at such a critical time in our lives. As she observed me having to move from one house to another like a "little gypsy," she had grown more and more convinced that somehow she and Uncle Clyde had to make it up to us. When he lost his job and found another opportunity for employment in Central Pennsylvania, she immediately saw the chance to clear her conscience of wrongdoing. Since they had accumulated a good amount of savings in the many years they had been employed in high-paying positions, he had no qualms about doing this.

Within one week the stone house became mine. It was placed in a trust, stipulating that it was mine to sell, rent, or keep at age twenty-one. Until that time, it was understood that it was mine to live in if I chose to do so.

Did I choose to live there? What a question. Of course, I chose to live there. Finally I had a home that I could call my own. Now the hospital would release Mom because the conditions were right for her discharge—even if it was on a temporary basis. I just knew in my heart of hearts that this was the answer to our dilemma. Mom would finally have a place to call home without the constant fear of being told that she was not welcome there.

I was elated. This was a red-letter day in my life. Finally our problems were behind us. I could breathe easily once again.

Mom did return home a few weeks later. My aunt and uncle had gone to New Holland, a small Amish community near Lancaster, Pennsylvania, a week before. They would be renting a furnished home until they found a house that they liked well enough to buy. Because of this decision, we were left with a fully furnished house. There was no need, at least for the present, to scrape up sufficient money to purchase necessary furnishings that we would need when my aunt and uncle were ready to move their present furnishings to their new residence.

When Mom had recovered totally and had found another bookkeeping job, there would be plenty of time to replace whatever things we needed. We could do this one item at a time if need be. It would be fun redecorating and replacing the things that had belonged to my aunt and uncle.

Finally, after four long and painful years of uncertainty and grief, the black cloud that seemed to hover over my head constantly was beginning to disappear. Behind that cloud, I could see the sun shining through.

CHAPTER 7

AN UNEXPECTED
TURN OF EVENTS

It was a warm spring day in mid-April when Mom was released from St. Joseph's Hospital. Swollen buds were beginning to burst from the branches of many of the trees in our yard, displaying their first hints of fragrant pink, white, and purple flowers. Various kinds of birds were happily chirping their melodic songs as they carried pieces of straw and other unidentifiable objects to their new, partially completed residences. The row of forsythia bushes along the driveway was sporting blooms of the brightest yellow I had ever remembered seeing. I was happier than I had been in several years. All was well with the world, with one exception.

Aunt Tammy had been taken to the hospital by ambulance earlier in the day. She had been experiencing breathing problems, and her doctor felt that it would be best for her to be in the hospital where she would have easy access to oxygen if she needed it. Her condition had remained constant for some time now—no improvement, but no further deterioration either. We were hopeful that she would be returning home in a day or two when the doctors found the source of this new symptom.

My family had never given up hope for her recovery. Many novenas were being made, and many rosary beads were frequently being prayed on as well. The hope was that a new cure for this horrible disease would be discovered in time to save her life. She had already been taken to the Mayo Clinic for a second time, but the visit did not prove successful.

Aunt Dar and Uncle Lenny had come in from their home in Lima, Ohio. Uncle Len had taken the day off, and they planned to stay over for the weekend because of the new development in Aunt Tammy's condition. They were anxious to join the rest of the family in welcoming my mother home from her long stay in the hospital as well. Since they had been responsible to a great extent for the good care she had received, they wanted to be present for her triumphant return to a new beginning toward normal life.

Even Aunt Millie and Uncle Pete, who hadn't been back home since last fall, were expected to arrive at any time. They were bringing Pat and Elaine with them as both the children were on Easter break. Of course, all the local family members were present for the gala event. My grandparents were thrilled to be surrounded by most of the family once again.

Uncle Jack had defrosted some of his deer meat, compliments of the large buck he had taken during the winter. This was a special treat that most of us enjoyed. He was the only person I knew who could prepare venison and make it taste delicious. Aunt Marcie took on the responsibility of preparing the remainder of the feast. She was an excellent cook and had no trouble preparing a variety of her favorite recipes for the large group.

Grandma, I noticed, was somewhat preoccupied during the festivities. Though she didn't mention Tammy, I felt certain that her prayers were being said for a good report from the hospital on her youngest child. Tammy had just turned twenty-six three weeks earlier.

With the exception of Aunt Harriet and Uncle Clyde (who were in New Holland making preparations to move into a rented home) and Uncle Hank (who was with Aunt Tammy at the hospital), our entire family was in attendance to celebrate Mom's homecoming.

The day could not have been more perfect. There was a gentle breeze that caused the fragrance of spring flowers to permeate the atmosphere. Aunt Marcie and Uncle Jack's vast variety of delicious foods prepared to perfection was enjoyed by everyone. Mom seemed exuberant that she was finally home with the family and away from the horrors of being in the hospital. She had been told by her doctor that she would once again be living in familiar surroundings that were now hers to call home. There would be no further uncertainty as to where she would be spending each day.

It was late in the evening when the last remaining family members reluctantly said their good-nights with the hope of meeting once again during the long weekend ahead. Mom and I were planning to visit Aunt Tammy in the morning. Aunt Millie and Uncle Pete said that they would accompany us. As their plans were to return to Cleveland the following day, this might be the only opportunity they would have to visit with Tammy. Aunt Dar and Uncle Lenny had promised Pat and Elaine that they would take them to the zoo the first time they had the opportunity to be together in Pittsburgh. The following day seemed to be the perfect time to fulfill this promise.

Everything seemed right with the world once again. Aunt Dar and Uncle Lenny stayed overnight with us, and we talked for quite a while before going to bed. Uncle Lenny reminded me of some of our previous conversations regarding right and wrong choices and the consequences resulting from those choices.

"Aunt Dar and I are proud of you, Mara," he said, sporting that boyish, crooked grin that characterized his unique way of expressing his satisfaction. "You've come through this battle like Aunt Dar and I expected that you would. You're a real trooper, and this situation with your mom has prepared you to face any future hurdles that life may have in store for you. We both hope that it will be a long time before you have to face anything as serious as this one has been. But in any event, we are both convinced that you will be prepared to handle whatever may come your way."

He will never know that I considered taking the coward's way out a few times in the past year. They wouldn't be quite so proud of me, I'm sure, I thought. But this was my secret, and I had no intention of sharing it with anyone. We said our good-nights and went to our rooms, anticipating a long, restful sleep. It had been a long and busy day, and we were all exhausted.

Sometime during the night, I was abruptly awakened by the sound of a piercing scream coming from the kitchen.

Terrified at what I might find, I bolted down the steps two at a time with my heart pounding furiously in my chest. I was confronted by my aunt and uncle attempting to subdue my mother, who was furiously attempting to escape their grip.

I gasped. "What happened? What's wrong with Mom? Was that you screaming, Mom?"

"Mara, your mom took the phone call. It was from Hank. Aunt Tammy died a half hour ago. Her muscles in her chest were no longer able to support her lungs and trachea. Her lungs collapsed, and she suffocated. The doctors think that she may have developed pneumonia. This is what started the process. There was nothing that they could do."

It seemed fitting that since the family was all here from Ohio, they would remain for the funeral, which was scheduled for Monday morning.

Aunt Tammy looked lovely. They had done a good job making her look like she had looked before this disease robbed her of her vitality and youthful good looks. I took a red rose from one of the many floral arrangements that had been placed near the casket.

Lifting up Rene, I put it in her tiny hand so that she could place it in the coffin beside her mommy's body. She was too young to know what had happened. She thought that Tammy was asleep. She leaned over in my arms and kissed her mommy on the cheek as she put the rose in Tammy's hand.

This was more than I could endure. I handed Rene to Hank, who was standing with me in front of the coffin. I made a quick exit to the ladies' room, where I stayed until I could recover my composure. My initial taste of death wasn't going very well.

Grandma and Mom did not go to the funeral home at all. Both of them were overwhelmed to the point of uncontrollable grief. We all took turns staying home with them during the two days of visitations.

What had promised to be a wonderful weekend with the family turned into an unbelievable nightmare. For most of us, this was our first experience with the death of a loved one. The loss and grief we were all experiencing were unbelievably painful. At least we had one another and that proved to be of some comfort. We spent most of our time reminiscing about Tammy's graduation from high school, her engagement party after Hank had asked her to marry him, and of course, the beautiful wedding and the even more beautiful bride. How proud Uncle Hank had been when he announced the arrival of their precious little bundle from heaven, Rene.

My own thoughts, though unexpressed, were dark and confused.

Why did you allow this, God? We were taught in CCD class that you are the giver and the sustainer of life. You kind of slipped up on this one, didn't you? Are you really the kind, loving Father that the nuns say you are? If this is your brand of kindness, I don't think I want any more of it.

We buried Aunt Tammy in a quiet little cemetery a few miles from where we lived. Only the immediate family and close friends of Tammy and Hank were present. After the usual prayers and eulogizing were completed, the pallbearers lifted the coffin into the open grave. Aunt Dar, at this point, burst into a frenzy of grief and unbelief and attempted to jump into the grave as the coffin was being lowered into the ground.

It took Uncle Len and two of my other uncles all the strength they could muster to restrain Aunt Dar. They immediately took her back to their car, which was parked with the funeral procession a few hundred yards away from the grave site. Uncle Len stayed with her and attempted to comfort her the best way he knew how during this terrible time of loss. Aunt Dar and Aunt Tammy were the two youngest children of my grandparents. Although Aunt Dar now lived out of town, she and Tammy had been inseparable growing up together.

The following morning, we said our good-byes to our family members who were traveling west to Cleveland and Lima and did our best to begin to return to some normalcy of life.

From the very beginning, Mom began to show increasingly familiar signs of mental disturbance. Tammy's death could not have come at a worse possible time. Within a few weeks, Uncle Len and Aunt Dar were forced to return to Pittsburgh where they had already made the necessary arrangements to have Mom recommitted to St. Joe's Hospital for yet another round of electric shock treatments. This time, nothing that her doctors attempted seemed to have much effect on my mother. Several months later, Mom was committed to a state mental institution for the second time.

I was left alone in what was now legally my home. My dreams had been shattered. Uncle Len's words continued to reverberate in my mind: "When you come to a crossroads in your life, Mar, weigh your choices. If you make the right choice, things will eventually straighten out, and your life will become normal once again. If you decide to take the other road, you could be opening yourself to a lot of heartbreak."

I pondered these words in my heart, and they would invariably lead me to compare my life thus far to that of my mother's life.

Often I would find myself going through family albums and seeing my mom's image captured on old sepia prints. She had been such a beautiful woman. I wondered what wrong choices she had made that caused fate to deal her such a horrible blow. Even in her late thirties and early forties, she had ceased to resemble that lovely young woman in the pictures. I vowed that I would not repeat the same mistakes that had brought her to this tragic end in spite of what future sorrows might invade my life.

CHAPTER 8
REACHING NEW MATURITY

The warm, gentle breeze of spring rapidly moved into summer with its increasingly hot temperatures and heavy downpours of rain. I could often observe through my kitchen window my industrious grandmother diligently caring for her young vegetable plants that were now beginning their rapid growth toward maturity. She worked alone this year. The small garden beside hers was unattended and had, once again, become overrun with weeds. I wondered what thoughts she entertained as she diligently planted rows of corn and hoed around her young tomato plants. Her heart must be broken at the tragic loss of Aunt Tammy. I thought that perhaps I was adding to that void in her life by not being by her side in my own little garden as I had been in previous years. She might appreciate the companionship more this summer than ever before. But my thoughts were not on gardening but rather on finding a way to make some money.

Before school let out for summer vacation, my final year in elementary school, I was given an opportunity that I couldn't pass up. My two best friends who lived on the other side of the field behind grandma's garden and our fruit orchard were getting working papers and had invited me to join them. A large and hugely popular dairy store, located at the entrance of our county park, was hiring young people for summer work. I had to be fourteen years old and ready, able, and willing to work, and I felt that I could meet the requirements. I needed some spending money. Aunt Harriet was taking care of my living expenses, but not much else, with the exception of twenty dollars every once in a while for incidentals.

If I wanted to buy new clothes or go somewhere with my friends that would cost money, I was out of luck.

My two best friends had just received precision roller skates for their birthdays which came in the spring. I would have to wait until Christmas or my birthday in January. The problem was that the three of us had signed up for advance lessons in freestyle and dance skating in September in preparation for entering competition next spring. If I could save enough money from my paychecks this summer, I could buy a pair of used skates from the roller rink and have them in time to begin lessons. The three of us were skating twice a week now and were all eligible to join the advanced classes to prepare for competition skating.

We loved skating but had to admit that the boys who skated at the rink were pretty interesting as well. We all looked forward to being asked to do the specials that came up throughout the evening so that we would be able to get to know them better. I found myself getting more interested in the opposite sex as the summer wore on. My days of playing tackle football and beating up on boys who invaded our camp sites in the woods were fast becoming history.

Doggedly, I pursued getting hired by the dairy store; and two weeks after submitting my working papers I did succeed in getting hired for summer work along with my friends. This was a great opportunity for kids who didn't have parents to provide them with spending money for their various activities. I was to receive two dollars per hour in wages and all I could eat during the eight hours that I was working. This meant that all the ice-cream cones, sundaes, and ham barbecues that I could stuff down my gut were mine for the taking while I was on my two fifteen-minute breaks and half-hour lunch break each working day.

Not only that, but this particular dairy store, being situated at the entrance to the park, was a hangout for teenagers. I could meet lots of guys here who came in for a sandwich or some ice-cream treat either before or after going to the swimming pool or the tennis courts. I was elated. Not only could I foresee getting those precision skates that I had to have, but I could extend my social life in the process. I was promised thirty hours a week if I was a good worker, followed all the rules, was friendly with the patrons, and able to take some of the abuse that the very nature of the job entailed.

I felt that I was more than capable, and I knew that I would be wildly successful in my first paying job.

By the last week of August I had saved sufficient money to purchase brand-new Chicago precision skates like my friends had. I was very proud of my success in pursuing my ambition, and prouder still that I had been successful in reaching a goal that I thought was out of reach. The skates cost three hundred dollars. My family was very pleased with my acquisition as well. They were delighted that I had chosen to work for the much-needed money rather than mope around the house all summer wishing for something that I couldn't possibly have. Although I was unaware of it at the time, this singular life experience at an early age established in me a work ethic that remained intact throughout my working years.

The most important thing that came out of summer vacation that year was the fact that I had very little time to indulge in pity parties and feel sorry for myself because of my mom's absence or the fact that I had a dad who deserted me. I missed Tammy as we all did. But once again, when a person is busy working and pursuing goals, there's not a whole lot of time to be sad.

My one regret throughout the summer months was that I had deserted my granny for the very first time. She worked alone this year in her garden. Her young sidekick was rarely seen in the garden area anymore. I attempted to cover the guilt by assuring myself that granny understood that I was growing up and had to begin to assume responsibilities if I wanted to get anywhere in this world.

She admitted that she did indeed miss my presence in the garden, but she was very proud of me for the accomplishment in being able to purchase the skates without help from family. Jokingly she added, "I know someone who doesn't miss you one little bit—Gracie."

When I entered my freshman year of high school following the summer's end, I tried to pull a fast one on my Aunt Harriet. In the absence of my mother, my aunt was the self-appointed guardian of my spiritual life. Living alone and without my aunt's knowledge, I faked Mom's signature on the application for enrollment in public school.

Since Aunt Harriet and Uncle Clyde were living in Central Pennsylvania, it took them almost an entire semester to get wind of the fact that I had defected. They put an immediate stop to this. My aunt, who was now employed as a plant nurse in the community where they had recently purchased a new home, had to handle my transfer to a parochial high school by mail. She was successful in this endeavor. She alerted my grandmother, who had pretended that she knew nothing about what was going on. Just to be certain that her orders were carried out Aunt Harriet called my Aunt Marcie, who lived in the neighborhood, requesting that she keep close tabs on me.

My orders were to show up at St. Felix Academy the first day of the second semester. There was to be no argument, no resistance, and no tears. This would prove to be the best thing that could happen to me as I approached my adult years, she assured me. Public school was out of the question. My grades had slipped somewhat during my first half of ninth grade, and there were definite signs that my attraction to the opposite sex was the primary cause of this. She had already signed the necessary papers and paid for the second semester in advance. My uniforms had been ordered, and I would be called to go to the department store in Pittsburgh for the necessary alterations a week before school began.

Mom was still not responding positively to any treatment she was receiving at the state hospital. As a matter of fact, when I visited her with any of my aunts and uncles, I observed that she had become unresponsive and almost zombielike in her approach to us. This was so disheartening to me, and at this point, I wondered if Mom would ever again be able to live outside those institutional walls.

My world was collapsing around me. I had a new boyfriend whom I had met at the public school I attended. I knew that when I was taken out of that school he would lose interest in me. Boys were like that I was finding out, much to my dismay.

In spite of the adversity facing me at the tender age of fifteen, my Aunt Harriet's words resounded over and over in my mind, that this would prove to be the best thing that could happen to me as I approached adulthood. This statement was yet to be proven.

I was suddenly jolted back to reality by the sound of spinning tires on slick ice and the screeching of brakes. Up ahead it appeared that the limo, in an effort to back into the graveyard and pull closer to the grave site for the removal of the casket, had miscalculated the turn. The left rear tire had evidently caught the edge of the road and had skidded into the ditch beside it.

Under my breath, I uttered a choice expletive that I felt was appropriate for the foolish move that would further delay getting this burial ceremony over with once and for all.

I glanced at my mother and my Uncle Henry who were anxiously watching the activity surrounding the limo.

"Who needs a comfort break?" I asked.

From the look on both of their faces, I knew that I had hit the nail on the head. We had been riding for almost three hours. My uncle's car had become quite cold when he turned off the ignition some time ago waiting for the funeral director's signal for us to leave our vehicles and move to Aunt Mo-Mo's grave site. It was cold in the car, so I assumed that it must be bitter outside.

"Uncle Clyde, I believe that everyone back here needs to use the restrooms. I'm going to go over to the church where the priest is standing and ask if we can use their facilities. It's been a long ride. I'll be back for Mom as soon as we get permission to go into the church. No sense making her walk over there until I know that he has no objection to our request."

"Okay, Mara. I'll take Henry with me as soon as you get an okay from Father," he responded.

Aunt Harriet had not as yet entered the conversation. She had not spoken to me during our drive here. I guess she thought that this was the punishment due me for my insolence at the church. Actually, I couldn't have cared less. There were times when Aunt Harriet could be very difficult to deal with. When she didn't get her way, there was literal hell to pay. I had found by experience that the best way to handle her when she was like this was to totally ignore her until she got over it.

I unlocked my door and quickly jumped out, closing the door immediately so that no cold air would be allowed to enter. It was bitterly cold outside. The wind was blowing from the north across Lake Erie, bringing gusts of frozen snow with it. I pulled my wool scarf tighter around my neck and began to make my way across the frozen path to the church. It was icy in spots, and I reminded myself to take extra precautions with Mom when I came back to get her. She was very feeble and not at all sure-footed anymore. Maybe if Aunt Harriet was able to get over her little tantrum, she would be willing to take one of Mom's arms and I the other so we could get her to the church safely.

"Boy, it sure is cold up here," I muttered to myself. *What I wouldn't give to have my flask with me right now. A good long pull on that baby would do wonders to warm me up in a hurry. It would help me to get rid of this headache too,* I thought longingly. *The horrible part of this is that we have to drive back to Cleveland before the day is over. I can't wait to get to my car and get my booze. I really need a good stiff drink after all this.*

I thought of Mo-Mo, her cold, lifeless body finally at rest in the coffin the pallbearers were now carefully removing from the back of the limo. The funeral director had skillfully and quickly been able to retrieve the trapped left wheel from the ditch, and the coffin was being placed under the tent in preparation for the ceremony. Many of the people who had been part of the long funeral procession were now leaving their cars and heading for the grave site.

I met the priest who was officiating at the service when I had approached the church a few minutes earlier. He told me that he had unlocked the doors and we were certainly welcome to use the facilities. He urged me to get my group to the grave site as soon as possible as the ceremony would be starting in a few minutes.

Hurrying back to my uncle's car, my aunt and I removed Mom from the backseat and helped her across the frozen landscape while Uncle Clyde walked carefully with an arm supporting my Uncle Henry.

It was a slow and painstaking walk for both of them but, as we approached our destination, I noticed that it would take a few minutes to gather the many people in attendance under the tent. There were several elderly people who had been part of the group attending the burial. They too were being assisted by family members in making the brief trip to the grave site.

Having completed our necessary visit to the church, the five of us slowly and cautiously made our way to Mo-Mo's future home where a large group of friends and relatives was now gathering.

For the first time that day, I realized that it was January 4, my birthday and Mo-Mo's burial. What a way to spend one's thirty-third birthday.

CHAPTER 9

TIME FOR A CHANGE

"Gee-whiz, Mom, can you believe that it's been almost a month since Millie's funeral? We haven't heard from any-one in Cleveland except for the thank you card from Elaine for the mass card and floral arrangement. Maybe they just want to be left alone for a while. I guess each of us has his or her own way of dealing with grief."

No response from my mother, as usual, as she sat quietly at the table sipping hot tea. I cast a sideway glance in her direction, hop-ing that she wouldn't notice me studying her. Since arriving home from the funeral last month, Mom had spent most of her time in her room.

Much more so than usual, I thought, a faint hint of alarm finding its way into my psyche. *I certainly hope this isn't the beginning stage of another mental breakdown. This has been quite a blow to her. I guess this is her way of dealing with the loss of a sister—her favorite sister at that.*

The loosely fitting housecoat she was wearing couldn't hide the frail frame it covered. She was beginning to look very thin these days.

Wow, I thought with a sense of utter helplessness. *All the meals she's been missing are beginning to take their toll.*

"Mom, I hope you'll join the family for dinner tonight. I'm having your favorite no-peek chicken and dumplings. What do you say? You need to put on some weight. You're beginning to look like you're walking around in a gunnysack. Pretty soon we're going to have to go on a shopping spree and get you a whole new wardrobe. Those clothes that I bought you for Christmas are a couple sizes too large."

"No, Mara, I don't want you to spend any more money on clothing for me. I have more than enough to wear. I do believe that I could eat a little something tonight though. I'm beginning to get my appetite back. You know, I've had a lump in my throat since we got that phone call from Elaine on New Year's Eve."

As I directed my attention from the dinner I was preparing at the stove our eyes met, and simultaneously we both burst into tears. I moved toward her in an effort to comfort her with a reassuring hug. Too late, however. She had bolted from her chair and made a fast retreat to the bedroom which had become her dark sanctuary since her beloved sister's untimely death. She evidently felt more comfortable in her room, where she could grieve privately without being observed by the concerned glances of her daughter and grandchildren.

Okay, I thought, *I'm not going to push. Maybe when I get the family around the table in a few minutes, I'll send one of the kids to knock on her door.*

My thoughts were interrupted by the sound of the garage door going up and the delighted squeals of our two younger kids coming in for dinner. They had thoroughly enjoyed an afternoon of sled riding and frolicking in the half foot of fresh snow. It had fallen during the previous night, displaying a sparkling new winter wonderland. I heard a snowball hit something hard, and instinctively I yelled at my son. His mischief making was all too familiar to all of us. When trouble was brewing, he was generally the culprit.

"Randy, how many times have I told you not to throw snowballs in the garage?" I yelled from the top of the steps. "If you break a window in one of our cars, there is going to be the devil to pay, and you are the one who is going to be doing the paying. When are you going to begin to listen to me?"

"Don't worry, Mommy. I didn't break anything," he responded with his typical cavalier attitude, which drove me to utter distraction.

I quickly changed the subject so as not to belabor the fact that we had had several similar confrontations in the past—all to no avail. "Where are your dad and Rachael? I thought I told you to round them up and let them know that we're ready for dinner."

"I did, Mommy," he responded, stuffing a snowball down his sister's sweater as she was taking her jacket off. The high-pitched shriek that emitted from deep down in Roni's frail tiny body confirmed what was occurring in the game room.

"All right, stop that right now, Randy. While you still have your coat and boots on, please go next door to the O'Conners' and let your father and sister know that I'm ready to put dinner on the table. Tell them to get over here on the double unless they want to eat cold food for dinner."

I turned to Roni. "Roni, you stay where you are, and Mommy will come down with some dry clothes for you to change into after I dry you off. Come on, kids, let's get moving. Dinner is almost ready."

Grabbing some fresh jeans and a sweatshirt out of the girls' bedroom closet, I bolted down the steps to the game room to find Roni standing in the middle of the room, shaking uncontrollably from Randy's latest prank. Her lips were beginning to turn a pale shade of purple. Hoping to spare her additional discomfort, I carefully removed the remainder of the snowball, which by now had worked its way down her back and into her underwear.

Sparky, our Toy Manchester, had awakened from one of his many daily snoozes by the fireplace. Having heard the ruckus downstairs, he had anxiously followed me to the game room to find his precious Roni in a state of distress. He affectionately licked her cold hand in an effort to comfort her in his inimitable puppy-dog manner.

Roni looked at me with that innocent, questioning expression that had become so familiar. "Mummy, why does Randy have to tease me all the time? He knows I don't want him to shove snowballs down my back. They hoit, and they're so cold."

"I know, honey," I replied sympathetically as I held a fresh tissue to Roni's dripping nostrils. I was painfully aware that winter was far from over, and this exploit would no doubt be repeated many times by my mischievous son before the first robin of spring made its initial appearance in our backyard.

Aside from that, bringing to mind my own escapades at Randy's age, I recalled, with a strange combination of horror and unexplained glee, some of the nasty things I had done to my cousin Janice when we were growing up. Concluding that he had come by it naturally, I shrugged it off as a mere childhood prank while, at the same time, I was painfully recalling the outcome of my own mischief making.

No doubt about it, I thought. *This kid is getting away with murder, and something should be done about it.*

Mom had been a strong disciplinarian, having to play the role of both parents. I often experienced the result of her anger and lack of restraint as she would paddle me for my repeated acts of disobedience that had been directed toward Janice. I teased that child at every opportunity; and Janice, being the tattletale that she was, never failed to report every ugly detail that brought her wailing to my mother.

I sighed inwardly, realizing that Randy was a chip off the old block. After all, the apple never falls far from the tree, I concluded to myself. The problem was, however, that Randy was not receiving the discipline he needed, and Roni was suffering as the result of it. To be sure, his dad was not big on discipline. Actually, Rand wasn't around the house enough to witness the chaos his son was creating. Not that it mattered. Any attempt at even the mildest form of discipline on my part would be immediately countered by an irate response from Rand. His son could do no harm.

"For Pete's sake, let the kid alone, Mara," would be his usual response. "He'll outgrow it."

My argument remained unchanged. "What do you mean he'll outgrow it? If this behavior isn't nipped in the bud, it will only get worse…and what about Roni? He torments her constantly. Doesn't she matter? It's all right that she is being terrorized by her brother daily and that she's too little to defend herself against him?"

"You're overreacting as usual, mamma bear," would be his all-too-familiar retort.

This was his pet nickname for me when he was pointing out my maternal nurturing with regard to my children, especially my baby Roni, who had become Randy's favorite target for terrorizing over the past year. He knew that this condescending approach infuriated me.

"Why don't you go and pour yourself a stiff one before we eat, sweetheart? It may mellow you a bit and get you in a better frame of mind. You can be such a bore when you take on a dictatorial approach to the many little issues of life."

This would be one of his anticipated remarks used expressly to point out my weakness for alcohol. Having driven home his point, he would attempt to end the argument with that self-satisfied smirk that I had come to despise.

"Mara, you're putting way too much emphasis on Randy's behavior. He's just a normal six-year-old boy, and that's what six-year-old boys do to their younger sisters when they are bored and need a little excitement in their lives."

I would become quite annoyed with chauvinistic comments like this and would attempt to keep the argument going by countering with a nasty response designed to deliver a scathing blow to his ego. "How would you know how a normal six-year-old boy treats his younger sister anyhow? You never had one, or a brother either. I guess that's why you're such a spoiled brat."

"It takes one to know one, my darling wife," he would immediately hurl back at me without missing a heartbeat. "One spoiled brat marrying another spoiled brat makes for a loud and lively union, doesn't it?"

Finally, in an effort to put the cap on the escalating argument, he would change the subject abruptly. "Have I told you lately how cute and vulnerable you look when you're losing an argument? You should know by now that you're no match for me. You women seem to have the same thing in common—all emotion, no logic. It makes winning an argument so easy."

"On the other hand," he would stress, "a real man always has total control of every situation. This is the reason that the male of the species is far superior to his counterpart in so many respects. Don't you agree?"

"No, I don't agree, Rand," I would respond, my voice rising in indignation.

Once again, he would have touched a vulnerable spot; and once again, to my dismay, I would be well on my way to losing another argument because I was allowing emotion to overrule logic. Before I could rally with the scathing response screaming inside me, he would clamp his hand over my mouth and slap me soundly on my posterior. I would be infuriated by this patronization.

It was obvious that he enjoyed this little exchange, and I would know predictably what was coming next. To counter my next move, he would quickly grab my arms and hold them firmly behind my back until I had regained my composure. When he felt my arms go limp, this would be his cue to release me with that same self-satisfied smirk on his face, which made me physically ill. With that done, he would dismiss any further discussion on the subject. He would leave the room with a quick gesture of his hand, indicating that the argument had ended and I had lost it once again.

This type of drama was becoming all too frequent. Looking back on the months before our wedding, I sometimes regretted that I had not chosen the abortion route that we had discussed as a possible way out of our dilemma. This certainly had been his choice. But that was one argument I was determined to win. I couldn't bring myself to end the life of an innocent and helpless baby. My Catholic background, sketchy though it was, had left an indelible mark on my conscience. This was terribly wrong. It was murder, and I knew that I wouldn't be able to live with myself if I gave in to his pressure.

It was becoming quite evident that this man much preferred being single than having to face the prospect of becoming a husband and father, weighed down by the many obligations of married life. Not wanting him to feel obligated to me, I gave him permission to walk out of my life. He had my blessing. I would go through with the pregnancy without his support and put the baby up for adoption. The stipulation would be that we would not see each other ever again.

He evidently pondered my words and came to the conclusion that I meant what I said. Though he had been able to win me over most of the time by his convincing arguments, somehow this time it was different. There was another life involved, and I had the courage, for once, to take a firm stand for my conviction.

Two weeks later, to my complete surprise, he announced that he would go through with the marriage. He had weighed all the circumstances and felt that this would be the noble thing to do. He did not want his child to be brought up by strangers. Needless to say, I was flabbergasted beyond belief. I had already made an appointment with an adoption agency to begin the adoption procedure.

His decision weighed very heavily on me. Did I really want to keep this man in my life? If I married him, I knew in my heart that I would be in for a lot of disappointments and very little love, if any. Rand was so absorbed in self-love there would be precious little left over for me or my child. On the other hand, I was relieved that now this tiny being growing inside of my body would be given a legal name and the security of having both a mom and a dad, something I never had growing up. I couldn't explain this new feeling getting stronger in me with each passing day, but I knew without question that I did not want to give up this baby. In spite of the complications involved in having a child under these circumstances, I had already put these concerns to rest.

Maybe, just maybe, Rand would adapt to married life and, in time, surprise me by becoming a model husband and father. If I worked diligently at becoming the model wife and mother, perhaps I could convince him that there was nothing as great as a conjugal relationship.

I was to learn, within months after we were married, that people don't change because the circumstances of their lives change. Real change comes from within, as I would one day experience for myself.

Nonetheless, I had spent many years, since Rand and I had married, involved in codependency groups, as well as attending regular AA meetings and other self-help classes in an effort to rid myself of the guilt and frustration I was experiencing. I knew that there were things in my life that were destructive to my marriage. Randy and Roni would soon be at the age where they would know that their mom had some serious problems. Rachael had already reached sufficient maturity to enable her to see the harmful effect of my drinking, though I took great pains to hide it. I was becoming desperate to find an answer to my problems. There did not appear to be one in the foreseeable future. Was it to be my destiny to be caught in a trap from which there was no way out?

CHAPTER 10

FROM BAD TO WORSE

"Oh God, what's wrong with me anyhow?"

Realizing that once again I had become lost in thought about a life that was out of control, I quickly turned my attention to my little Roni, who was looking up at me with such a pitiful expression on her face that I wanted to throw my arms around her and hug her shaking little body close to me. Evidently, she had retrieved a bathroom towel while I had been preoccupied with my own thoughts, and she was holding it out to me.

"Mummy, my back is still wet. Will you dwy it for me so that I won't be cold anymore?"

"Of course, sweetheart. You'll be okay in a few minutes. After I dry you with this towel, I want you to go to your room and put on a clean top. Then I would like it if you would knock on Nana's door very gently and ask her if she's coming out for dinner."

Roni's demeanor changed instantly when I made this request. Just seconds ago she had been concerned that she couldn't get warm because of Randy's snowball escapade. Suddenly she forgot about her own problem, and she became very thoughtful and somber. She looked at me with a genuine expression of anxiety.

"Mummy, Nana won't come out and eat with us. I just know she won't. You asked her a lot of times to come out of her room for dinner, and she wouldn't. She doesn't eat much anymore since Aunt Mo-Mo went to heaven. Nana is vewy skinny. When I don't eat my cawwots and peas, you always tell me that I'll get sick if I don't eat my vegibals. I think Nana is going to die pretty soon and go to heaven like Aunt Mo-Mo did. I don't want my nana to go to heaven now."

I was genuinely taken back by this display of concern coming from my youngest child. Evidently, the recent death of a beloved aunt was having its effect on Roni. I realized that all my children were shaken by the death of Aunt Mo-Mo. They had never had the experience of losing a close member of the family to death. It was evident that my two older kids were processing this event by the questions they asked me about Mo-Mo and the circumstances surrounding her death.

Roni had remained quiet during these past several weeks since Mo-Mo's passing. I knew that this subject would have to be dealt with eventually. I was waiting for Roni to open the conversation. It looked like the time had arrived, and I immediately captured the moment.

"You know, Roni, it takes time to get over the death of someone we truly love. This time is called the time for grieving. It's a good thing to go through this because it helps us get rid of the sadness we feel now that this person is no longer with us. We can cry as much as we feel like crying because we know that we will never see this loved one again while we are here in this life. When our sad thoughts about losing this person begin to change to happy thoughts about all the good things we loved about this person, our grieving time is almost over.

"When this happens, we will be begin to live normal lives once again. We won't be so sad anymore. You know, sweetheart, none of us will ever forget Aunt Mo-Mo and what a wonderful lady she was.

So many people loved her because she was kind to everyone she met. She did many good things for so many people. She loved you, honey, and that is why you—all of us—will miss her. But as I said, after a while, we need to put away the tears and start to smile again and move on with our lives.

"Don't be worried about Nana. She is taking a little longer to get over Aunt Mo-Mo's death. But, honey, you must remember something very important. Nana and Aunt Mo-Mo were sisters like you and Rachael are sisters. They grew up together, and they knew each other a lot longer than any of us knew our aunt. I'm sure that Nana needs this time alone to stop being sad about not seeing Aunt Mo-Mo anymore and to begin thinking about all the good times they had when they were younger."

Even while I was explaining this situation to Roni, I was being gripped with that old familiar feeling of dread. The last time that Nana had to face the death of a sister, Tammy, the youngest sibling of their large family, she had suffered her longest mental setback since the onset of her illness. She had ended up, once again, in an institution where she remained for several years. Had it not been for the fact that all the state hospitals were forced to close their doors for lack of funding, Nana may have remained in that awful place to this day. The very thought of this made me shudder.

As I watched my little girl's facial expressions, I could see that she was very intent on grasping my every word with the limited reasoning of a four-year-old child. I believed that in time Roni would come to her own conclusion about these more-difficult experiences that life presents to each of us. Moms are here to give their kids a little boost in the right direction. As children mature, they have to put the finishing touches on their own life experiences.

Uncle Lenny and his words of wisdom to me when I was a young teenager suddenly came to mind. I had often thought of the things he said to me about making right choices as we come to the various crossroads of our life. Unfortunately, I had made many wrong choices. Getting involved with alcohol was one of them. Marrying Rand was another. For the very first time, I realized that it was the alcohol that brought about my relationship with Rand.

Turning my attention back to my child, I found Roni looking at me with a mixture of understanding and puzzlement. I held my breath, waiting for her response and hopeful that the explanation I had given her was sufficient at this time to answer her questions satisfactorily.

"Mummy, where is heaven? Did Aunt Mo-Mo go there?"

"Well, uh, yes, of course, she did, honey."

"Mummy, do you think that our nana will die pretty soon because she can't stop crying for Aunt Mo-Mo? You said that even if we're sad because someone we miss so much is gone, we have to stop crying and be happy again. Why won't Nana come out of her room and eat dinner with us? Mummy, Nana is not happy anymore, and Nana looks vewy sick. Do you think that Nana wants to go to heaven with Aunt Mo-Mo now?"

"Sweetheart, didn't I tell you that Nana will be all right? It's just taking her a little longer than the rest of us to get over Aunt Mo-Mo's death, that's all."

This conversation had taken on a depth of understanding in Roni that amazed me. It also made me realize how inadequate my responses to her questions had been. How could I tell her where heaven is? How do I know who will go there and who won't go there? I couldn't lie to her, but I didn't have these answers. How could I tell her that Nana was a special case, that she was very different from most people because of the unfortunate life that she had lived?

"Sweetheart," I responded, placing my hands on her cold cheeks, "there are some things that even moms and dads can't answer. I can only tell you what I know. When you grow up, you will understand some of these things much better."

I was becoming very uncomfortable with this discussion, and I wanted to bring it to a rapid conclusion. Roni had touched on some questions I had pondered for years. I deliberately turned my attention to the dinner that was waiting on the stove to be served.

"If we all don't get around the table soon, we'll be eating cold food tonight or, even worse, burned food, honey. So we can talk about this a little later, okay, sweetheart?"

This was my excuse to steer her in another direction, a direction with which I was more comfortable.

Concluding with what I hoped would satisfy my child's insatiable curiosity to understand things that were beyond her realm of comprehension, I attempted to end the conversation by reiterating that everything would work out all right in time. She was too little to take on such a grown-up problem.

Roni was much too tenacious to be dismissed this easily. She was on a roll now. The silence since Mo-Mo's passing was over. She was thoughtful for a brief moment, but it was evident that she was putting some things together in her mind. This time it came in the form of a statement rather than a question.

"Mummy, God can take Randy to heaven whenever He wants to, except I don't thinks that God really wants him in heaven. Randy is vewy, vewy bad, and you said that only good people go to heaven. I don't think that Randy is bad enough to go to that other place either, but I wonder and wonder where he will go."

"I don't want God to take Rachael to heaven," she continued. "She is my good sister. She helps me make my bed in the morning before she goes to school, and she always lets me play with her Barbie and Ken dolls. And when it's too hard for me to get their clothes on, she helps me do that too. I love my sister, and I don't want God to take her away from me."

As I looked deeply into those enormous, questioning blue eyes, I realized that I was looking into her soul. Our conversation had triggered something of great importance to both of us. I had the assurance that Roni had figured something out that was so important for her to know. Her summation of sibling relationships was a clear indication that she now understood why her Nana was so sad. Her immature mind was processing both of these sibling relationships. She had figured out all by herself that the love she had for her sister was the same kind of love Nana had for Aunt Mo-Mo. Now she understood, at least in part, why her Nana had been grieving for such a long time.

I assured her that God wouldn't take Rachael to heaven just yet. But even as these words were spoken in feigned reassurance of my child's deep concern, my thoughts returned to the horrible accident that had occurred at the other end of our street just a few days after Christmas. I didn't know this family except to wave to them as we occasionally passed each other in our vehicles. On one occasion, while walking our dog, we stopped to introduce ourselves.

This family had just moved into the neighborhood in time to celebrate Christmas. They had been thrilled at the prospect of owning their first home with a large fenced backyard where their two children could finally have a safe place to play. They had lived in an apartment fairly close to the city limits of Pittsburgh. Due to the crowded conditions in this complex, Marty and her husband, Fred, were understandably relieved when they were finally able to find an affordable home in our neighborhood, one that would meet the immediate needs of their growing family. They had impressed me as a caring, conscientious couple who put their children's welfare at the top of their priority list.

Three days after Christmas tragedy struck that family. While backing out of the driveway, Fred had failed to see his four-year-old son in his rearview mirror. Evidently, the child had been in Fred's blind spot. Assuming that the youngster was still inside the house with his wife, he was, perhaps, a little less cautious than he might have been.

We heard the ambulance that day but didn't find out until later in the evening that little Freddie Jr. had died on the way to the hospital as a result of cerebral hemorrhage.

Once again, I could feel anger and resentment welling up from somewhere deep in the pit of my stomach.

"You let this happen, God," I murmured in disbelief.

How could you allow something as horrible as this to happen, and especially at this time of the year? What kind of devious pleasure do you derive from this? Shame on you for being such a Christmas Scrooge. You took from those loving parents one of their two most precious possessions. Worse than that, because of the circumstances of the little boy's death, you left the heartbroken daddy with an overwhelming sense of guilt from which he will probably never recover.

I just don't understand you, God. I'm pretty certain that I could never serve you under these circumstances. I heard from the nuns that you are a God of love, but you are also a God who administers justice when it's deserved. I sure don't see it that way. Did Fred and Marty really deserve to lose their precious little boy? I don't think so.

My attention once again returned to the matter at hand. Roni was dry and comfortable now and happy that her questions had been satisfactorily dealt with, at least for the moment.

"Okay, little girl. You knock on Nana's door and see if she will come out of her bedroom and have dinner with us."

Returning to the kitchen, I put the finishing touches on dinner, hoping that Roni would be successful in convincing her nana to join us. My mother seemed to favor our youngest child slightly more than the two older ones. Perhaps it was Roni's winsome ways that had captured Mom's heart, or maybe it was just that she was the baby of the family. Whatever the reason, I hoped that Roni would have success in drawing Nana out of her shell long enough to have some dinner with us.

Just then, I heard the garage door drop down with a loud bang.

Rand has got to adjust the chain on that thing before it snaps in two, I told myself. *It would be disastrous if one of the kids got it in the face with the loose end of a flying chain. Back to the orthodontist for new braces for Rachael maybe, or possibly some facial stitches for one of them. I don't know why he procrastinates until something nasty happens. He's always so preoccupied with whatever it is on his mind these days. He doesn't seem to get anything done around here anymore.*

I attempted to brush all the negative thoughts from my mind as I spooned the steaming chicken and dumplings onto a large platter.

"Come on, guys, dinner is being served," I called loudly enough to be heard throughout the house. "Roni is trying to convince Nana to come to dinner tonight because her nana is getting 'vewy, vewy skinny.'"

Rand, having come into the kitchen, threw me an all-too-familiar glance as he removed his jacket. "Maybe she'll starve herself to death and bring one of my fantasies to a good conclusion," he commented wryly.

"Stop it. Let's not start on my mother again. You knew what I had to deal with when you so graciously agreed to marry me, so make the best of it, okay? Rachael is right behind you on the stairs, and she doesn't need to hear you ranting about my mother again. It makes for a very uneasy situation, don't you realize that? Or don't you give a damn?"

Without responding to my irate question, Rand slid into his chair as Randy and Rachael joined us in the kitchen and took their places at the table. Nana—led by a chattering, victorious Roni—came from the direction of the hall and joined us. Finally, we were all together for a meal. Roni was very proud of herself. She had single-handedly convinced Nana to have dinner with us.

It had been a while, I realized. *Maybe things will begin to return to some semblance of normalcy.* As I passed the platter, there were varied degrees of satisfaction expressed as the Reuben family was being treated to one of its favorite meals.

"Rachael, since it's Friday, you and Randy don't have homework to do this evening. I'd like for you two kids to pick up around the house for me, please, after we finish with dinner. Mrs. Drummond and Mrs. Bingham will be here at seven-thirty. We're going to make final plans for the Girl Scout Cookie Sale. We still have a lot to do, so we're going to have to hustle to get everything ready for the opening day of the sale next week. Mrs. O'Conner will be here a little later. She has to wait for Kathy to get home from cheerleading practice so someone will be there to watch the kids."

Roni, as always, never wanting to be left out of the action, volunteered her services. "I want to help too, Mummy. What can I do?"

"Don't worry, little girl. You did such a good job getting your Nana to have dinner with us tonight. I have a very important job for you to do before the ladies get here. We'll talk about it while we clear the table and get the dishes in the dishwasher."

With dinner over, Rand reminded me that he would be playing cards with his poker group later in the evening. "I'm sure glad I don't have to hang around here listening to a bunch of cackling hens trying to put an event together. It's beyond me how you women get anything done when you're all talking at once," he added condescendingly.

"Don't you ever have anything nice to say about women, Rand? I really believe you have an intense dislike for the opposite sex. Please try to keep in mind that we ladies do fill a very important function in our society, whether you care to admit it or not. Oh yes, and since when do you need an excuse for your Friday night activities, my darling husband? If my memory serves me correctly, you haven't spent a Friday night at home with the kids and me since we've been married. Why are you so demeaning when you discuss my friends? You got something against women in general, or is it just me in particular?"

This same argument had been regurgitated many times in the past, so I was not surprised by his predictable response.

"Just women in general, and you in particular, my darling wife, love of my life. Women were made for men's pleasure. Their places are in the kitchen and the bedroom. They need to be more sub-servient and keep their opinions to themselves, if indeed they have any opinions noteworthy of discussion. I haven't found this to be the case very often in my lifetime."

He concluded his demeaning comments by tweaking me on the behind as he left the room abruptly. That familiar feeling of repugnance once again gripped my inner being, but I attempted to stifle my growing outrage. Roni was patiently waiting in the dining room to carry out her contribution to the evening's event.

"Okay, sweetie," I called to her from the kitchen. "How about I give you some napkins, and you can fold them around the silverware like I showed you last week? If you need help, I'll be with you in a minute to finish the table settings. You did such a good job, I believe that I'll assign you this job permanently."

Mom had immediately retreated to her bedroom after finishing her dinner, and I could hear the two older children bickering over chores in the living room. The shower began to run, and I knew that Rand was preparing for his evening out with the boys.

I was beginning to feel washed out. I reminded myself that I hadn't had any alcohol for several hours, and I needed a little boost now to get through the remainder of the evening. The ladies might be here for several hours as we had much to do yet to prepare for the sale beginning in a few days.

This is a good opportunity for me to get a refresher, I reasoned as I headed for the buried treasure I had hidden in my briefcase in a dark corner of my bedroom closet.

As I took a mammoth swig from my half-empty bottle of Scotch, it occurred to me that I was repeating this practice more frequently in the recent weeks since I had left my job. It was easy for me to drink at will during the day when Rand was at work and the kids were in school. Mom was usually in her room and rarely came down to the laundry where I usually spent most of my mornings. There was never a fear of detection during these times. But after dinner—well, this wasn't a good idea. I had no idea when one of the kids might walk in and catch me in the act. That would be a disaster.

I had high hopes that being home all day would help me cut down on my drinking. The stress I encountered at the office would be gone. The position I held as credit manager was one of tremendous responsibility. I had not considered the amount of pressure I would be under at home. Attempting to balance the varied functions of running a household smoothly and managing three active, healthy children with varying needs was much more of a challenge than I had anticipated. I had worked for the same company for many years, returning to my position after Rachael was ten weeks old, and I had continued with this company ever since. But this business of overseeing a family and household was a whole different story. It was unfamiliar and challenging.

My kids were being cared for by either family members or adult sitters in my absence. I was limited to evenings and weekends with them. It didn't take me very long to realize that being a full-time mom was much more demanding that I had ever imagined. But I wanted this more than anything else in the world. It bothered me greatly that my children were being brought up by other women. Though I knew that I was far from perfect, these were my kids, and I wanted to raise them my way.

What a wonderful day it was when Rand had finally given his consent for me to leave my position. I sensed that it was very difficult for him to do this. I was commanding a very adequate salary by this time, and I had begun to move up the corporate ladder after many years of faithful service with the same employer. Rand was not at all happy that he would be taking on the total financial responsibility for our growing family. On the other hand, he was aware that he was dealing with an alcoholic wife. He had threatened on many occasions to commit me to a hospital where I could get "dried out" and get professional counseling.

Something had to be done about my condition. I certainly wasn't getting any better.

I had turned in my resignation the early part of December. My final day on the job would be New Year's Eve. Aunt Millie passed away late that evening. Her untimely death and the subsequent trip to Cleveland a few days later to attend the funeral certainly didn't give me a good reason to lessen my intake of alcohol. My New Year's resolution had been squashed before it had even begun. I promised myself that I would begin again as soon as things returned to normal.

Unfortunately, things were not returning to normal. My secret drinking was becoming excessive at times and—sadly, I realized—much more frequent. I was beginning to have severe headaches and, the next day, hangovers, which didn't adapt well to raising three noisy, active children. I would become cross with them on occasion for no obvious reason. When these times would occur, the guilt would certainly always increase. The fault was mine. My children were just being normal kids. They had no clue why their mom was becoming so upset with them. It appeared that history was repeating itself. I often thought about my relationship with my mother just before her initial nervous breakdown.

Is this what was happening to me?

Somehow, someway, there had to be an answer to my dilemma. I could not allow this to happen.

Rand and I seemed to be more at odds than ever, and our relationship was beginning to become the object of much concern to the children. I sensed that they were feeling uneasy about our frequent arguments. From what I could ascertain, while I was bringing in a large part of the family finances, Rand was attempting to "put up with my idiosyncrasies."

Now that I had exchanged my successful career for becoming a full-time wife and mother, I began to sense a great amount of resentment on his part because the entire financial burden had fallen on him.

Certainly, I was keeping my end of the bargain, I thought. I kept a clean and organized house—at least as organized as possible with three active children invading it each day after school. All the taxiing required for piano and dance lessons for the girls, dental and doctor appointments, T-ball practice for Randy, and the miscellaneous errands that had to be run in an effort to properly maintain a household were being taken care of by me. Dinner was always ready when Rand arrived home from work. His clothes were clean, and his white dress shirts, which he wore daily, were neatly pressed and ready for him when needed. Indeed, this was a full-time job if done properly, I was finding out. I certainly wished that my husband would realize this fact.

Certainly, I was the first to admit that I was far from perfect. My ability to handle money left a lot to be desired. Having commanded a very respectable salary for so many years, money was no object to me. After making an adequate contribution to the necessary household expenses, I lavished it freely on the children's needs and wants. Because of this, Rand took over control of the budget shortly after I left my job. That was fine with me. I had enough to do. The big problem was my attraction to alcohol.

Rand was a weekend drunk. That really didn't interfere with family life too much because he wasn't home that often. He worked on Saturdays, golfed on Sundays when the weather permitted, and took weekend trips to nearby lakes and streams for fishing periodically, which was his all-consuming passion. Friday and Saturday evenings were given to his favorite pastime, barhopping. I had found this to be very upsetting for the first several years of our marriage, but when I finally realized that I was stuck with a married bachelor, I resigned myself to the unfortunate fact. It gave me more time to spend with the kids, which I really enjoyed. I got busy catching up with the years I had missed being with them because of my job.

There was much to be desired in our relationship, to be sure, but I tried to look on the bright side. Rand was a good provider. Though the children didn't get everything they wanted, they certainly didn't lack for the things that were important for them to have. I was grateful for this.

Thinking about my neighbor next door, Vicky O'Conner, I realized that I really didn't have too much to complain about. Vicky and Ernie had five children ranging in ages from thirteen years to eighteen months. Ernie had a drinking problem, but it was compounded by a serious gambling habit as well. Although Vicky didn't complain much, as she and I developed a closer friendship, I knew that there were times that she worried whether the children would have sufficient food and clothing. Ernie meant well, and he loved his children. But when he stopped at the racetrack before doing the grocery shopping for the week, he would come up short more often than not.

I knew that I had to find a way to stop drinking. It was so destructive in so many ways. I felt that a social drink now and then was all right. Unfortunately, I couldn't stop with just one or two. There was something driving me, something that caused me to lose count and, ultimately, to lose control. How did this happen? When did it start to become a problem? I wondered. I had tried everything that I felt might help me rid myself of this curse in my life—if not for myself, then certainly for my children's sake. Nothing seemed to work, but surely, there had to be an answer. I needed desperately to find that answer.

CHAPTER 11
THE DEVIL IN DISGUISE

My troubled thoughts were interrupted just then as Rand emerged from the bathroom dressed like he was about to conduct a business meeting with all the big brass in his company.

"I thought you said that you were having a friendly little poker game with the boys tonight," I questioned. "Aren't you afraid you'll spill a beer on that new suit you bought last week?"

"Not that it's any of your business how I dress when I leave here for my night out with the boys, my inquisitive little wife. But just to appease your curiosity, it's Bernie's thirty-eighth birthday, so the guys and I are taking him out on the town after we finish with our card game. Don't wait up for me." He added, "I expect that it will be a long night."

He blew me a kiss as he started down the stairs to the game room. Recalling something that needed reinforcement, something that we had previously discussed, he turned abruptly to remind me of our appointment with the "shrink," which was fast approaching.

"I want you to get mentally prepared for this meeting. I can just imagine that this is placing you in an embarrassing situation. Having to admit to a total stranger that you have lost control of your life because you can't leave the bottle alone will be tough enough. But when one adds to the situation that this weakness of yours is creating chaos for your husband and three children, well, Mara..."

He purposely allowed his comment to fade away, knowing that I would complete it myself with an appropriate concluding thought.

"And, Mara," he added, "don't even think of cancelling this appointment. I told you before, and I'm telling you now, that this condition of yours has to be dealt with. I'm not putting up with any more of this nonsense. If you should decide that you don't want to go along with this, I want you to know that I will leave you and the kids in a heartbeat. We both know that I do my share of elbow bending too, but the big difference between you and me is this. Alcohol does not control my life as it does yours. Good night, my darling wife. I'll see you tomorrow. Keep your chin up, sweetheart. This is the only viable solution I know of that may help you resolve the mess that you've made of your life."

As abruptly as he had reminded me of the dreaded appointment coming up very soon, he moved quickly down the remaining steps and moved toward the door leading to the garage. I suspected that he was not in the mood to listen to me raise an objection to this plan. He had much more important things on his mind this evening. He certainly was not going to waste any time getting involved in another argument with me, which was certain to go nowhere.

I stood at the top of the stairs wanting to scream in an effort to release the pent-up emotions of the past few weeks. Instantly I thought the better of it when I glanced in the kitchen and saw Roni busily searching the cabinet drawers for more clean silverware.

How in God's name am I going to get through this evening? I desperately wondered. *I need to have another shot or two of Scotch to take the edge off, but I don't dare attempt that, not now. One of the kids will surely catch me in the act. Not only that, but the ladies will be here in a few minutes. I've just got to get a grip on myself somehow and get through this night.*

With all the remaining willpower I could muster, I deliberately erased all thoughts of this most recent confrontation with my husband regarding his solution to my drinking problem and I forced myself to look ahead to the meeting, which would begin shortly. I had planned a brief time for coffee and dessert. Then we would get right to the business at hand.

Sherry Drummond had reluctantly offered to take on the responsibility of overseeing the cookie sale, though she had five children of various ages and a wayward, disagreeable husband at home. Her good friend Carly Bingham had offered to help Sherry with the sale. Carly's father was the pastor of the black Baptist church on the other side of town and lived across the street from Sherry. Living close to each other, they felt that they would be better able to coordinate their various tasks connected with this event.

I was grateful for their help because I had attended a Girl Scout leadership weekend with both of them the previous summer. I observed how interested they were in the Girl Scout Association and how satisfied they were with the activities that this organization offered to girls. Between the two of them, they had four girls who had been regular attenders of the troop that I had just recently taken over. I had worked with these kids for a few months and had been impressed with their intense interest in scouting and with their leadership abilities. Both women were delightful to be with. I looked forward to working with them in the future. They both seemed to be at total peace with the world and shared an intangible quality that I couldn't quite put my finger on.

Vicky would be dropping in a little later. As assistant leader, she wanted to keep abreast of the plans being made for the sale. She had agreed to help out with the sale if needed but wasn't overly enthused. I realized that Vicky had a lot on her plate and that it would be difficult for her to devote much time to this event. She always made herself available to attend and help oversee regular troop meetings. With a maximum number of girls allowed in any given troop, I needed all the help I could get with the various activities in which we were involved. Vicky's obvious love for children endeared them to her. She worked well with them and was able to bring the best out of each girl, regardless of the large variety of personality differences. In my opinion, she was the best choice I could have made to be my assistant leader.

On the other hand, I could see that Sherry and Carly were well organized and fully equipped to handle anything that needed to be done to make this upcoming sale a successful venture. As the meeting came to a close, I was fully persuaded that I had the right women working with me to have a successful troop.

My only problem with Sherry and Carly surfaced during our initial meeting when I had taken over the troop the previous September. I had resolved that I would be very careful to direct any conversation away from matters that did not pertain to scouting.

I had invited the women who had girls in our troop to come over to my home for a time of getting acquainted. Of course, I wanted them to know the women to whom they were entrusting their girls every week and to be convinced that we had the girls' best interests at heart. Vicky and I would be diligent to fulfill all the requirements outlined in *The Leader's Handbook*. We would follow the badge program to the letter, enabling the girls to pursue their interests and expand their knowledge of each project they took on. We would teach them, to the best of our ability, to be honest, diligent in all they did, and learn to work well with others. Above all, we would help them realize that they needed to develop an allegiance to God and country so that when they grew up to be adults, they would become useful citizens, good wives and mothers, and assets to society.

In turn, we requested that when we had scouting activities planned, we would be able to count on some of them to join us as chaperones for day trips or weekends away. The Association required that for each eight girls we took to camp, one mother would be required to join us. With the full load of forty-five girls allowable for a troop, most of whom would be accompanying us on the camp outings, we might have to call on as many as seven or eight moms.

The attendance at that meeting had proven to be very disappointing. Only a few women—along with Vicky, Sherry, and Carly—showed up. I was obviously upset and really surprised that more moms really weren't all that interested in getting involved with their children's activities.

Carly had been the first to comment when she noticed my disappointment. "Mara, you have a lot to learn about group participation. My mom has been trying for years to get our members more involved in helping out with our activities at church. Most people just don't want to take time out of their busy schedules to do this. They want the benefits. They just don't want to make any contributions of time. It's human nature, I guess."

"That's a different story, Carly," I responded. "I certainly wouldn't consider volunteering my time for church work either. That's just not my thing. I'm Catholic, and I let the nuns handle those things. That's why they joined the convent in the first place, and that's what they get paid for.

"On the other hand, one would certainly think that the majority of moms would jump at the opportunity to participate in any worthwhile secular activity their daughters were involved in. It seems to me that it would be a great way to develop a stronger tie with their daughters. It's a way to let them know that they are taking an active interest in their lives."

"Mara," Sherry had interjected, "I surely don't want to be disagreeable, but to my way of thinking, there is no better way to teach your children eternal values than to get them involved at an early age in the church. I agree with you that scouting prepares kids for this life, but growing up in a church that teaches our children that they can know God personally prepares them not only to live this life successfully but, more importantly, to know where they'll spend eternity."

Vicky had taken it all in but, up to that point, had remained silent. She obviously hadn't wanted to get involved in a controversial subject like religion.

I had been very uncomfortable with the direction the conversation had taken during that first meeting. I certainly had not called the meeting to talk about religion. I had decided to nip it in the bud tonight should the subject come up once again. I truly liked and respected both Carly and Sherry, but I had no interest in having them bring up the subject of religion when they attended a leadership meeting for the Girl Scouts. For this reason, I determined to get the troop business taken care of and end the meeting quickly when this had been accomplished.

Being careful not to deviate from the subject in question, I carefully discussed with the ladies all requirements needed for a successful sale, assigned leaders for the various groups, and had a brief question-and-answer session for those present who had never helped with a cookie sale.

The meeting ended in record time with much being accomplished. As the women left my home, each expressed gratitude once again for Vicky and I having the fortitude to take on this mammoth job of helping to shape their daughters' lives. They told us how much the girls enjoyed being members of our troop the past several months and how proud they were of their accomplishments thus far. A few of the moms volunteered their services for the coming camp outing in June.

When I finally said my last good-night, I felt a mixture of gratification and weariness grip me. I turned to see Vicky standing behind me and observing me closely as I closed the living-room door.

"Honey," she exclaimed with that soft, fluid Southern accent that I so loved. "Ya'll are certainly a devil in disguise, aren't you?"

"Now what in the world do you mean by that remark, my dear friend?" I responded, somewhat surprised by her unorthodox description of me.

"Mara, I would like to talk to you tomorrow morning, if ya'll plan on being home. I've got somethin' important on my mind I've been wantin' to discuss with you for quite a spell now. I know it's late, and you look pretty tuckered out. If it is okay with ya'll, I'll be over around ten in the morning."

"Of course, Vicky, that will be fine. I just, for the life of me, can't imagine what could be of such earth-shattering importance. But you have definitely aroused my curiosity. I'll be all ears, you can be sure."

"How do you think the meeting went? Did I cover all the bases?" I asked, abruptly changing the subject.

"The meeting went fine, honey. Now, ya'll run along to bed. Ya'll look like you could use a good night's sleep."

As she blew a kiss and closed the door behind her, I thought about how fortunate I had been to have Vicky as a next-door neighbor. They had moved into the neighborhood only a year before, but we had become friends almost immediately. I was enthralled with her soft Southern accent and her matter-of-fact attitude about life in general. Even though her ongoing struggle with her husband's drinking problem, plus an extremely tight budget, were things she had to face on a daily basis, she seemed well able to cope with both problems. I was extremely envious of her amazing strength which, on the other hand, I was greatly lacking.

Evidently, their earlier life together had been one that any young woman might envy. Ernie had a brilliant mind and a business savvy to match it. He had begun a local newspaper in the small community outside of Phoenix where they had made their home.

Within a very short time, the paper was getting rave reviews for its timely and brilliantly written editorial commentaries. Ernie was off and running—well on his way to a successful career doing what he loved to do. Just as he was nearing the pinnacle of success, something disastrous happened.

Vicky was reluctant to talk much about it at first. Evidently, it was the source of much pain and disappointment to both of them. What little she shared with me early on in our relationship had something to do with a man whose name was Bob, whom Ernie had hired to handle the marketing and the bookkeeping. Ernie was pleased with Bob's performance and was considering the possibility of offering him a partnership in the business.

Ernie felt the need to expand at this particular time as the business was growing more rapidly than he had expected it would. He needed more equipment, a larger building, and one or two additional people to handle the overflow. He knew that Bob had just recently come into a rather sizable sum of money, obviously inherited, and it was Ernie's intention to offer him 50 percent interest in the business if he wanted to buy in.

As fate would have it, before he had had the opportunity to do so, Ernie arrived at his office one morning to find the doors padlocked. There had been an official-looking notice affixed to the front door in his absence—indicating that, due to accrued unpaid bills and overdue taxes, he was being sued by his creditors for all delinquent monies. After a much-frenzied investigation, he arrived at the unhappy conclusion that Bob had been embezzling funds from the business.

Evidently, this shock was too much for Ernie to absorb. All his hopes and dreams had been dashed to pieces in an instant. As a result of this sudden reversal in his life, he had gradually turned to alcohol to soothe the savage beast raging inside him. It was at this point in time, after several moves and subsequent failures in new fields of endeavor, that Vicky and I had met.

She had informed Ernie that she was finished with the many moves she had to endure. At that point, they had three small girls, the youngest being a toddler. She was not willing to continue to go on like this and insisted that the family return to the Pittsburgh area where her mom and dad lived. She felt that she needed support from her parents and her younger siblings.

Regardless of Ernie's decision, she was taking the three girls and leaving for Pittsburgh the following weekend. Ernie knew that Vicky had drawn a line in the sand. He must comply with her decision or return to his single life once again. He loved his wife and children, so he decided to put an end to his useless struggle to find himself in the faraway state of Arizona.

Both Ernie and Vicky had lived in the Pittsburgh area when they first met and subsequently married several years before. Vicky was a Southern belle, born and raised in Alabama. When her dad was given the opportunity to take an excellent position with a large manufacturing concern in the Pittsburgh area, the family jumped at the opportunity and moved north. This had been Vicky's home for the seven remaining years that she had been single, and she was content to live with her family.

Vicky had attended high school in the Pittsburgh area, had made many friends, and secured her first job in downtown Pittsburgh. She considered herself a northerner and was disappointed when, after marrying Ernie, they had moved to the southwestern part of the country, where Ernie felt that his opportunity to attain success in his field of endeavor would be more promising.

It was at this point in time that Vicky and I met. They had rented a home right next door to ours with the intention of buying it once Ernie's business got off the ground.

As our friendship blossomed, little by little, she began to share her situation with me. In many ways, our lives paralleled. I could empathize with her as she confided in me her distain and disappointment at the unwelcome turn of events her life had taken.

I was not quite so desirous of sharing my life with Vicky. True, both our husbands were alcoholics and, as a result, were quite capable of creating chaos in our families. I was hesitant to reveal to her that I was having a major struggle with the bottle as well. I knew that Vicky would not touch any form of alcohol, and when she saw me take what I wanted her to believe was a social drink, I could detect a faint look of disapproval on her face.

While I was working during the week, we saw each other infrequently. After I retired from my position and was at home with the family, there would be more opportunities for us to develop our relationship. She and I would be working together with troop activities. Our older children were already playing together. I welcomed the opportunity to spend more time with her, but the prospect frightened me as well. How would I be able to hide from her the fact that I had the same problem that her husband, Ernie, had fallen prey to?

I was very careful not to place myself in a situation where she would be able to detect this problem in my life, or so I thought. I felt that I was a master of disguise when it came to hiding my big secret. Taking an honest look at her situation, I readily understood why she despised drinking as she did. It was a constant source of pain in her life and that of her children. If she were to become aware that I too had succumbed to this debilitating habit, my fear was that she would drop me like a hot potato. Having had the good fortune to find such a friend as Vicky, I certainly didn't want our friendship to end on such a note.

After I got the kids off to bed for the night, I went into our bedroom and took a good long swig from my old familiar friend Mr. Scotch. I wondered what Vicky had meant when she said that I was "the devil in disguise." It never occurred to me that perhaps she already had some inkling that I had a drinking problem. Had I given her cause to come to this conclusion?

Well, tomorrow morning will come soon enough, and the mystery will be solved, I concluded. *Right now I feel like I could use a good night's sleep. I really haven't slept well for the past few weeks. I certainly can't understand why this should be. I'm working a lot harder at home than I ever did while I was managing a credit department.*

I quickly changed into my pj's and hit the bed with a sigh of relief. I was so exhausted that I thought I'd be asleep before my head hit the pillow. I was wrong. Though my body was exhausted, my mind refused to fall in line with it.

I wonder what Vicky was referring to when she said that I was a devil in disguise, I pondered, staring at the black ceiling above me. I mentally scanned the previous weeks when we had spent significant time with each other. Other than attending midnight mass together, which turned into an utter fiasco, I couldn't put my finger on anything that may have caused her to detect that I had an addiction. After all, that was a solitary occurrence; and disgusting as it had been, it certainly couldn't have given her a clue to my condition, or could it?

A lot of people celebrate Christmas by attending office parties. This is just part of the big picture for those of us who are involved in corporation life. That particular party was much more than a reason to celebrate the holiday. It was a farewell send-off by my colleagues, many of whom I had known for years. I would be leaving my long-term position in a week to become a stay-at-home wife and mother. They knew that this had been my desire for some time now, and they were merely helping me celebrate the coming of the long-awaited event. In addition to that, they were aware that I was under pressure awaiting the news from Cleveland that one of my favorite aunts had passed on. They wanted to help me take the edge off with a few extra drinks.

Sometime later, as I tossed and turned, continuing my rationalization of this situation, I fell into a deep sleep. The reoccurring dream, which had often found its way into my subconscious mind over the past few weeks, once again repeated itself. In my dream, I knew that I was struggling to find the underlying meaning to it. There were familiar clues that I halfway remembered, but I couldn't put them together to complete the picture.

The dream was always the same—the blurred but brilliant kaleidoscope forming ever-changing patterns behind the manger scene. The familiar figures of Mary, Joseph, the wise men, the shepherds, and their sheep blurred by the central figure of the infant Jesus lying in the manger on a bed of straw. His arms were outstretched, and the tiny index figure of his right hand appeared to be pointing directly at me, beckoning me to come to him. The dream always ended at this point.

I awoke in the morning somewhat refreshed, but I was baffled once again, having no clue as to the events that had occurred on Christmas Eve while Vicky and I were attending midnight mass. The entire day into the evening had been surreal. It was like a giant jigsaw puzzle with a bunch of critical pieces missing.

CHAPTER 12

MY SECRET DISCOVERED

*R*ight on time, as always, I thought as the sound of the doorbell interrupted the serenity of our usually chaotic home on a Saturday morning. *That Vicky is certainly amazing. Five kids and a husband to feed, the house to pick up, a couple loads of wash and folding to do—and she's here, and not a minute late. How organized can one woman be?*

The kids had been anxious to build a huge snowman in the backyard. The snow was just right for snowman building this morning. It had not snowed for three or four days now, and what was still on the ground had hardened to just the right consistency for forming balls. After breakfast, I bundled up the two younger kids and stuck extra mittens in each of their jacket pockets, promising that I would join them after Mrs. O'Conner and I finished some very important business.

Before leaving for work, Rand had agreed to place the smaller snowball on top of the larger one to form Mr. Snowman. Randy, of course, was in charge of completing the larger one, and Roni the smaller one. If everything was finished and ready for assembly, Rand would finish the job when he returned from work at lunchtime.

Under my breath, I whispered a little prayer that he would come right home as promised today instead of making his usual stop at the bar next door to his office. Normally he worked all day on Saturday, but because of construction vehicles blocking the street parking around his building, he expected the floor traffic to be light. He had already alerted his sales staff that they were getting the afternoon off.

Randy and Roni were already hard at work in the snow, attempting to outdo each other as their tiny snowballs grew larger and larger, when the doorbell sounded. Randy, of course, was winning—I observed—as I glanced out of the kitchen window before opening the door for Vicky.

Rachael had been invited to a girlfriend's home for the day to play a new board game her friend had gotten for Christmas. I had extracted a promise from Randy before he was permitted to leave the house—no throwing of snowballs and no snowballs mysteriously finding their way down Roni's jacket. The penalty for disobedience would be his immediate removal from the yard to his bedroom for the duration of the day. I knew that two of his little friends would be joining them shortly to assist in the "great snowman" project, so I didn't anticipate any trouble.

After breakfast, Mom retreated to her room. She wasn't interacting much with the family these days. MoMo's death had set her back considerably. Having had to deal with this type of mental illness, I knew that I just had to have the patience to wait it out. At least she was beginning to eat normally again. That was a step in the right direction.

I had put together a caramel pecan roll before breakfast to go with our coffee. This was one of Vicky's favorite delicacies, and I certainly enjoyed doing something nice for her when I had the opportunity. She deserved it. I knew that she had a lot of heartache and sadness in her life; and whenever I had the chance, I tried to do something, no matter how seemingly insignificant, to brighten her day.

As I opened the door, I was greeted by a very serious Vicky, which was completely out of character for her. *Oh boy*, I thought warily. *I wonder what's going on under that mass of red curls. Is this concern for me, or did something happen at her house to cause this somber change that I detect?*

"Hi, girlfriend," I greeted her cheerfully, attempting to inject a little joy into the atmosphere. "I made your favorite breakfast roll this morning when I got up. Thought you'd like a slice of it with your coffee."

"Ya'll didn't need to go to the trouble, Mara. I didn't come over to eat this mornin', but then again, you might cut me just a wee bitty piece for dunkin' in my coffee since ya'll went to the trouble to make it. I just can't turn down your caramel pecan roll, honey. It's so yummy."

As I placed the steaming coffee and rolls on the table, I studied her face carefully.

"I know you well enough to see that something is really bugging you, Vicky. Is everything all right at home? Did Ernie make it home in one piece last night? Are the kids okay? What's going on?"

"Mara," she responded, so seriously I hardly recognized her voice, "everything is all right at my house—well, as good as can be expected. My question to ya'll is this. Is everything all right at your house?"

"Look, Vicky, you're not one to pull any punches, so why not get right to the point?"

"Okay, sweetheart. I will do just that. Rand told me a while back that he was lookin' for someone to stay with your children and your mom for a spell because ya'll were goin' away. I asked him where you were goin', and he told me that he was plannin' to take you to a place where ya'll could get help with your drinkin' problem. He asked me if maybe my younger sister, Lori, might be interested in the job. He didn't know how long you'd be away, so he couldn't give me a definite time frame until he spoke with your doctor.

"'I heard you tell Mara how much Lori likes children,' he had said. Aside from that, he knew that she was fresh out of college and hadn't started to look for work yet. The money he was willing to pay might come in handy, he had surmised."

I looked at her in utter disbelief. She could see that I had no idea what my husband had planned for me.

Vicky had broken the ice, and there was nothing in the world that could stop her now from pulling out all the stops. "You know, Mara, I wasn't sure about ya'll for a long time. I should be able to spot a habitual drinker a mile off. After all, I live with one, don't I? But I couldn't be sure. I really never saw ya'll drink much. It was Christmas Eve when we went to church together that I really began to think that maybe ya'll had a real bad problem. Then a few days later, when Rand came over to our house to get your kids, he told me what the problem was."

"Honey," she continued without stopping to take a breath, "do ya'll realize that ya'll made fools out of both of us in church that night? Do you remember anything at all about Christmas Eve?"

Without giving me an opportunity to answer, she supplied one for me. "I doubt it," she continued.

She was fired up now, and I knew from experience that I had to let this fire run its course and burn itself out naturally. Nothing I could say in my own defense would be of any value. Actually, there wasn't anything that I could say in my defense. I didn't remember much after putting Randy to bed. Kathy came over to stay with them when her mom picked me up. After that, most of the evening was one big blur.

Vicky continued her interrogation. She wanted me to know, in no uncertain terms, that I had been totally out of control and that she had been asked by the ushers to keep me quiet, or they would be forced to escort me out of the building. If she was attempting to shame me out of my wretched habit, she was certainly giving it her best effort. She was filling in all the nasty details of my outlandish behavior. Being married to a habitual drinker, I'm sure she realized that, no matter how much shame we alcoholics may feel as the result of our actions, it's going to take a lot more than that to get rid of the wretched habit.

"Do you remember singing the Christmas hymns so loud that everyone in the church could hear you? A man who was sitting a few pews in front of us turned around and told me to shut you up. 'Does she think she's the lead soloist for this mass?' the gentleman had asked indignantly.

"Mara, honey, ya'll have no idea how humiliated I was in that service. It was packed out, or I would have gotten ya'll out of there quicker than a bunny finds his hole when he's bein' chased by a fox."

Vicky was ranting now. She had begun to enumerate each embarrassing incident that had taken place during the Christmas service. Although I was looking directly at her and could hear the steady drone of her voice, it seemed to fade into the background as my mind went back in time to the events of that infamous Christmas Eve afternoon and evening.

There had been an office party at work. Hors d'oeuvres and martinis had been ordered in around lunchtime, and the party was in full swing by the time it was suggested we close shop and beat the last-minute traffic home. This gathering, much to my surprise, turned out to be not only our regular annual Christmas office party but also a farewell send-off for me. I had only one week to work before leaving my position permanently to become a full-time wife and mom. As old friends from other divisions of the company dropped by to say their good-byes and wish me well, the time passed quickly.

The janitor came by at one point and reminded us that it was Christmas Eve for him too. He would be happy if we would leave the office so he could get his job finished and get home to his family. Reluctantly, we gathered our gifts and other personal belongings and left the building. Someone suggested that, since it was only five in the evening, we should drop into one of our after-work haunts and have one last nightcap for Mara. By this time, none of us was feeling any pain, and as a result, the party was getting a little rowdy.

It was after seven when I arrived home. Kathy was becoming frantic as she had lost control of the kids. In just a few more hours, the jolly fat man in his red suit would be squeezing his rotund frame down our chimney. The children were becoming excited in anticipation of the soon-coming holiday and everything that went with it.

"Mrs. Reuben, you said that you would be home by five o'clock. My mother called twice and reminded me that I promised to help finish trimming the tree before she left for midnight mass. She asked me if you had left a number where you could be reached. I told her that you had not given me a number. She was pretty upset about the whole thing. I could hear it in her voice."

"Okay, honey, let me pay you. I want to give you some money for the extra two hours and also a Christmas gift from the Reuben family to their favorite babysitter."

"Before I leave," Kathy volunteered, "I think that I had better tell you what happened here while I was watching the kids. Randy knocked the tree down a couple hours ago chasing Roni and the dog around the house. Rachael came home from her girlfriend's house a few minutes later, so we all worked really fast to put it up and looking good again before you got home. I'm glad you were late, even though Mom isn't," she added. "We did a nice job, don't you think?"

"Actually, it was all pretty exciting," she continued. "It gave everyone something special to do to keep busy, and there were only two ornaments broken out of all that mess. Too bad that one of them had to be one of those old-fashioned glass ornaments that your grandmother gave you. Randy told me not to tell you, and maybe you wouldn't miss it. I told him that I couldn't do that. When I began to babysit last year, Mom told me to report to the parents everything important that happened while I was in charge."

"I appreciate that, Kathy. You did the right thing. Here is your extra money and twenty dollars for your Christmas present. I hope your mom isn't too mad at me for being late," I added, escorting her to the door.

I was doing the best that I could, but I was aware that I was slurring my words. I hoped that none of the kids would notice. "You run along now, honey. I know your mom is waiting for you." I managed to get out an almost unintelligible, "Sweetheart, I hope youanyourfamily have a very {hic} Merry Christmas, all right?"

Kathy looked at me with a faint smirk on her lips. I vaguely recall that, at that moment, I had an almost uncontrollable urge to slap that smug look right off her face. She was a nice girl, but how dare she be able to detect that I have had too much to drink? I thought that I was doing a pretty good job of disguising my condition. I had even made it home without a police escort.

"Merry Christmas everyone and thank you, Mrs. Reuben. Randy wasn't too bad today, except for the Christmas tree incident," Kathy added as she stepped outside, closing the door behind her.

After a few choice expletives directed at my son, warning him of the serious consequences of his behavior, I made my way carefully to the bedroom to change into something more comfortable. I was feeling a little unstable on my feet and certainly didn't want the children to notice anything out of the ordinary about me.

The girls reminded me that I had promised to help them with the last batch of cookies before bedtime. The two younger children always left a plate of cookies and a glass of milk for Santa. They thought that Santa would be extra hungry tonight because he would be working "overtime."

"Did your dad call?" I asked the girls as I followed them to the kitchen, tying an apron around Roni's small frame.

"Daddy called when we were fixing the tree, Mummy, and I told him that it was all Randy's fault that the tree fell down because he was chasing me and Sparky around the house with his air rifle. Daddy didn't say anything about that. He just wanted to know if you got home yet. I told him, 'No, Mommy's not here yet, and it's dawk outside.'"

Randy appeared in the doorway as Roni was ending her dissertation on the events of the last few hours. "You're such a little tattletale, Roni. I'd like to belt you across your mouth for that," he said, his arm raised to take a shot at her.

"Randall Charles Reuben, go to your room this minute. Christmas Eve or not, I've had enough of this from you. Can't we even celebrate the birth of the Christ child without all this fighting and confusion?"

Rachael, who had been quietly observing all this, made a comment that cut into me like a knife. "Mommy, do you think Jesus wants grown-up people to celebrate his birthday by getting drunk? You're drunk again, and I know that Daddy is at a party with his friends from work, and he's getting drunk too. He promised me he'd come home early and help me wrap your present, and he broke his promise again. It's almost bedtime, and he's not here yet."

I stood for an instant, dumbfounded by my oldest child's accurate observation. I might be able to fool my two younger kids, but Rachael was now old enough to see that the dysfunction in our home was caused mainly by alcohol.

My God, I thought. *Things are out of control here. My son is out of control. My marriage is out of control. I'm out of control. What in the world am I going to do about this situation?*

At that moment, the phone rang. I felt relief at this convenient interruption. At least I could put Rachael's probing question on hold until I could think of a good answer to give her, assuming there was a good answer.

"Girls, start getting the ingredients ready for our cookies, and I'll be with you just as soon as I see who's on the phone."

I turned to Randy. "Randall, I want you to get your teeth brushed and get into your jammies immediately. I'll be in to get you tucked in as soon as I get off the phone. Do not make me tell you again. Now go," I commanded.

He disappeared into the bathroom like a bolt of lightning. Apparently, the sound of my voice was sufficient to let him know that there would be no argument regarding bedtime tonight, Christmas Eve or not.

Answering the phone, I heard Vicky's concerned voice on the other end. "Hi, honey, Merry Christmas. Is everything all right?" Vicky drawled in that soft Southern accent. "I've been watchin' out of the window for your car to pull into your driveway. Ya'll are late gettin' home, sweetie. You didn't forget about midnight mass, did you?"

Not giving me time to answer, she reminded me that we would have to leave at ten-thirty if we wanted to get seats.

I responded with some trite explanation for my late arrival. Even as I heard the feeble excuse roll from my lips, I knew that I wasn't fooling this gal. After all, wasn't she married to a full-fledged alcoholic? Wasn't she, of all people, aware of the endless times her Ernie had disappointed her by being late for an event they had planned? Many times, he had failed to show up at all, leaving her to face family or guests, embarrassed beyond belief with the same tired, worn-out excuses she had used many times before in an effort to justify his absence.

"No, Vicky," I lied. "I didn't forget about church tonight. I'll pick you up about twenty after ten, okay?"

"Honey," she replied hesitantly, "if it's all the same to ya'll, how about lettin' me do the drivin' tonight? After all, church was my idea, and beside that, it sounds to me like you got a real snoot full at your office party today."

Normally I found Vicky to be both amusing and genuinely concerned as she would mildly chide me on the few occasions that she knew I had been drinking. Her engaging yet direct approach to life was refreshing. It was softened by her easygoing attitude and that engaging accent of hers. Nonetheless, she was a dynamic little redhead with some real firepower—charming but deadly serious—as her well-intentioned remarks hit home with total accuracy.

Tonight was an exception. I was becoming increasingly irritated with her as she prodded me about my drinking. The pleasant buzz I had experienced throughout the day was beginning to wear off. In its place, I could feel a whopper of a headache moving into my head.

Randy was yelling at me from his bedroom. The girls were in the kitchen arguing about who was going to use the gingerbread-man cookie cutter first, and Rand wasn't home yet to look after the children.

I'd better have them all in bed and asleep before he gets home, I reflected. *He won't be in any shape to deal with a bunch of excited kids on Christmas Eve. What the hell! He can't deal with them when he's sober.*

Turning my attention to Vicky, I said in a mildly agitated way, "Okay, my anxious friend, I'm good to go. But if it will make you feel better, you can do the honors tonight. I'll be ready when you get here. Just give me a toot on your horn. By the way, Rand is making his Christmas Eve rounds as usual. If he doesn't get home before we're ready to leave for church, could you send Kathy or Linda over to stay with the kids until he gets here? The two little ones will be in bed. Let me know, okay?"

I hurriedly hung up the phone before I gave her time to respond. I knew that there would be opposition to this request. What teenager wants to babysit on Christmas Eve? I was certain that one of her two older girls would be home with the three younger children while she and I were at church. Perhaps Linda would be willing to come over for a short time. Rand and Ernie were both of the same mind when it came to celebrating the holiday, and it didn't have anything to do with spending a quiet evening at home with family.

As I glanced toward the kitchen on my way to tuck Randy in for the night, I reassured the girls that I would be with them in a few minutes to help with the cookies. In the meantime, I told them to take turns rolling the dough. This should keep them busy during the time I would spend with their brother.

Randy was in bed, much to my surprise, running his Matchbox race cars along an imaginary mountain road that he had made with his blankets. He looked at me with that sincere expression of repentance that had melted my heart so many times in the past. He was certainly a charmer when he wanted to be and accurately named for the daddy whom he adored and emulated.

I was determined this time that Randy would not go undisciplined for his threat to harm Roni, especially when he had been the instigator of the action that had caused the problem to begin with. I would use this situation as an object lesson. This was Randy's first year in CCD class, which was taught at our church for all children whose family were members in good standing. Perhaps I could reinforce a principle that he had already studied in one of these classes, the importance of being obedient to one's parents.

Before I had a chance to begin my little sermon, Randy—once again with a pleading voice and tears running down his face—promised that he would never be mean to his sister ever again.

I had heard this tale of woe many times in the past, and this time, I was going to remain steadfast in dealing with the situation. His feigned sincerity and skillful persuasiveness were not going to win me over. This child needed discipline in his life, and I was going to administer it. I felt that I had the upper hand under the circumstances. There were things at stake for Randy. Not only was he being left out of our traditional Christmas Eve reading of *The Christmas Carol* with his sisters, but he would miss out on the freshly baked cookies as well. I suspected that he was much more interested in the cookies than he was in Charles Dickens.

As I was determined to carry out this disciplinary action, it seemed to be the perfect time to talk to him about spiritual things, as well relating them to his behavior with his younger sister.

"Do you think that God gets angry with us when we promise to be good over and over again and then we break our promise to him?" I asked as I pulled his comforter over his shoulders and removed his race cars from the bedding.

"Oh, Mommy, don't be dumb," Randy responded. "Daddy says that God doesn't have time for little things like this. He's too busy with big things like wars and bank robberies and all that important stuff. Daddy says that he's not even sure that God is real. He says that he has to see something before he believes it, and he has never seen God. Daddy says that even if God is real, He sure isn't interested in kids when they fight with each other. He's got more important things to do."

Without further comment, I kissed Randy good-night and left his room with an uneasy feeling in the pit of my stomach. I just didn't understand my husband. He constantly undermined every religious value that I attempted to teach our children. His dad was an Orthodox Jew, raised according to the teachings of the Torah. I was certain that Pop had attempted to instruct Rand in these teachings; but he had confided in me, during one of our conversations on religion, that Rand from his early teen years was resistant to religion and its many rules and regulations. He had absolutely no interest in the subject.

Perhaps it was the anti-Semitism that seemed to be prevalent in the community where Rand had been raised, or perhaps it was something entirely different. Pop had no way of knowing because Rand had never discussed it with him. All I knew was that this was just one more obstacle in our marriage that I had to circumvent, and it appeared that I was fighting another losing battle.

Recently, he had adopted an agnostic point of view toward God, and it was evident that he was influencing his son in this direction. I had been amazed that he even permitted the children to attend CCD classes. His response to that was very noble. He felt that it would be better for the children to be given the opportunity to investigate all sides of the issue for themselves. When they were old enough to make their own decisions on the subject, they were free to do so.

I certainly did not agree with this line of reasoning. It had always been my contention that we, as responsible parents, were to raise our children according to our own belief system. If they strayed from the faith when they became adults, at least we had done our best to lead them in the right direction. Since Rand had no particular belief, the least he could do would be to allow me to instruct them in Catholicism. This, at the very least, would give them something to believe in. Something was better than nothing, wasn't it?

By this time, my head was throbbing. My pleasant buzz had worn off. Over the years, I had prided myself on the way I handled alcohol. Too little was not effective in creating the effect I desired and left me feeling tired and dull. Too much—as I found I was experiencing more often than I cared to admit—put me in a position where I was no longer in control. To my way of thinking, I had found the happy medium. Tonight was evolving into a situation that might sorely test my theory.

As I left Randy's room and started for the kitchen, I thought about the half-empty bottle of Chivas Regal hidden away in my briefcase.

That's it, I thought. *A few ounces of Scotch will get me through the evening.*

I could hear the girls' laughter coming from the kitchen. I looked behind me to be absolutely certain that Randy had not followed me out into the hall for another trip to the bathroom. Mom had retired to her room hours ago, the babysitter had said. All clear. I opened the closet door and groped in the semidarkness until I felt the familiar soft leather of my briefcase. Inside, hidden under my training manual and other file folders from the office, was the coveted bottle of instant liquid joy.

I opened it quickly and raised the bottle to my lips. The smooth amber liquid slid down my throat effortlessly, releasing a familiar warmth throughout my entire body. Along with that familiar sensation came a renewed spurt of instant energy, which I so desperately needed to get through the next few hours. As I leaned against the closet door to await the full impact of the Scotch, I heard Rachael's impatient voice calling me from the kitchen.

"Come on, Mommy, everything's on the table to finish the cookies. I even rolled the dough like you showed me, but it's too fat in some places and too thin in other places. I think you'll have to fix it a little bit before Roni and I use the cookie cutters to make shapes. The buzzer just went off. Hurry up, please."

"Okay, Rachael," I responded. "I'm going into the bathroom for a minute. Then I'll be right down. What's the big hurry anyhow? We have plenty of time."

"Yah, Mummy," Roni added, her voice rising in excitement. "These are Santy's favowite cookies, and I got a cawwot from the frig for Rudolph. I weally want Chatty Cathy for Christmas. Do you think Santy will bwing me Chatty Cathy for Christmas, Mummy?"

I was attempting to buy some much-needed time to allow the alcohol to do its job. While in the bathroom, I ran my toothbrush over my teeth and gargled with some mouthwash in order to take away the smell of whiskey from my breath.

Briefly reviewing the events of the day, I vaguely recalled that I had been having too much fun to think about Vicky and the promise I had made to go with her to midnight mass. I had thought about it earlier in the week. Then it left my mind completely with all the hustle and bustle of the holiday absorbing my extra time and energy. It had been my intention to leave the office early. One drink with the gang—that would be it. I still had a few last-minute gifts to wrap for the kids and a few close friends.

The girls had one more cookie recipe they wanted me to help them with. I would get home in plenty of time to take care of the few remaining chores that still needed my attention in preparation for Christmas morning. The kids and I had started a tradition a few years before. We would turn the tree lights, the mantle, and the outside lights on and gather around the tree. I would read a portion of the Dickens's classic *The Christmas Carol*. Rachael liked to assist me with part of it. She was an excellent reader and liked to show off a little to her siblings.

While we were reading, the kids would be enjoying some of the freshly baked cookies that had just come out of the oven with their mugs of hot chocolate. We made certain that we put a few of those cookies and a glass of milk on the coffee table for Santa, and Roni made doubly sure that we didn't forget the cawwot for Rudolph.

After the kids were settled for the night, I had planned to take a long, hot shower and a couple of aspirins and go to bed early, giving me ample time to sleep off the lingering effects of the booze consumed during the afternoon. I was planning a large family gathering for dinner tomorrow evening, and I wanted to be up for it. I knew from previous years that Rand would not be home until much later.

As was frequently the case, things had not turned out as planned. I had arrived home two hours later than expected. The telephone call from Vicky had jolted me back into reality. Being strong on commitment, I couldn't let her down. Vicky, in the brief time since we had become friends, had always been there for me when her many obligations would allow. I knew that she had a lot to cope with. An alcoholic husband and five children would be enough to try any woman's soul. Yet when I couldn't come up with an appropriate assistant troop leader to help me with the troop I had agreed to lead last year, Vicky came to the rescue.

No, as horrible as I was beginning to feel, I determined that I would not let her down. I was going to church come hell or high water. At that point, my thinking became confused, and images were becoming blurred.

The first thing I was consciously aware of was the fact that Kathy had come to my rescue to look after the children until either Rand or her mother and I got home. I noticed that the cookies were in neat rows of Santa Clauses, gingerbread men, and Christmas trees. They were on the kitchen table all beautifully decorated with icing and colored sugar.

Roni was fast asleep, I noticed, as I opened the girls' bedroom door and took a quick look in the direction of her bed. She was sleeping soundly, as was Randy. Rachael was in the kitchen with Kathy, helping take the clean dishes and utensils out of the dishwasher and put them away. Vicky was impatiently waiting in the foyer for me to put on my coat. I noticed that she had a very strange look on her face. She was watching me intently.

At that moment, I remember thinking, *I must have had help from Santa's elves this evening. I sure don't remember doing any of this.*

Vicky grabbed my coat from me and began to help me get it on as she handed me my gloves and scarf from the container in the coat closet.

"Why don't ya'll sit down in your armchair, and I'll help ya to get your boots on, honey. It is bitter cold outside. You'll be okay when a blast of that frigid air hits you in the face. We sure can't dillydally, though. We're already fifteen minutes later than we planned on leavin'. The car is all nice and cozy. That's the good news. I had to leave it on the street because your driveway is a sheet of ice. I think that I'll grab your arm, and we can hold each other up, okay? If we walk through the yard where the snow is higher, we'll be less likely to slide on the ice."

⇒⁺⁺⇐

"Hey, Mara, come back to me, honey. Ya'll haven't heard a word I've said, have ya?"

"Yes, I have too, Vicky. I've heard every word you've said. As a matter of fact, much of the account you've given me regarding the Christmas Eve service has triggered something in my brain. Finally, I'm beginning to fill in the blanks. Just hearing you talk about all this has enabled me to have some instant recall. I don't remember everything that happened that night, but much of it is coming back. If I can eventually put all the missing pieces together, I believe I will be able to understand what that dream I've been having is all about. Remember that dream that I told you about?"

"Mara, ya'll scare me. What are ya talkin' about? Just because ya'll have the same dream over and over again, that doesn't necessarily mean it's somethin' important. Who do ya think ya'll are anyhow, a fortune-teller or a tea-leaf reader? Or maybe you think you're the prophet Daniel—you know, that Jewish guy in the Old Testament who was able to interpret dreams?"

She did not wait for my response. Vicky had other things on her mind this morning, and the secret code to unlock the meaning of my recurring dream was not one of them.

"Listen to me, honey. Ya'll have a serious problem. I'm in agreement with your husband. Ya really do need help, and the sooner ya'll get it, the better. Your kids are going to suffer for this if you don't cooperate with Rand. I know that he's far from perfect, but he has your best interest at heart. Well, maybe not just yours, honey, certainly his too, and the kids'. Don't forget about your poor mom. Who would be willing to take care of her if ya'll were no longer able to be here for her? There's a whole lot at stake here, Mara.

131

You've got a mountain of responsibility, so ya'll had better start thinkin' about what ya'll are going to do to get your life straightened out."

"I'm here for ya'll, honey," she continued. "Maybe God moved me and my family right into the house beside yours because He knew that I would be able to help ya through this someday. I've been aware over the years, since my Ernie has developed this problem that God has given me the strength to get through each day no matter what happens. He's also taught me how to deal with an alcoholic mind-set. Mara, not everyone can do this, but believe me, I can. I've had a lot of practice."

I looked at Vicky with a new appreciation. Sitting across from me was a real friend.

There are friends, and then there are friends. It's all relative, I thought. This one's a keeper. She's not going to abandon me because she can't deal with the fact that I'm just one more thorn in her side. She's true blue, really loyal, and I am so fortunate to have someone like her to walk through this with me, someone who truly understands my dilemma.

I could feel hot tears stinging my eyes as my body began to shake violently from the sobs that were gripping my entire being.

"I'm going to take your advice, Vicky," I said between sobs. "I'll keep that appointment with the shrink, or whoever it is that Rand has scheduled me to see. I can't do this myself. No one knows it better than I do. I've tried everything to shake this addiction, and nothing works. I've got to try it Rand's way. It could mean that I'll be away from my family for a while, but if it works, then it will be worth it, won't it?"

Vicky got up from her chair and quickly moved to my side of the table. She put her arms around me and gently wiped the tears that were now running down my face.

"Mara," she said firmly, "ya'll have just taken the first step to total recovery. Ya'll admitted that you need help. I'm waitin' to hear these same words from my husband's mouth, but more important-ly, from his heart. When this happens, my troubles will begin to come to an end, just as yours have begun to come to an end this morning."

CHAPTER 13

A MOST UNUSUAL CHRISTMAS EVE

The first weeks of February brought cold winds, intermittent snowstorms and school closings for the kids in our district. This turned out to be a blessing in disguise for Girl Scout Troop 344. While the schools were closed, some of the more energetic kids in our troop were busy knocking on doors throughout the community with a variety of tasty Girl Scout cookies to sell. For the most part, they were welcomed by housewives who seemed to be glad to buy from any girl who was willing to defy the elements in order to get a sale.

Sherry, Carly, and I put in many hours tallying sales, ordering cookies, and generally speaking, overseeing all aspects of the sale. During the time the sale was in progress, the three of us got to know one another much better. Observing these two ladies as we worked diligently with the girls, I was impressed with the way they encouraged our scouts to do the best job that they could do. During this time, I gained new respect for both of them. Once again, as I had observed at our initial meeting, I saw that same quality emerge in each of them which I had so admired and secretly envied.

A week after the sale ended, I was notified by the home office of the Girl Scout Association of America that our troop had taken top honors for having sold the most cookies in the district. It was no surprise to me when I was also informed that Sherry's daughter, Chris, and Carly's daughter, Pam, had come in first and second for the highest volume of cookies sold. The prizes to the top two sellers were monetary gifts of two hundred and one hundred dollars, and the troop to which they belonged would also receive a two-hundred-dollar award for having produced such outstanding scouts.

I called Carly immediately with the news. I knew that I would be seeing Sherry in a few days to count the money from the proceeds of the sale. I would tell her personally when we met.

Carly told me that Sherry and Chris had both been praying that the troop would be blessed for all their hard work. "It looks like God has answered that prayer," she said, "but he also blessed Chris and Pam in a special way. Outside the providence of God himself, Sherry confided in me that she could not afford to send Chris to camp this summer, and this is what Chris wants more than anything.

"Sherry just doesn't have that kind of money. From what you have told me, it looks like God has favored both girls. Chris now has the opportunity to attend camp if this is how she would like to use the two hundred dollars."

"'So you think that God had something to do with this, Carly?" I asked in total disbelief.

She responded without hesitation, "Of course, I do, Mara. God is interested in everything his kids do. If what we are praying for is a concern to us, it certainly is a concern to him. He is our Heavenly Father."

"I tend to disagree with you, Carly, but you are entitled to your opinion."

Once again, I changed the subject abruptly, not at all comfortable with the direction it was taking. "Incidentally, Carly, don't say anything about this to Sherry. If you don't mind, I'd like to tell her the good news myself. The money from the proceeds of the cookie sale will be delivered to me this afternoon by one of the people from our downtown headquarters.

"I have to count it again and then have Sherry count it to be certain that the totals are the same. Since she is my cookie chairman, this is necessary just to keep everything on the up-and-up."

That evening I was able to reach Sherry on the phone. "I'm wondering when it would be convenient to stop by so we can count the proceeds from the sale," I asked. "It shouldn't take more than an hour or so, Sherry."

"How about Monday after dinner, around seven-thirty, Mara? Does that suit your schedule? I was prepared for this because you had mentioned something about me keeping you accountable for the money when I volunteered for this job."

"Sounds good to me, Sherry. I'll see you then. Bye now."

I wanted to end this conversation as quickly as possible. The subject of religion, which always seemed to surface during our conversations, made me uneasy. My religious beliefs or lack of them were my business. I really didn't want to discuss this subject with anyone.

Nonetheless, try as I may, the dialogue that Carly and I shared during our phone conversation continued to resound in my mind throughout the remainder of the day.

I wonder if God would be willing to answer a prayer for me like Sherry seems to believe he did for her and Chris. Maybe I'll give it a try. It sure can't do any harm. One thing I know for certain. I need to get rid of this drinking problem before it ruins my life and my children's lives as well. But I don't want to have to be hospitalized in the process. It would mean being away from the kids and from my mother. They need me to be here.

While I was considering the possibility of writing out such a prayer so I wouldn't leave out anything of importance, my mind again returned to the Christmas Eve service at our church.

I recalled that sometime during the mass, I already had some kind of a conversation with God, something about making a deal with Him. I vaguely recalled that I challenged him to reveal himself to me, but only on the condition that he was who he professed to be. If he was willing to do that, I would make it my business to get my life together and begin to live the way he wanted me to live.

I must have been half out of my mind with booze to suggest such a thing to God. How could I possibly have had the audacity to think that he would be agreeable to something like that, especially coming from a drunk like me? Yet somewhere hidden deep down in some unseen, unknown part of me, I seemed to sense that something of profound importance was taking place, something that would greatly impact my life in the days to come.

"Have I heard that voice before? Oh yes, I remember. That was the same voice that had communicated with me as a child, giving me direction for each critical step I was about to take during those very dark years of my early life."

It was not an audible voice but a sound, an echo, something unfamiliar to me. It was coming from my innermost being. It seemed to be a part of me, and yet somehow separate from me. I couldn't explain it. The thought suddenly dawned on me that this indeed could be God's way of giving me direction as he had done so many years before.

I searched my mind frantically in an effort to remember what else had transpired during the service. I vaguely recalled that my attention was focused on the manger scene at the front of the church. It was beautifully lighted by green and red floodlights and surrounded by tall stately pine trees that had been adorned with a myriad of colored lights. The entire scene was a hazy blur of colors running together like a many-faceted kaleidoscope. The alcohol had done a thorough job on my brain. I had reached the saturation point. Still, this was reminiscent of the recurring dream that had haunted me for weeks.

Instantly, I went back in time to that cold winter morning when Aunt Harriet and I saw from a distance a scene similar to that which now captured my total attention. The Nativity scene, that wonderful reenactment of the birth of the baby Jesus, had been placed in front of St. Catherine's church for the viewing pleasure of the faithful. How vividly I recalled the deep sense of disappointment I felt when we arrived at the church only to find a group of cardboard figures supported from behind by wooden stands. In my eight-year-old naivety, what I expected to be real people and their live animals were nothing more than poster-board facsimiles.

I recalled glancing around the crowded church when I noticed my neighbor Marcia decked out as usual in her full-length ranch mink coat. How often she reminded me and anyone else who was willing to listen that her husband, Joel, carefully selected each skin and then had each one perfectly matched with the one to be placed beside it in preparation for the final assembly of the garment. No doubt about it, it was a gorgeous coat. But that's all it was—a fur coat.

Marcia and I were nothing more than passing acquaintances. I couldn't stand her materialism, and her affectation was something for which I had no time or stomach. She only attended church to show off her wardrobe. Worshipping God and listening to his Word were of very little concern to her. But were these things really any more important to me?

At that point, I turned my attention to what was presently occurring in the sanctuary. One of my favorite Christmas hymns, "Oh, Come, All Ye Faithful," was being sung by the congregation, and I began to join in. I must have been singing a little louder than I should have been because an usher came to our pew and threatened to have me physically removed from the service if I wasn't able to get control of myself.

Vicky, faithful friend that she was, went to bat for me, promising the usher that she would take full responsibility for my behavior. If another outburst were to occur, she would get help and take me out of the church. I remembered at that moment that Vicky must have deeply regretted her insistence that I accompany her to the church that evening. What a risk she ran, knowing full well that I had been drinking for most of the day.

Just then, out of the corner of my eye, I caught a glimpse of a neighbor whom I hadn't seen for some time. Jack and I were both members of the PTA and very much interested in the scholastic progress of our children. For some reason, Jack had been absent from the monthly meetings and other school events recently. Rumor had it that he was having marital problems, and possibly there was another woman involved.

As our eyes met, I observed that these rumors might very well be credible. On his arm was an attractive blonde-haired woman considerably younger than his wife. Both had obviously been celebrating the holiday in a big way and enjoying each other's company immensely. Immediately upon recognition, Jack turned his glance away from mine.

Funny thing, I remembered thinking. *It doesn't appear that Jack wants to be recognized with a woman who is not his wife. Well, if that's the case, then what in the hell is he doing in church with her on Christmas Eve? Didn't he realize when he brought her here that there was a likely possibility he would be seen by people who knew him? After all, this is a small community. Many of us run into each other frequently.*

Then again, maybe he planned it this way. Maybe this is his coming-out party. He should be home with his wife and children, especially tonight of all nights—but then, I should be too. So should Rand and Ernie. I certainly don't have the right to judge this man when my own life is every bit as loathsome. What a bunch of hypocrites some of us are. We're trying to pretend to be something we're not. We're attempting to cover our sins with a blanket of phony self-righteousness. God must be sitting up there in his heaven regretting that he ever made us.

My eyes returned to the manger scene. I remembered that I glanced at the lifelike statue of the baby earlier in the service. For an instant, I thought that I had seen His finger move in my direction, beckoning me to come to him. I shook it off immediately, realizing that I had consumed way too much alcohol.

I was hallucinating, I assured myself. *This is nothing new.*

I had experienced this phenomenon before. Still, I continued to stare at the image of the tiny infant lying on a bed of straw.

It appeared that the mass was coming to a conclusion. I wondered why Father John had not preached his usual Christmas sermon. I thought it very strange because he always had a sermon on Christmas Eve. As the overhead lights dimmed, the organ began the opening chords of the familiar hymn "Silent Night." As I continued to fix my gaze on the baby once again, I thought that I saw movement in the manger. Even the straw was moving slightly as the child repeated his invitation to me. A piece of straw fell out of the manger and dropped to the floor.

I turned to Vicky at that instant, and with an impatient gesture, I told her that I had to get out of the church immediately.

"What's wrong, honey? Ya'll got to use the restroom?"

"No," I said impatiently. "I just have to get out of here. Come on, if you're going with me. Let's go."

"Mara, what in the world is wrong with ya'll? Ya look like ya'll have seen a ghost. I saw ya fussin' in your seat a few minutes ago. What did ya'll see, or should I say, what do ya'll think ya saw?"

"Never mind, Vicky. You wouldn't believe it if I told you."

"Look, honey, mass is goin' to be over in a minute or two. Can't ya'll wait a little longer? That way, we won't have to push through the crowd. Back in the vestibule, there's standin' room only. A few people have already gone, but it's still crowded. Besides," she added as an afterthought, "I'm not goin' with ya'll. Ya'll are goin' with me. Remember, I'm drivin' tonight."

"Okay, you're the boss, Vicky. I guess I'll just have to wait," was my curt reply.

Exiting the church a few minutes later, we saw a few neighbors who lived on our street and a few parents of girls who were in our troop. We stopped to wish them a merry Christmas. Before I had a chance to speak to anyone, Vicky quickly directed me to where she had parked her car and, just as quickly, whisked me inside.

"My goodness," she said breathlessly. "It must be below zero, and that wind makes it seem colder than that. I better drive very careful. It was slippery gettin' here, and it will probably be just as bad or worse gettin' home. Ya'll feel better now that you're out of church? If I didn't know ya so well, I would venture to say that the good Lord was dealin' with your soul in there," she jokingly remarked.

"You hit the nail on the head, Vicky. That is exactly what He was doing."

We arrived home a few minutes later without incident. Vicky was able to get up my driveway without skidding.

"Rand must be home, honey. Someone salted your driveway. I'll help ya'll get into your house, and then I'll be on my way. Looks like Ernie made it home too. His car is parked on the street. He's probably waitin' for me to pull in ahead of him."

"Vicky, you know something? I don't think I'm going to need any help getting into my house. I feel perfectly fine. My head is as clear as a bell."

"Yeah, uh-huh. I've heard that one before," she responded in total disbelief.

Not wanting to insult me, Vicky hesitated for a minute, giving me the opportunity to prove to her that my last statement was accurate. I opened the door, and while carefully avoiding a patch of ice close to the car, I slowly but cautiously made my way toward the garage door.

She waited behind the wheel, watching my every move, ready to jump into action if needed. I glanced back slowly as I reached my destination, using my automatic door opener to enter the house through the garage entrance. I waved and blew her a kiss, mouthing the words, "Merry Christmas" and, "Thanks for the ride, sweetheart" as I entered the garage. The last thing I saw before closing the door was the amazed look on her face.

Entering the living room, I saw Rand asleep or unconscious on the sofa. I wasn't sure which. He had removed his suit coat, his tie, and his shoes and had rolled up the sleeves of his dress shirt, which was noticeably wrinkled. The lights were still lit on the tree and mantle, and when Vicky dropped me off in the driveway, I noticed that the outdoor lights were still on as well.

The house was quiet. Evidently, Kathy left when Rand got home to relieve her. Rachael had gone to bed. It appeared that her request had been carried out by her daddy because there was now a solitary package under the tree, which had been decorated with Christmas wrap. The tag on it was addressed "to Mommy, from Rachael, Randy, and Roni."

Well, what do you know? I thought. *I guess my bachelor husband still has a little honor tucked away under that debonair persona he likes to display. He certainly doesn't impress me with it, as if that mattered.*

Seeing the single package under the tree reminded me that I had things to do yet this morning before going to bed. Santa Claus had not yet dropped in for his annual visit. I heard the cuckoo clock in the hall sound the quarter hour and was surprised to see that it was later than I realized. The clock indicated that it was now 2:15 a.m.

If I'm going to play the fat man in the red suit, I'd better get on with it, I told myself.

Returning to the game room, I unlocked the door of the small enclosed area under the steps where the much-awaited gifts were hidden. Rand had built this several years before to serve as extra storage space. It came in handy at Christmastime as he had added a lock to the door. I was the only one in the house who had the key to the hidden treasures within during the Christmas season.

Hurriedly, I began to remove the packages. Carrying the larger ones up the steps, I placed them under the tree. Several trips later,

I had successfully transferred all the remaining gifts to the living room and stacked them appropriately in front of the larger ones.

Now it's beginning to look a lot like Christmas, I observed as I ate one of Santa's cookies, which were placed on a small plate sitting on the coffee table. I took the glass of milk to the kitchen, where I dumped the contents down the drain and left the conspicuously empty glass on the counter. Checking to see if everything was in order, I saw Roni's cawwot placed carefully beside the half-empty plate of cookies.

Whoops, I thought, *don't want to forget that.*

By this time, I was beginning to get a little hungry, so I disposed of Rudolph's cawwot the quickest and most efficient way I could think of. I ate it.

That red-nosed reindeer would be very upset with me, I thought with a chuckle.

Returning to the kitchen, I transferred all the Christmas cookies that were on the table into a large cookie jar, which was shaped like a rotund snowman. I put them on the top shelf of the pantry, out of sight and out of reach from my family of cookie monsters. Once again, I wondered who finished making these cookies and had decorated them so attractively. I didn't remember having had anything to do with it. The thought occurred to me that, when I got the opportunity, I would ask Kathy if she and Rachael had finished the job for me. That's something that young girls like to do, especially when there are no adults present to monitor the number of cookies that seem to disappear from the batch with regularity.

I was getting sleepy as I mentally marked off my list of "things to do before Christmas day."

One more item to take care of, and I'm off to bed, I said to myself, very tired now but very happy as well that everything was finally in readiness for the big day.

Relieved that I made the stuffing for the turkey and had the foresight to do the baking the night before last, I considered sleeping a little later in the morning than I normally did on a Christmas morning. Since I was a little ahead of schedule, I would stay in bed until our excited little tribe invaded our bedroom with their familiar war cry of, "Come on, Daddy and Mommy, let's open our gifts and see what Santa put in our stockings."

Putting the finishing touch to the last-minute gifts that I had not wrapped, I hurriedly placed them under the tree with the other packages. I then attempted to awaken my very unconscious husband, without success. He had not moved one inch either way since I had first seen him stretched out on the couch. I grabbed a comforter from the closet and covered him with it.

"Merry Christmas, my darling husband," I whispered softly under my breath. "Back on the couch again. It hasn't been the first time, and I am sure that it won't be the last."

I turned off all the lights and headed for the bedroom, sneaking a peek at the cherubs as I passed each of their rooms. As I crawled into bed, the thought occurred to me that I was stone sober. I remembered that I told Vicky that my mind was as clear as a bell. I could see that she didn't believe me, but it was true. Then when I saw the astonished look on her face as she watched me get to the garage without incident, I realized that there was something different about this picture.

With the amount of liquor I consumed over the previous twelve hours, it was amazing that I was still on my feet, let alone in control of all my faculties. Something strange had happened during the Christmas Eve service that I couldn't comprehend. But then again, I was grateful for whatever had taken place. I was tired, but I had a feeling of well-being. Everything was ready for Christmas morning, and I would be awakened by the children without suffering the usual hangover. All the plans I made for the day would be carried out without difficulty. I would be able to enjoy Christmas with the family this year, the first one in many years.

CHAPTER 14

THE BEST NEWS OF ALL

The dreaded third week of February had arrived, much to my chagrin, along with a fresh covering of new snow and ice, making the roads difficult to travel. On Friday, I was scheduled to have a consultation with a physician from Allegheny Hospital, some miles north of the city.

Perhaps we would have several inches of additional snow by then, preventing us from keeping this appointment, I hoped, not really expecting fulfillment of this wish.

Don't be your usual wimpy self, Mara. You know that you've got to keep this appointment in spite of the embarrassment that it might cause you. Aside from that, you promised Vicky you would go through with this, I reminded myself.

As I was backing my car out of the driveway, I attempted to wipe all thoughts of this upcoming event out of my mind. At this moment, I had some more good news for Sherry and Carly and their girls which I was anxious to share with them.

Glancing at the clock on my dashboard, I realized that I had just enough time to reach Sherry's home by seven-thirty. Given the fact that the roads were icy in spots, I would need the extra few minutes to arrive on time.

It's going to take a little while to count the cookie money and complete the paperwork involved, I mentally calculated. *When we're finished with our business, I will surprise her with the news that their girls are going to be interviewed by the* Pittsburgh Post *for their part in the annual cookie sale. As the icing on the cake, I'll let them in on the unexpected surprise involved as the result of their outstanding salesmanship. Of course, the reporter will plug Troop 433 too. This always speaks well of the participating community involved and its many worthwhile programs. It's a win-win situation for all concerned.* The kids were going to be delighted with this news, and I believed their moms would be as well.

I don't want to forget to tell both of them they will each need a recent picture in their uniforms by next week, I reminded myself. *I can do that tomorrow evening during the meeting. That will be the perfect time to share the news with the rest of the group. Honors go to those who put forth the most effort.*

Being extremely cautions of the hazardous road conditions, my thoughts yo-yoed back and forth between the events of Christmas Eve—which had been bizarre, to say the least—and the anticipated death of a beloved aunt a week later.

I wonder how Pete and the kids are getting along, I thought, *especially poor Matt. I will drop them a note this week to let them know that I'm thinking about them. Maybe I could say that I've asked God to comfort them in this time of great loss.*

No, *I'll scratch that. That just isn't me, and it isn't true anyhow. It would sound so phony. I might be a lot of things, but I'm not a phony, that's for sure. On second thought, I do recall that I had felt very much like a phony during the mass on Christmas Eve.*

But then again, I did attempt to pray one day last week, if that's what one would call praying, I reminded myself.

It had been a particularly bad day for me. A call from school regarding Randy's behavior, followed by another argument with Rand about our son's lack of discipline, had left me in a foul mood. Of course, my only recourse was to go a little heavier on the beer and Scotch throughout the day, numbing me to some extent from the stress I was under.

Half stoned by the time that evening rolled around, I remember going into our bedroom and closing the door behind me. The kids were in bed for the night. Mom had gone to her room a short time before, and Rand was in the game room. One of his friends had dropped by, and they were watching a hockey game on TV.

I remember thinking about the upcoming appointment with the doctor that I would be forced to keep in another week. Out of nowhere came this overwhelming desire to talk to God about my life and this upcoming situation in particular. It wasn't even a prayer, at least not like any prayer I had ever heard being offered to the Almighty. It was just a regular conversation like I'd have with one of my friends.

You know, God, I said to Him. *I know you're real. You're not a myth like some people believe, a figment of one's imagination. You're the Creator. You made everything on this earth and everyone who has ever lived here, and that goes back a lot of years. You created me thirty-three years ago and put me down here to live for some reason unbeknownst to me. You didn't create me to be a drunk, and you didn't force me to marry a man whom I should never had married. You certainly didn't have anything to do with the two abortions I consented to in order to save an already-disastrous marriage. I also know that you didn't have anything to do with the immoral lifestyle I lived while I was single. I had the free will to do whatever I wanted to do, and I have been suffering the consequences for those wrong choices ever since.*

What I want to know is this. Why did you make me? What is my purpose here? I learned a lot of religion when I was in school, but a lot of it didn't make much sense to me. It wasn't relevant to my life then, and it's not relevant now. I always learned from the nuns and the priests that you are the supreme ruler of the universe. It that's correct, then why are so many people I know so screwed up? If we're made in your image, then how come we don't look or act anything like you?

In church that night, I know that it was you who sobered me up when I saw the statue of the baby Jesus move His finger and point it right in my direction. That really freaked me out. I never saw anything like that before. Now, that was relevant. He was inviting me to come to him. Why did he do that? What did he want with me? Did he want to remind me of all the terrible things I have done over my brief lifetime and warn me that he's going to send me to hell if I don't straighten up? Why would he choose to communicate with me? I'm nothing but a drunk. I'm not even worth His effort, whatever it was that he was trying to tell me.

One important thing you did for me that night, God, was show me myself in other people. When I looked around the church and recognized some people I knew, you showed me that I'm a hypocrite just like them. We are taught that we have to be in church for mass every Sunday and holy day. What do we do when we get there? We look around to see whom we know and see how they're dressed, as if that mattered. We women are especially guilty of that. Then we check them out to see who accompanied them to church. Could it be that there's something going on between one of the married couples we know because one of the men happened to be with a woman other than his wife? This could be the juicy beginning of a nasty rumor, which would no doubt spread through the area like a raging forest fire.

It could destroy the reputation of an innocent couple who had always enjoyed credibility in the community, couldn't it? Didn't these gossipers give any thought to the children of this couple who could be seriously damaged because of vicious tongues directed at their parents? Why did it create sheer delight in these troublemakers to discredit others without adequate proof of what they were saying? Did they stop to consider the possibility that one of these mysterious visitors could have been a relative from out of town visiting their family for the Christmas holiday?

Halfway through the services, we begin to glance at our watches impatiently, hoping that the priest won't be long-winded with his sermon. We will be having a little neighborhood get-together to bring in the holiday after church. We need to get out of here in a hurry tonight. After all, it is the season to be jolly, and we must get home and finish preparing the food that we plan to serve to our friends and neighbors.

Where are you in all of this, God? Do we even take time to just thank you for our good health, for our kids, for a roof over our heads and plenty of food to eat, for good-paying jobs that enable us to have these things?

So what do we do? It seems like we keep playing this game year after year and hoping that one day we'll do something worthwhile, something that might merit a ticket to heaven when we die. How can we know if we're good enough by your standards? What do you use as a measuring stick, God, to determine who will make it to heaven and who will suffer the eternal torment of hellfire?

Most of the people I know are a bunch of sinners just like I am. The faithful who attend church and receive the sacraments on a regular basis have been led to believe that these are the things that are going to enable them to stay out of hell when they breathe their last breath. I know a lot of people think that just because they're following the rules, they're going to be exempt from your judgment. Something tells me that this line of reasoning is simply not so. They're merely going through the motions. Their heart's not in it. Jack may still be an adulterer or not. Marcia's still wallowing in her self-importance, thinking that she's a cut above the rest of humanity. And I am still a drunk, not even able to take care of the kids you gave me some of the time.

What's the answer to this human dilemma, God? Do you really care about the humanity you created? If you do, and you're not just playing a malicious game with us, I sure would like to hear from you. If you can give me some valid answers to some of these questions that constantly plague me, I'd be more than willing to serve you. Is it too much to ask you to reveal yourself to me and remove the blinders from my eyes? Surely you didn't leave us without an answer to these many problems that confront each of us as we stumble through life, or did you?

My thoughts were interrupted as I saw that I was approaching Sherry's street. As I made the turn, very cautiously avoiding a patch of frozen ice, I noticed that her area had not as yet been plowed or salted.

Seems like they always leave this part of town until last when taking care of road maintenance, I observed.

I had never been to the Drummond home, and I was looking for the fifth house on the right-hand side of the road. Sherry had identified their home by telling me that the trim on the house was blue, and there was a picket fence with a gate on the left side of the house that led to the backyard. I was relieved to have such accurate directions as all the houses looked alike. They were small white clapboard Cape Cod dwellings that sat back several hundred feet off the street.

These houses, I had been told, were built in the early 1900s when bituminous coal mining was the primary occupation of families living in the immediate area. There were several large veins of coal within a few hundred yards of Sherry's street. A mining operation was opened in order to remove the coal from this area. These houses were built at that time to house the overflow of families coming into the area seeking employment.

Well, I said to myself, *the houses are really small, but at least the kids have a huge level front yard where they can play in safety*. I remembered Sherry having told me that she and her husband Sharky had five children. As I parked my car in the driveway, I noticed the white picket fence that Sherry had given me as a landmark to identify her home.

"Hi, Mara," she said warmly, welcoming me into her home. "Come in and get out of the cold. Are the roads bad? I haven't been out since this afternoon, and they were beginning to get a little slippery then," she added. "You can put your boots on that little rug I have by the door, and I'll hang your coat in the closet beside it. I want you to meet my boys before I send them up to bed. They get a little rowdy in the evening, and I want to get the house quiet so we can take care of business without interruption."

"Chris is across the street at Pam's house. They're working on a badge together. I told Carly to keep her overnight because you were coming over, so I could keep you honest with the cookie money." She chuckled. "When they found out that you'd be here to help me count the money, they wanted to help. I told them that would not be acceptable to the Girl Scout Association, and besides, they will be with you tomorrow night during your weekly meeting. April's babysitting this evening but will probably be home before you leave. My husband's not home tonight either."

Her three boys were delightful. Each one in turn came over to me and shook my hand heartily. "Hi, Mrs. Reuben, nice to meet you, ma'am," they greeted me with three of the broadest smiles I had ever seen.

I was overwhelmed. Her boys were as pleasant and as mannerly as they were good-looking. They were disciplined and polite just like their sisters.

The boys said goodnight to me and hugged their mom and then headed upstairs to their bedroom.

"Sherry, I'm impressed," I commented as I saw the last of the three brothers reach the top of the stairs. "You and your husband are doing a fantastic parenting job. What a wonderful family you have!"

"It's very important to me that these children be raised in the proper way. It's quite a job at times, but the credit goes to the Lord. I couldn't do it by myself," she commented.

Oh boy, here we go again, I thought. *I really like this lady. I just wish she wouldn't have to bring God into the conversation all the time.*

"Yes, uh, of course, that is important," I halfheartedly agreed. "Well, we better get down to the task at hand. I don't want to keep you up all night counting money."

"It would be a welcome change, Mara, even if it isn't my money. I never have enough of it in my possession at one time to have to sit down and count it. This might prove to be fun."

"I'll say this, Sherry, there's plenty to count, so have all the fun you want to have."

She led me into the large well-equipped kitchen, where she had everything in readiness for the job ahead of us. A large oak table had been pushed to the center of the room where we would both be able to walk around it easily if the need arose. A calculator, several coin wrappers of various denominations, a mechanical coin sorter, a tablet of scratch paper, and several sharp pencils were neatly laid on the table for our use.

"Well, you never fail to amaze me, girlfriend," I exclaimed with awe. "You are ready for this job, to be sure. Had I been as prepared as you are, it probably wouldn't have taken me three and a half hours when I made the initial count. With this kind of organization, we will be finished in no time. By the way, before we get involved in this, remind me when we finish to share some good news with you. I'm pretty excited about it, and I believe that you, Carly, and the girls will be happy to hear this. It concerns all of you in one way or another."

"Now isn't that ironic?" she responded, an expression of mild surprise moving across the features of her pretty face. "I have some good news to share with you as well."

"You've aroused my curiosity, Sherry, but I'm not going to succumb to the temptation of asking you what it is right now. If you're not in a big hurry to kick me out of your house, we can share our good news with each other when we're done with this monster."

"That's a good plan, Mara," she replied, pulling one of the chairs away from the table for me to sit in.

I looked at her wall clock just then to take note of the time. I was anxious to see how long this job would take to complete. Having the competitive spirit that I had, I was curious to see if she could beat my time. I assumed that she would probably be able to do this because of her fantastic organizational skills. She also had some tools available for this job that I did not have at home. The time was five after eight, I noted.

The task was completed in record time. The total Sherry had arrived at matched mine to the penny. I completed the paperwork that was required, made out the deposit slip, and we both signed off on it. All the coins and paper money were neatly placed in a large leather bag the bank had supplied for this purpose. The amount of time required for Sherry to accomplish this was under two hours. I glanced at the clock once again. The time was now five minutes before ten.

"Wow!" I exclaimed. "That was amazing."

"Not really, Mara. You forget that I have five lively children and a hard-to-please husband to care for. That requires moving quickly most of the time, honey. It's just a habit that's been cultivated over the years."

Yes, that's true, I thought. *Vicky's lifestyle is very similar. She gets a lot accomplished in a short period of time too.*

"I think you're shortchanging yourself, girl," Sherry continued. "You have three children of your own, a husband, and a mother whom you have to care for—not to mention that big house you live in and the Girl Scout troop you lead. I know there's a lot of work connected with that alone, not to mention everything else you do. Come on now, don't try to kid me, Mara. I think you're just trying to be humble."

"No, not really, Sherry. I do have all those things to take care of, but that doesn't mean that I get them done all the time." I thought regretfully, *If she knew the reason that I don't get things done as I should, she would probably pull her girls out of my troop faster than a heartbeat.*

"Well, I know one thing for sure," Sherry commented. "Whatever our speedometers register, our husbands don't appreciate all the energy we women have to exert in one day, and that is no joke."

"Now that we're done with the money, let's you and me relax a little while and have a piece of the lemon meringue pie I made this morning. Would you like coffee with it, or maybe some hot chocolate? That's my favorite on a cold winter night."

Enjoying the pie, which was excellent, and a cup of hot coffee with my new friend, I shared the good news I had just gotten from the Girl Scout headquarters.

"Carly and Rich will be thrilled about this. They know that their Pam is quite an achiever, and this will be one more proof of it, not that she needs any more proof. All of our girls know who they are and what they are capable of doing. April only missed the monetary prize by about twenty dollars in total sales, you said, but she's still very happy about her honorable mention. Maybe next time she'll try just a little harder. I'll be sure to remember to tell Carly to have a recent picture of Pam in her uniform. Rich has a great camera, and I know that he'll be happy to take the pictures of the girls. He likes to show off his photographer's skill."

Hmm, I wondered, *where does Sharky fit into this picture? I haven't heard his name mentioned all evening, with the exception of Sherry telling me that he wasn't home tonight. It's kind of reminiscent of my relationship with Rand. O Lord, I hope not. Surely she can't have the same problem that I have, can she? I deserve what I got, but Sherry is such a wonderful person. She deserves a lot more in life. I wonder what this is all about.*

At this point, my curiosity overcame my good sense. This was certainly none of my business, but nonetheless, I was determined to find out if this fantastic lady I was sitting across the table from had the same problem that I had.

"So tell me, Sherry," I began, "your husband's nickname is Sharky. That is most unusual, even for a nickname. How did he come by that handle?"

"It's no secret, Mara. Everyone in this area knows all about my husband. Sharky is a high roller. He's a gambler, specifically a poker player. That's how he got his nickname. He's good at what he does, or at least he used to be before he began drinking. That's why his friends called him Sharky when he was in his prime. The name has stuck with him. He plays a lot of poker, high-stakes poker—and he plays often, most every night or until he runs out of money, which-ever comes first. He used to—"

"Oh, uh, please, Sherry, no more," I said, interrupting her story midway through a sentence.

Suddenly I felt I was intruding on a personal matter. I was hear-ing things I had no business hearing. Why did I bring up her hus-band in the first place? If Sherry wanted me to know about her marriage and her personal life, she would no doubt have brought up the subject herself.

"I'm so sorry. I didn't mean for you to tell me your life's story. None of this is really any of my business."

"Mara, you have to let me finish."

Then she said something that caught me completely off guard: "I'm compelled to tell you my story. You have to know."

"What do you mean 'you're compelled'? What or who is com-pelling you?"

"God is, Mara. He wants you to know some things tonight that you've never known before."

"What are you talking about, Sherry? Why do I have to know these personal things about your marriage?"

"All right, Mara. I guess that I had better begin at the begin-ning. That makes good sense, doesn't it?" she asked.

I was becoming somewhat nervous about the direction this conversation was taking. I thought of the flask of whiskey buried under several papers in the glove compartment of my car.

Boy, do I wish I could get to it right now, I thought desperately. *I need something to stabilize me. This is not what I had planned for this eve-ning. This woman is going somewhere with this conversation, and I don't want to go there.*

I thought about bringing this dialogue to an abrupt halt. I glanced at the clock above the stove once again. I would tell her that it was getting quite late and that I didn't want to keep her up any longer. After all, she had those three little guys of hers who were going to need their breakfast before they left for school in the morning. I had two of my own who would require my attention as well. I would suggest to her that maybe we could continue this conversation sometime in the future when it would be more convenient—when we would have more time.

I mentally searched my long list of excuses. Was there one I could use in this situation that would sound sincere enough to allow me to leave without appearing to be rude? Sherry was a delightful person, and I certainly didn't want to hurt her in any way. As a matter of fact, I was hopeful that tonight would be the beginning of a solid friendship between the two of us. I weighed these things in my mind for what seemed like an eternity while I observed her calm, confident composure.

Although I thought she was a very attractive woman when we first met at the Girl Scout leadership outing last summer, right now, as I took a closer look, I realized that she was beautiful. Her features, which were finely chiseled, were perfectly placed in a heart-shaped face, which was framed by a thick, lustrous abundance of warm-brown somewhat curly hair. It was cut in a simple but attractive style. Her full lips were beautifully shaped, and they appeared to be turned up ever so slightly to form a faint hint of a perpetual smile, friendly and warm. Her skin was a rich, deep tan and flawless in texture. Without question, it was her eyes—dark and alive with radiance—that totally captivated me.

Surprised by the words that came from my lips, I heard the sound of my voice break through the few seconds' lull in our conversation as I responded to her question, "Yes, Sherry, I guess it would be a good idea if you were to begin at the beginning."

Sherry cleared our dessert dishes from the table and quickly refilled our empty cups, passing the cream and sugar to me. At that moment, April, removing her parka and gloves, came into the kitchen. She greeted me warmly and then left the room just as quickly as she had entered.

"I'll see you tomorrow night at meeting," she said excitedly from the hall. "I finished two of my badges last week, and I'm anxious to show the girls what I discovered."

"That's great, April," I responded. "It's encouraging to see my scouts so enthusiastic about their badge work. That scouting program gives you girls a lot of opportunities to expand your knowledge of so many things."

"Yes, it does, ma'am. Good night."

"Good night, April," I responded as I heard her bolting up the steps to her bedroom, two at a time.

Sherry sat down once again, and as she looked at me intently, those large, piercing eyes appeared to penetrate my very soul. "The Lord has told me a few things about you, Mara."

I looked at her with a new awareness of what she was talking about. Up until Christmas Eve, I would have thought this to be impossible. God communing with a mere human being? "Ridiculous, no way," would have been my response. Now I knew better. God, in his own time and in His own way, had communicated with me through the statue of the infant Jesus.

"So what did he tell you, Sherry?" I asked expectantly.

"He told me that you were experiencing many difficulties in your life and that he loves you and wants you to know that you don't have to carry these burdens anymore. He will carry them for you because they are much too heavy for you."

"Really? And how can he do that?" I questioned, leaning forward in my chair.

"How can he do that? You must surrender your life to God, Mara. His Son died on the cross to take away the sins that are causing you so much difficulty. He took the sins of the whole world, yours included, in His own body when he hung on the cross. By dying, Jesus became the sacrifice that God the Father required to forgive those sins. This is the only sacrifice that was acceptable to God.

"That's why Jesus had to die. He who knew no sin became sin for us, the Bible tells us. We are taught that if we do good works throughout our lifetime, we will eventually make it to heaven. This is a lie out of the pit hell, Mara. Our good works are nothing more than filthy rags. They are not acceptable to God."

I was in awe by the things that Sherry was speaking to me. I had never heard anything like this before. The intensity with which she spoke made me realize that she believed, with every fiber of her being, everything that she was sharing with me.

"One more important thing to complete the picture, Mara. This sacrifice that Jesus made for us is not general. True, he did die for the sins of the whole world. But at this point, it becomes a very personal matter. Anyone seeking this wonderful gift of salvation, like you may be doing right now, must ask Jesus to forgive her sins. You don't have to name them. He knows what they are. Just ask him to forgive you. If you are sincere in doing this, he will come into your life and forgive you for everything you have ever done that has not been pleasing to God. He will help you live this new life that he has given to you."

I was hanging on every word that Sherry spoke. I looked at her, and she seemed to radiate an inner peace that I so longed for. I sensed something electrifying in the room. Something or Someone had joined us. This was a very special moment, one that I knew I would remember for the rest of my life. Sherry reached across the table and gently took my hand. Her radiant smile penetrated the very depth of my being.

"Would you like to ask Jesus into your heart right now, Mara? I can help you do this if you don't have the words."

I knew that this was the answer to my dilemma. I was absolutely convinced that the prayer I said to God just a few nights ago had just been answered by this beautiful lady sitting across from me. But this was all so new. I just heard from Sherry's lips things I had never heard before. I needed time to process this information.

"Sherry, I believe what you have told me is true," I replied. "I know now why you are so radiant all the time, why you have such inner peace regardless of what you may have to face in your life. The little you told me about Sharky and your marriage proves beyond a shadow of a doubt that you are living proof of what Jesus can do for a person when he changes that life. Actions speak louder than words. I can see that you are living the life you have been given by Jesus. It's beautiful, Sherry. But I must think about all this before I commit to it. This is all too new to me. I'm on unfamiliar ground. You understand, don't you?"

"Yes, of course, I do, Mara. But remember this. The Bible says that today is the day of salvation. Don't wait too long to make a decision. The enemy of your soul would like to erase from your memory every word that has been spoken here tonight. He wants your soul, Mara, and if he can make you forget this conversation, he will have a foothold in your life. He wants to take you to hell with him."

Although this last statement scared me, I did not want this evening to end. Nor did I want to leave this presence that I had sensed in her kitchen since Sherry began to speak about spiritual matters. I believe that Sherry sensed this.

"Mara, I know the hour is late. Your husband will probably be wondering where you are. I don't want to keep you any longer than you want to stay. Before you leave, though, I have a few little booklets that I'd like you to take with you. You can read them at your convenience. Have you ever read the gospel of John? If not, it's important that you do. Read it once every day until you begin to gain insight into it. It's very powerful. I'll be right back," she said as she disappeared into the hall.

I sat back in my chair and breathed deeply. I hadn't realized how intense this last hour or so had been. Glancing at the clock, I was shocked to see that it was ten after four in the morning. Where in the world had the time gone? It was just a little after eleven the last time I looked. I got up realizing that we must end our time together, fantastic as it had been. I went into the living room and retrieved my coat and gloves from her closet. While I was putting my boots on, Sherry came from the direction of her bedroom carrying a canvas bag containing several books and other pieces of reading material.

"Take these with you, Mara. I want the hardcover books back when you have finished reading them. The rest is for you to keep."

She gave me a warm hug at the door, and the evening ended with a statement that I buried in my heart: "I love you, Mara, but remember this. Jesus loves you even more, so much that he died so that you could live forever and spend eternity with him. I'll be praying for you until we see each other again. Do be careful on your way home. It looks like the roads are really getting bad. Don't lose your balance on the ice with that bag of money. That would be disastrous."

CHAPTER 15
A DIFFICULT DECISION

As I made my way slowly but steadily up our slick driveway, I used my remote control to open the garage door at the same time. I knew that if I were to slow the car during the ascent, I would begin to slide. No doubt it would delay my opportunity to pull the car safely into the garage. I would either have to start over again or park the car on our off-street parking space. The last thing that I wanted to do was to leave my automobile outside for the rest of the night. Rand would be livid. This would only add insult to injury. All the way home from Sherry's house I rehearsed what I would say to him when I finally made it into the house. I hoped that he would be asleep and I could sneak into bed without a confrontation.

I looked up at that instant and saw the spotlight go on in the front of our house. Rand was awake! He was standing in front of the picture window in our living room looking down at me. The look on his face let me know that no matter what I rehearsed in the way of an excuse for my lateness, it would fall on deaf ears.

Safely inside the garage, I turned off the ignition and grabbed the large bag containing the cookie money and the smaller canvas bag that Sherry had given me containing some books and other written material. I entered the game room to find Rand standing in the center of the room, arms crossed over his chest and fully dressed. The look on his face was coldly placid. As always, he was in control. At least, that is the impression he appeared to convey. It was difficult to determine just what he was thinking at this moment. It only took a minute for me to find out.

He began to approach me as I stood in the doorway. Noticing that the expression on his face had not changed, I considered having a possible escape plan prepared if the situation should warrant it. Rand was not given to physical violence. He was so totally effective with verbal abuse there was no need for him to become physical. This morning, however, I wasn't at all sure that he would remain true to character.

"Where have you been all night, my lovely wife? The bars close at two o'clock, and it is now 4:45 a.m. You've got some fast-talking to do, so you had better get on with it—and don't lie to me. I'm going to check your story."

"Why would I lie to you? I've never lied to you in the past. Do you think I would start now?" My voice was calm and self-assured, not at all in character with my normal response when confronted with this type of situation.

"All right, my dear," he replied authoritatively. "You get your story ready. I'm going to call the township police and let them know that you made it home in one piece, and I presume with no accidents to report. Is that correct? As I watched you pull into the garage, I took a good look at your car, and it appeared to be in good condition. I don't suppose that you killed anyone while you were wandering around the icy streets, or did you? No one in his right mind would be out in this weather, especially at 4:30 a.m., so I'm not concerned that anything like that could have happened. When I get off the phone, you can tell me just exactly what you've been up to these past eight hours. It should make for an interesting story."

"I'd be glad to enlighten you as to my whereabouts, Rand. I did leave a note and phone number with the babysitter. Perhaps she forgot to give it to you," I suggested.

"The girl didn't give me a note or a phone number or whatever it was that you supposedly gave her," he responded, an attitude of skepticism in his voice.

On my way to our bedroom to change into my pj's, I heard him on the phone with the officer on duty at the park office. Evidently, he had been planning to accompany one of the policemen in an effort to find me most likely stranded on the road somewhere, or worse. Since he knew which bars I frequented, he suggested to the officer that it might be helpful if he were to ride with him in the patrol car. Locating me might be a little easier that way.

I'll have to call Mandy sometime after school today and see why she didn't give Rand the note I left with her. This could have simplified matters quite a bit, I conjectured, more than a little irritated at the apparent oversight on her part.

I had called Vicky when I realized that I would need someone to stay with Mom and the kids while I was at Sherry's home. I rarely left the house on a Monday evening, but since Sherry requested that I bring the money to be counted on Monday, I wanted to comply with her request. Rand remained at work after closing hours on Monday evenings in order to catch up with paperwork for the Tuesday-morning sales meeting with his superiors and sales staff.

Quite often he and one or two of his salesmen would stop at the bar next door for a few beers after finishing their work. He rarely stayed there very long, however. Tuesday morning came early, and he needed to be in bed early Monday evening in order to be mentally prepared to chair the coming meeting.

Securing a sitter for a Monday evening had been difficult. Both of Vicky's girls were busy with school activities; but at the last minute, a friend of Kathy, whose name was Mandy, called me and agreed to sit for a few hours. I told her that I wasn't certain how long I would be gone but that my husband almost always arrived home by ten o'clock.

Mandy arrived on time. I was always skeptical when using a new babysitter. Randy would be anxious to take on someone new and test her to the umpteenth degree to see what she was made of. The girls, though curious, were no problem. In fact, Rachael was quite helpful under certain circumstances. Mandy appeared to be mature for her fifteen years and had some limited babysitting experience.

Kathy had recommended her, so this made me feel somewhat better. She seemed levelheaded and listened carefully to my last-minute instructions before I left the house. I had given her a note with Mrs. Drummond's phone number, indicating that this was where I could be found if an emergency should arise. As I was leaving the house, I added that I hoped it would not be necessary to call me for any reason other than for a dire emergency because Mrs. Drummond and I would be counting money, and an interruption such as a phone call could be very disconcerting. I remembered telling her to be sure to give the note to Mr. Reuben when he got home.

I wonder what could have become of that note, I mused. Rand had not mentioned having seen a note that would indicate where I could be reached.

At that moment he entered the bedroom. This time, that calm, assured composure of his had become somewhat ruffled. He looked at me with absolute disgust as he grabbed my arm and pulled me closer to him.

"Let me smell your breath, my sweet little cheat," he said between his teeth, each word enunciated slowly and clearly so that there would be no mistake as to his intent.

"Look, Rand, what is this all about anyhow? I'm not on trial here, and you have no business treating me like this. You haven't even given me the opportunity to tell you where I have been and why I am so late getting home. If this situation were reversed, and I was interrogating you as to your whereabouts—which, by the way, is a common occurrence—there would be all kinds of hell to pay."

"Don't attempt to turn the table on me, Mara," he continued. "I told you before that a woman's place is in the home. A dutiful wife should be found either in the kitchen or in the bedroom—in either case, meeting her husband's needs. Don't try to compare me with how you would like to see a marriage function. Men are men. We are a special breed unto ourselves. The warrior-hunter is a part of our intrinsic nature. Don't attempt to change it."

"Where did you get this archaic viewpoint you have on marriage?" I continued. He started this argument, and this time, I was going to have my say. "Can't you see that your attitude toward married life is a big part of the reason that our marriage is on the rocks? Wives aren't meant to be servants. They are meant to be partners in this relationship."

"Listen to me, sweetheart," he continued, "and listen well. Any so-called man who caves to his wife's demands is a wimp. It appears that there are a lot of this kind around these days. It's disgusting, to say the least. Why these cream puffs walk around with rings in their noses while their wives crack the whip over their backsides is beyond me. It is disgusting and degrading.

"Get this into your pretty little head. You are not married to a wimp. If you have any designs about making me into one, you can start looking for someone who will be more willing to bend to your demands. As I recall, I told you before we were married that I would have my weekends free to do with them as I pleased, and I have not changed my mind one iota. This is what is sticking in your crawl. I've known that from the very beginning of our marriage. But don't forget, my dear, I did warn you, didn't I?"

What's the use? I thought. *This is going nowhere, just as all our previous arguments on this subject had met the same fate. We're at a serious impasse. I must find a way to get control of this drinking problem. Once I get on my feet again, I have to reach down deep for the inner strength that I know I have in order to get this man out of my life once and for all. This is a toxic relationship, and the longer the kids and I are exposed to this environment, the worse things are going to get for all of us.*

Rand tightened his grip on my arm. I attempted to break free, but he would not release me.

"You're hurting my arm, Rand. Why are you doing this?" I demanded to know.

"I'll tell you why I'm doing this, Mara. I want to know what was going on last night. Who were you with? Obviously, you weren't drinking. There's no smell of alcohol on your breath. Who were you with, and what were you doing for eight hours?"

"If you'll let go of my arm, I'll be glad to answer any questions that you may have. I have nothing to hide. But up to this point, you haven't given me a chance to explain where I was or what I was doing. Oh, and by the way, I have sufficient evidence to prove every word of what I am about to tell you."

"Oh, you do, do you? You're pretty cocky this morning, little girl. I notice that you haven't turned on the waterworks yet. As a matter of fact, you seem to be talking some sense for a change. So go ahead, talk to me. Tell me all about your evening, if you can."

"Oh, I can, all right," I shot back, resenting his implication. "If you showed any interest in my life, you would have remembered that last week I told you I was going to my cookie chairman's home this Monday evening. She was to recount the proceeds from the sale in order to keep me honest, no hanky-panky with the money you know. Our totals had to be the same."

"And…," he said. I finally captured his attention.

"The totals matched to the penny. So we signed off on all the paperwork required by the Girl Scout Association, sorted the coins, bagged the total amount, and made out a deposit slip."

"How long did that take?" he inquired, continuing his interrogation.

"We finished around eleven o'clock, as I recall. Sherry made a lemon meringue pie earlier. She invited me to stay and have pie and coffee with her. She wanted to share her good news, she said."

"Until four-thirty in the morning?" he responded skeptically. "You don't really expect me to believe that, do you?"

"You know something, Rand? I really don't care if you believe it or not," I replied, becoming increasingly annoyed at this line of questioning. "I told you exactly where I was and what I was doing during the time in question, and that's all I have to say."

"You're not getting off the hook that easily, my sweet little deceiver. What kind of a fool do you take me for? Do you really believe that you and this Drummond woman, whom you don't even know that well, spent more than four hours talking about her good news? You're going to have to come up with something better than that. But, out of curiosity, what was this 'good news' all about that so captured your attention you found it necessary to stay out all night to hear it?"

"Her name is Sherry," I said, in defense of my new friend, "not that 'Drummond woman.' She told me about Jesus and how he came into her life many years ago and changed her. She had a difficult marriage, Rand, like ours in many ways, and didn't know where to turn—again, like me. Because she knows him, her life has changed completely. She's radiant, Rand, and totally fulfilled. She doesn't have much in the way of earthly goods—her husband has seen to that—but she has peace and contentment in her life because of Jesus."

"Oh, come now, Mara, don't fall for everything you hear. You are as vulnerable as a child. Are you aware of that?" he continued. "I suppose that you're going to tell me that this Jesus came into her life and miraculously changed her husband too and that now they are living happily ever after."

"No, I'm not. Jesus came into her life, not her husband's, because Sharky wanted no part of Jesus. He refused to be changed. It was Sherry who changed. After her conversion, she began to see that no matter how bad her situation might be, Jesus would see her through her difficulties. She believes this, and that is where her peace and security come from."

"Did you say her husband's name is Sharky? Sharky Drummond?" Rand asked, his interest suddenly aroused by this new information I had given him.

"That's right. Sharky Drummond is Sherry's husband," I confirmed.

"Well, what do you know about that?" he responded, totally amazed.

"Do you know him, Rand?" I asked.

"We've met a few times," he admitted, rather sheepishly. "It's been several years since I've sat at a gaming table with him. We first met at a private poker club. That was before the booze got to his brain. He was some kind of a poker player back in those days. I couldn't touch him with a ten-foot pole. He cleaned my clock many a night."

"That's where I was until four-thirty this morning, at his home with his wife," I reminded him. "I'll give you their phone number if you want to check on me. Like I said, my trusting husband, I have nothing to hide."

"You know what, sweetheart," he said with a sudden change of heart. "I'm going to let it go this time, but don't let anything like this happen again, not on my watch. You don't need to be sliding around on icy roads all hours of the night. Remember, you have responsibilities right here, a husband, three kids, and a wacky mother. The problem is, in your present condition, you can't take care of what you've got. So don't go out looking for more."

"One other thing, Mara," he continued, changing the subject. "Our appointment with Dr. Reynolds is coming up in a few days. I want you to be mentally prepared to cooperate with him fully. I'm not in the least bit interested in anything that your friend Sherry has to say about the great change that has occurred in her life. If you ask me, that's nonsense. People can talk themselves into just about anything they want to believe, so just let that kind of thinking alone, all right. You need medical and psychiatric help with your problem. I'm willing to see you through this, just once, though. Don't screw it up. There won't be a second chance.

"Right now, how about some bacon and a couple of eggs over medium? You know the way I like them. Better make a fresh pot of coffee too. I went through one pot already over the past few hours. I guess you realize by now that your antics have kept me up most of the night," he added as an afterthought. "I don't know how I'm going to get through the sales meeting in a few hours, and you can take all the blame for that, my dove."

Having showered, dressed, and eaten breakfast, Rand left for work a short time later. Only then did I realize how exhausted I was. I would have to get the two older children up for school in another two hours. But two hours of sleep right now would certainly be appreciated. I set the alarm for seven-fifteen and jumped back into bed. It seemed like only seconds had elapsed when I sensed a strange presence entering the room. Was this a dream or a vision? What was happening here? Was this real? I was lying in bed, and as I looked toward the door, I saw a massive, hulk-like figure enter my bedroom and then close and lock the door.

I lay frozen in absolute terror as this horrible creature looked directly at me and began to move slowly toward the bed. It was massive in size, the head almost touching the ceiling. It was green like the Jolly Green Giant, but the face was ugly and deformed. The teeth were square and separated by large gaps between them. Two tiny horns protruded from its enormous head. As it approached the bed, I saw in the dim light of early dawn coming from outside that it had a huge chain in its enormous, muscular arms. The chain was like one used on transport carriers to secure automobiles and small trucks.

I could not move. I attempted to cry out, but I couldn't even open my mouth to emit a scream. As this monstrous thing drew closer to the bed, it began to fashion the chain in the form of a lasso. I realized at that instant that its intention was to encircle the chain around my neck and take me captive or possibly kill me. I attempted to scream once again. This time, I heard my voice utter the name of Jesus. "Jesus, help me," I cried out. At that instant, the monster stopped what it had been doing with the chain.

As I watched in utter amazement, it began to shrink. In a matter of seconds, this enormous form collapsed to the floor and was no bigger than one of Roni's rag dolls. I heard a strange noise like that of a candle being blown out. I looked at the floor on my side of the bed where I had just seen the shrunken form of the monster. In its place was a thin stream of smoke or fog or some similar substance that I could not identify. In a second or two, that also disappeared, leaving the room exactly as it had been when I first entered it.

My first sensation was that of wetness. I felt my pajamas. They were soaked. So was my pillow and pillow case, the sheet on which I had been lying, and the blanket that covered me. Everything was soaked. Had I lost control of my bladder in the terror of the moment? No, I thought. This was perspiration, lots of perspiration. It was wet everywhere I touched. I wanted to get up immediately and get the bed changed. I needed a change of nightclothes. I remember looking at the clock on my night table. Only fifteen minutes had elapsed since I had come to bed.

This whole thing seemed like a horrible nightmare, but one such as I had never experienced. I remembered thinking how glad I was that Rand had not been home to witness this. No doubt, he would have had me committed by now and not wait for Friday to do it. I attempted to get out of bed. My legs were like jelly. They wouldn't support my weight. I sat on my side of the bed for a few moments to get my composure. Try as I did, I could not erase from my memory the horror I had just experienced.

I was now wide awake. Little by little, I was able to return to some semblance of normalcy. Once I regained the use of my legs, I walked slowly to the closed door. It was locked.

"Strange," I said to myself. "I know that I didn't lock my door." On occasion, I would go back to bed after Rand had gone for the day, as I did this morning. I never locked our bedroom door, knowing that sometimes Roni would hear me moving about. She would invariably join me for a little snuggle time when she found that I had gone back to bed.

Something that Sherry said last evening continued to echo and reecho in my brain: "Don't wait too long to make your decision, Mara. Because if you do, always keep in mind that you are gambling against a worthy adversary, Satan, who wants nothing more than to take you to hell. He wants your soul and will stop at nothing to get it. Remember what the Word says: 'Today is the day of salvation,' not tomorrow, not next week, not when I get good enough to ask Christ into my life—or 'This is a big decision. I'll have to give it serious thought.' Rather, 'Today is the day of salvation.'"

CHAPTER 16
A SLATE WIPED CLEAN

The weekly meeting went well. Chris and Pam were elated to find that all their hard work was rewarded. Not only had they been acknowledged for their outstanding salesmanship, but there was to be a monetary reward given to each girl as well.

I observed both of them carefully. They didn't brag about their achievements. On the contrary, they appeared to be humbled by the accolades they had received. Because of their attitude, they were accepted by the rest of the troop as having deserved the honor bestowed on them. There was no jealously, and nothing negative was spoken about them. Instead, the troop, without exception, gave them the honor that was rightfully theirs. This was a magic moment for both Vicky and me. We were extremely proud of our girls and glad to be a part of an organization that used activities to instill principles. Our purpose, as adult leaders, was not to preach—because kids don't like to be preached to—only to guide, encourage, and offer assistance when it was needed. The girls, merely by observing the results of the activities in which the troop was involved, were able to form their own conclusions.

After the meeting I dropped Vicky and Patty off at their door. Rachael and Patty had become good friends in recent months.

Why not? They were the same age, lived next door to each other, and both were redheads. Vicky and I had to separate them at times as they were both born leaders, each thinking that her way was the only way. But we knew that our girls were drawn to each other, and we expected some head banging from time to time because their personalities were so alike.

Rachael pleaded with me to allow her just one half hour with Patty before coming home. She and Patty wanted to compare notes on a badge they were working on. Vicky said that it would be okay, but only for a half hour. Both girls still had homework to do before going to bed. Rachael jumped out of the car and followed Vicky and Patty into their house with the promise to be home when Mrs. O'Conner told her to leave.

I pulled my car into the garage, turned off the ignition, and sat quietly for a moment, enjoying the peace and tranquility of a much-needed moment alone. This morning's confrontation with the Jolly Green Giant had left my nerves frazzled all day. I could hear Rand and the kids upstairs, but they weren't aware that I was home. I reached into the glove compartment, removed my flask, and took a long swallow.

That familiar feeling of warmth and immediate relaxation hit me as the alcohol traveled quickly into my bloodstream and found its way to my brain. I followed with my breath spray, realizing that I would be in close contact with Randy and Roni in a few minutes as I got them prepared for bed. I hoped that Rand would have the process started as I really wasn't in the proper frame of mind for all the usual bedtime rituals.

Savoring these few moments while the Scotch took its full effect, I once again began to review the events of the previous night. Sherry quoted many scriptures to me during the hours we were together. There was no way I could possibly remember all of them.

How in the world could she have memorized all those scriptures? I wondered, in awe of her knowledge of the Bible.

This brought to mind that, as a child I had always wanted to have one of those mysterious black leather-bound books like the priests read from during part of the mass. I had been very curious as to what it contained. Neither the nuns nor my family members encouraged this. As I grew older and began to earn my own spending money, a small paperback copy of the Bible was one of my first purchases. I remembered I was glad I hadn't invested more money in it than I did because I couldn't understand a word of it.

I had started with the first book, Genesis, and I quit after struggling through three or four chapters. It made absolutely no sense to me at all. There was no one who could teach me how to understand it either. No one in my family had owned a Bible except for Granny, and hers was written in German. It was only on rare occasions that I would even see Granny's Bible.

I dare not approach one of my teachers at school because she would give me the same answer that I had heard before. I was treading on holy ground and had no business even attempting to understand it. It needed to be left in the hands of the clergy, who were inspired by God to interpret it. They, in turn, would teach it to the congregation during the gospel reading portion of the mass. I put my little paperback Bible in my bookcase with some of the books I had finished reading and it stayed there forgotten for many years collecting dust.

But Sherry knew how to interpret it, of that I was certain. Hadn't she told me things that I already knew? I knew that I was a sinner. Hadn't I slept around in my single years with many men, some of whom had wives? These were the sins of fornication and adultery. Hadn't I allowed my husband to influence me to give written permission to an abortionist to destroy two helpless tiny lives that were growing inside of my body? This is something I swore I would never do because, though the popular term for this deplorable act was *abortion*, God had a much less polite word for it. It was *murder*.

And now, wasn't I paying the price for having done these unthinkably evil things by the guilt I was carrying around like an iron ball and chain attached to my ankle? Wasn't my out-of-control drinking the result of attempting to erase the memory of these actions? To be sure, it had a numbing effect. But when the effect of the alcohol wore off, not only did the guilt return more intense than before, but accompanying it was a nasty hangover that would stay with me for many hours.

Yes, of course, she was correct in quoting that particular scripture, I readily admitted to myself. *No one knows better than I what a horrible sinner I am. Just because I'm a respectable, married woman now with a husband and three children, that doesn't make me any less a sinner. On the outside, I may be fooling some people, but God knows what is on the inside. He knows everything, seen and unseen, present and past.*

I continued to search my memory for other things that Sherry said and other scriptures that she had quoted. I needed an answer to this mess I had made of my life. Somehow, I believed that the answer lay within the pages of the little pocket Bible she referred to from time to time during our conversation. She used this book to point out these scriptures to me.

There was something else that I remembered. She said that "the wages of sin is death." I stopped her when she quoted that and asked her to explain what that meant. At that moment, I recalled that she looked at me with those beautiful, penetrating brown eyes of hers and explained it so simply that even a child could understand.

"Mara," she said with that gentle, compassionate voice I had come to love as the evening wore on, "that simply means that we earn wages for the things that we do, whether good or bad. The wage that we receive from sin is death. That doesn't mean that we necessarily die the moment we commit sin. You claim to be a sinner, and you haven't died, have you? No, of course not.

"It means that when we come to the end of our life and are still holding on to that sin, we will receive our wage for it, and that wage will be death. When the Bible refers to death, it is speaking of eternal separation from God. God is in heaven, and with sin on our soul, we cannot go there to be with him. He is a holy God and cannot look upon sin. There is another place where sinners will go. Do you know where that is?"

"Of course, I do, Sherry. That place is hell, and that appears to be my destination," I concluded. "But that's a fair move on God's part because that's what I deserve."

"Now wait a minute, Mara," she had hastened to add. "I'm not finished yet. That's the bad news. But next comes the good news. You mustn't jump to conclusions. Hear me out. The remainder of that scripture says that the gift of God is eternal life through Jesus Christ, our Lord, and that is the 'rest of the story,' as Paul Harvey would say, Mara."

We continued to talk on into the night, so engrossed in the subject we were discussing that both of us lost track of time. This was all new to me. I never heard anything like this before. Then she asked me if I would like to receive Jesus as my Savior.

"He is the gift of God being offered to you right now, Mara," she said. "He took your sins into his own body and allowed them to be crucified to that horrible cross. He was the only one that met his Father's requirement to take away sin because he was the perfect sacrifice. He never sinned, and that was the only acceptable sacrifice for sin that God would accept. Your part in this is to ask him to forgive those sins and to surrender your life to him. With His help you will be able to do a complete turnaround. He will wipe the slate clean and help you live for Him."

This seemed too easy. Is this all I had to do, or was there more that Sherry had not talked about? I trusted Sherry and all that she said. It was obvious that this experience had changed her life. I envied her peace of mind and loving disposition, which was so much a part of her nature. Could I expect this kind of change to take place in my life, or would it be different? It was at this point that I hesitated. This was a life-changing and extremely important move. I told her that I would need time to think about it.

I've spent every waking moment since our conversation attempting to process all this, I thought, getting out of my car. A strong conviction had begun to grip me. I was becoming more and more convinced that this was what I needed to do. What more did I need to think about before taking that step of faith Sherry talked about?

On the other hand, I reminded myself, *this would change my life. I know it would. I would have to give up my drinking buddies at Sammy's.* I had been spending my Thursday nights at the neighborhood bar with them for some time now. We always had such fun getting a buzz on together. Aunt Marcie and Uncle Jack would be disappointed as well if they didn't see me there anymore. They were both beer drinkers and frequently stopped at Sammy's for an evening out. Since I had to be home with the kids most school nights, we didn't have the occasion to see each other very often anymore.

Then what about the couples' poker club that Rand and I belonged to? We rarely went anywhere together, but this was something he agreed to do with me. We both enjoyed playing poker even though I usually ended up having too much to drink by the end of the evening. Rand would become verbally abusive and would invariably chastise me on the way home.

"You are a total idiot, Mara," he would say. "Bob and Ray are just waiting for you to start playing sloppy poker so they can take your money, don't you realize that? If you could just leave the booze alone while you're playing cards, you would do much better by the end of the evening. I guess that's like talking to a rock, though," he would add sarcastically.

Considering the pros and cons involved in making a decision like this, I started up the steps toward the kitchen. I momentarily put all this out of my mind. Randy, Roni, and Sparky were waiting for me at the top of the stairs, happy to see me as always. Rand had gotten them both ready for bed, so I took over at this point. We talked briefly about their day at school, and I asked to see their homework to make sure that it had been completed properly.

I reminded Roni that she would have to get up early with Randy and Rachael as she was spending the day with one of our neighbors a few doors away. Loretta was a friend of mine, and I had promised her that I would bring Roni to her home to play with their three-year-old daughter, Jenny. Roni was anxious for this meeting as well. She was getting to the age where she wanted to venture out into the great unknown on occasion to meet new friends and broaden her horizons.

Tomorrow will be the perfect day for this, I thought. *I've got so many stops to make. I'll be running most of the day. Roni loves to go with me, but she doesn't hold up too well after a few hours. Hopefully I'll be able to get everything finished and pick her up at Loretta's on the way home. That way we can be here when Randy and Rachael get home from school.*

After the predictable forty-five minute ritual of getting everyone settled in their beds for the third time, I knocked on Mom's door and asked her if she would like to join me for a cup of tea. She declined my invitation as she said she was in bed for the night.

Just about this time Rachael came through the garage and darted up the steps, two at a time. "Golly, Mom, this is going to be a fun badge to work on. Patty has already collected some of the stuff to start on it this weekend. Can she come over on Saturday, and we can work on it together in the game room? We have that big table down there that we can spread all of our stuff on."

"Of course, honey. But right now, I happen to know that you have not finished your math homework yet on account of the Girl Scout meeting, so you better get to it. I'll make you a sandwich that you can eat while you're doing it. If you need any help, call your dad or me. One of us will help you if we can."

"I'll have that cup of tea with you, mamma bear, since your mother's in bed," Rand said. He was standing behind me as I closed the door to the girls' room. I had not expected him to come up behind me like that, and it startled me.

"My, my," he exclaimed, somewhat surprised. "You are certainly jumpy these days, my love."

"You would be jumpy too, if you had to face what I have to face in a couple of days," I responded, somewhat irritated that he didn't have the sensitivity to realize the reason for my anxiety.

"That's what I want to talk to you about, Mara. Come on down to the kitchen. I'll make you a cup of tea, and maybe Rachael would like a bowl of soup to go with that sandwich. How about that, Rae?" he called to her on his way to the kitchen.

"We can get this over with very quickly, mamma bear. Then we'll go to bed early tonight and both catch up on some much-needed sleep. I might even give you a back rub, if you're lucky. That should help relieve your anxiety if nothing else does."

Same old pattern, I told myself, that old familiar feeling of resentment beginning to overwhelm me as he turned on the Reuben charm. *He's always Mr. Charming before bedtime. The rest of the day, I'm nothing more than an old tennis shoe that he can shove out of his way at will.*

No, I can't start anything right now, I thought as I restrained myself from making a few choice comments that were on the tip of my tongue. *This isn't the time or the place for that. I must use common sense. I will not allow myself to get emotional. Rand doesn't respond to emotional women, so it won't do me any good. I must remain coolheaded and as logical as possible. I'm going to comply with his request and keep my appointment with that shrink he wants me to see on Friday. I don't know where he got the idea that I wasn't going to go through with this. Whether this guy can do anything for me remains to be seen. At least I'll keep my end of the bargain.*

He brought our tea to the table and sat down across from me. "All right," he began, assuming his no-nonsense mannerism, "your Aunt Marcie will be here at nine o'clock on Friday morning to look after your mother and Roni. Of course, the older children will have already gone to school. Marcie's only stipulation, when I asked her if she could come over on Friday, was that she needs to be home by three-thirty. She has some kind of appointment later in the day that she can't miss. I told her that our appointment was at ten-thirty and that we would have plenty of time to get home so that she could be on her way. So that part of the day is covered."

"Now," he continued, "how are you feeling about this? You are going to cooperate with this doctor fully, aren't you?" His eyes narrowed as he shot me one of his dark, threatening looks. I was not intimidated in the least, much to my astonishment.

"Look, Rand," I began, my voice even and controlled, "I will cooperate to the extent that I can. First of all, it's very possible that our chemistries won't mix. You know how important it is to have a good physician-patient relationship. That is something that remains to be seen. Once we get past that hurdle, then I will do my utmost to cooperate with him. I will be as honest with him as I know how to be and will not withhold anything that would be helpful to him in determining what type of treatment he might have in mind."

"Having done all that," I continued, "he must understand that I have three young children and a mentally challenged mother at home who need care. He's going to have to weigh everything in the balance and come up with something that will take all these things into consideration. Is that fair, or am I being unreasonable?"

"I really can't answer that question, Mara. We'll have to see what he has in mind after he examines you. My concern is that you'll go off the deep end like you do with me on occasion and screw everything up."

"Well," I countered, "I can't make any promises about that. You are the type of person that I find it very easy to 'go off the deep end' with. Hopefully, this doctor has a little better bedside manner than you do, if you know what I mean?"

He changed the subject abruptly. "How about the blood work that you had done last week? Did the lab send that directly to his office, or will you pick it up tomorrow while you're out?"

"He should have that in his possession by now, but I will check to make certain that this has been done. I have that on my list of things to do," I assured him.

"Okay, sweetheart," he concluded with a deep sigh as he leaned back in his chair and looked at me intently. "Just remember what I told you. I am sick and tired of having to live with a drunk. You owe me a lot more than what you're contributing to this marriage, and I feel like I've been shortchanged. I don't like to be shortchanged. So make this work for everyone concerned—the first time.

"I'm not going to play ring-around-the-rosy with you. I hope you understand that. If things don't change around here very soon, you're going to see some changes that you hadn't counted on. This is not an idle threat. You can take this to the bank. Let's go to bed now, Mara. We both have a full schedule tomorrow."

CHAPTER 17

A WISE DECISION

The morning dawned bright and clear with not a cloud in the sky. Frost had formed in the corners of our large picture window in the living room. This told me that it was an extremely frigid morning because this was a rarity. The large plate-glass window was dual glazed, and the temperature had to dip to single digits before this occurred.

Rand had gone to work earlier than usual. On most mornings, he opened the building and checked all the offices and restrooms for broken pipes or anything else the cold weather might have done to disrupt the regular flow of business.

I could not fathom the thought of having Randy and Rachael standing in the bitter cold waiting for a bus that might be late anyhow, so I bundled them up with extra gloves, earmuffs, and scarves for their return home later in the day and drove them to school. Most of the parents who waited on our corner for their children's bus to arrive had the same idea, so there weren't many little people to be seen this morning.

After dropping them off, I returned home to get Roni up and dressed so I could drop her off at the neighbor's house for the day.

I noticed that no one in my household had been in any hurry to get out of bed this morning.

Too bad, I thought. *But I really have to move fast today.* I delayed going out earlier in the week due to the weather. But it appeared that I had chosen the coldest day of the year to do all of my running around.

Well, at least it isn't snowing. The cold I can handle. The snow I can handle, but I sure don't like the icy roads after a freezing rain, I thought, attempting to convince myself of the fact that I would be cold and uncomfortable much of the day jumping in and out of the car.

Let's see now. How will I get Mom and Roni out of bed this morning? They both need some breakfast before Roni and I leave here.

Okay, I said to myself as I began pulling the Belgian-waffle maker down from the top shelf of the pantry. *This is the most popular breakfast in this house. So today, in order to get those two out of the sack and into the kitchen, it is going to be Belgian waffles with sausage and pure maple syrup.*

The strategy worked well. Empty stomachs were filled, and the kitchen was reorganized in record time. I got Roni tightly bundled up, and away we went—Roni to meet a new friend, and I to get a multitude of chores taken care of.

I had three baskets of ironing that I wanted to deliver this morning. I called each of the ladies I ironed for, found that they would all be at home, and told them I'd be delivering their freshly ironed clothing sometime this morning.

We had a very well-stocked bar in our game room which had seen a lot of activity over the years—evidently, much more activity than Rand cared to see in recent months. When my drinking became a major problem, he cleaned out the bar, hid the bottles, and left me with nothing to satisfy my insatiable desire for alcohol.

When the money budgeted for food and cleaning items became depleted prematurely, he began to make out the weekly shopping list and allocate just enough money to cover what was on the list. All I had left was my car, and he would keep the gas tank filled so I would not require money to do it myself.

Drunks are very resourceful people. I had a car, I could drive, and I liked to iron. So there was the answer to my problem. It was hidden in plain sight. I would find women who hated to iron and were willing to pay money to have it done. I did an excellent job and never wanted for repeat customers. When I got my pay, I would immediately head for the state store and convert the dollar bills into bottles of whiskey.

In the summer months, I preferred to drink beer. It didn't take me very long to calculate how many ironings I would need to do each week to support my habit. Since I was fast as well as good, I did these extra jobs in my spare time, not neglecting my own household duties. When the children needed me for any legitimate reason, I was there for them. Dinner was always on the table when Rand came home from work, and for the most part, the meals were well planned, nutritious, and enjoyable.

I despised housework with a passion, but because Rand would bring clients home for dinner on short notice, I found it necessary to keep a neat, orderly house. Because Rand was in middle management, he was required to wear a suit, tie, and dress shirt each working day. He preferred white shirts, so white shirts it was. There was always a fresh one ready for him when he needed it.

He put in long hours on the job. He was ambitious and willing to go the extra mile, always having one eye on a promotion, and he knew that there was plenty of opportunity for advancement. He was already on the middle rung of the corporate ladder in his company at the young age of thirty-eight and was presently working his way to the top, one step at a time. He was blessed with good business sense and was a top-notch salesman. Moving into middle management last year provided him with additional opportunities to prove his administrative worth to the company. Prove it he did, but not without cost to him.

As my drinking increased, I noticed that he was spending more time in bars as well. He did not drink on the job—this was a no-no and detrimental to anyone in his position. He could usually be found at home on weeknights, but from Friday after work through the wee hours of Sunday morning, it was an entirely different story. The kids and I rarely saw him during that time. He was either out somewhere, getting ready to go out, or just coming home from being out; and usually, when he did come home, he was drunk.

When I first began to take in ironing, I lived in mortal fear that Rand would find out where I was getting the money to continue my drinking. It seemed like I always had extra baskets of clothing in the laundry room. Would he be perceptive enough to put the puzzle pieces together? No, he never noticed. The laundry was my domain. He rarely came into that room unless he wanted a freshly ironed shirt or to take a quick shower in the powder room if the upstairs bathroom was occupied. Perhaps he had become so immune to seeing me partially inebriated that he began to look the other way.

After delivering the ironing, I went to the nearest state store and restocked my dwindling supply of alcoholic beverages. Being in the neighborhood where I opened the Girl Scouts' account, I thought it wise to get rid of all the money that was in the trunk of my car. It wasn't mine, and I had total responsibility to see that it was taken to the bank and deposited as soon as possible.

It would just be my luck to get rear-ended by some woman who wasn't paying as much attention to her driving as she was to applying her lipstick in her rearview mirror, I thought. I had an ugly vision of a smashed Pontiac rear end and the canvas bag of bills and coins strewn all over the street. I stopped at the bank immediately and deposited the cookie money.

I needed to get the grocery shopping out of the way next. It was an easy matter now that Rand was making a list of food and cleaning items that we needed. It was a lot quicker, but not nearly as much fun. He robbed me of the challenge of searching for sales so that I would have an excess of food money to buy a bottle of liquor now and then. Well, no matter. I had my source.

After this, I had three more stops to make, and I was ready to head for home. It was becoming colder as the sun began to get closer to the horizon. Having completed these final stops, I glanced at my watch to see how much time, if any, I had left before picking up Roni at three-thirty. I was amazed to see that I was an hour ahead of schedule.

This is great, I said to myself. *It's easy to hide bagged liquor bottles with the groceries, but a twenty-four bottle case of sixteen-ounce Schmidt's is another story altogether. With Roni in the car with me, it would be difficult to get a case of beer out of the trunk without her seeing me. I don't want to leave it in there. The way the temperature is dropping, I can have a real mess if these bottles begin to freeze. I'll just drop these things off at home before I pick her up. I have plenty of time. I might just open that bottle of Brandy, as a matter of fact. That will really warm me up on a day like this.*

For no reason in particular, I decided to return home another way. Turning into a familiar street that I often traveled on my way to the mall, I happened to notice something out of the corner of my eye. Down in the hollow, on the left side of the road, sitting back several hundred yards from the street, was a tiny white-frame church. It was sitting in the middle of a lot that had to be at least ten acres in size.

Now, that is a strange sight, I thought. *Why would anyone want to build a tiny church like that on such a huge parcel of land? I've been on this road hundreds of times, but I never noticed that church before. I wonder if it was just recently built.*

I couldn't get over it. *Why should I be so curious about something like that? New buildings are going up all the time. This area is relatively new, and there is a lot of new developing going on. Why in the world would I concern myself with something like that?* I wondered as I began to speed up a little. I was so curious about this church that I actually slowed the car so that I could get a better look.

Crazy woman, I thought, *and you haven't even had a drink today.*

Arriving home moments later, I pulled the car into the garage and lowered the garage door. I didn't want to have a car just happen to go by at the moment I took the case of beer into the house. *Who knows? It just might be Vicky or one of the many neighbors I know fairly well. Anyhow, I want to keep the car warm for Roni. I'll be picking her up in a half hour.*

I began to unload the groceries and other packages I had purchased during my shopping expedition this afternoon. Reminding myself that I had four bottles of various kinds of liquor tucked away in the grocery bags, I decided to get all the alcoholic beverages and the case of beer separated from the groceries and into the laundry where I could hide them in some of my favorite spots.

The three laundry baskets that I picked up were in the backseat of the car. I would have to get them out as well. Roni's car seat was in the back, so I would have to move those clothes baskets out of the way so she could climb into her seat.

First of all, I took the laundry baskets, one at a time, into the laundry. I had a long metal folding table against the garage fire wall, where I did my folding and placed my ironed garments. I stuck the baskets under the table where they would be out of the way until I was ready to work on them. This also proved to be a good place to keep things that required some kind of an explanation if found because they were more difficult for Rand to spot.

Next, I put all the grocery bags on the landing of the steps leading to the dining room. I removed the liquor that I stashed in some of the bags and took the bottles into the laundry.

I had better put these away now so I won't forget them, I thought. I would have to do some pretty fast-talking if Mom or Rand or one of the kids saw them sitting out in plain sight. As I thought of Roni, I glanced down at my watch. It was 3:17 p.m. I still had a few minutes before I had to leave the house to pick her up.

What is that fragrance I smell? I wondered. *It smells like lavender or something similar to lavender. I wonder where that is coming from. Maybe Mom came down here for some reason while I've been gone. But she doesn't use cologne at all, let alone one that smells like this one. It's lovely. I wish I knew where I could buy some just like it. It's light and subtle, but it has such a fresh and beautiful fragrance.*

I dismissed all thoughts about this mysterious odor, which seemed to be coming from the laundry. I had more important things on my mind right now. I checked the car for a final time. Satisfied that everything had been removed, I returned to the game room and did one more quick inspection.

"Roni can help me with the small packages when we get home, and I'll carry the groceries to the kitchen then—uh oh," I said aloud. "I almost forgot the case of beer." It was sitting in the middle of the game room right where I left it.

I picked it up and headed for the laundry once again, wondering where I was going to hide it. I had pretty well exhausted all my secret places.

As I reached the door to the laundry, I stopped suddenly. I could still smell that lovely lavender fragrance, but there was something else going on in there that I couldn't identify. As I stepped into the room, I felt a presence. Something or someone was in here. I thought about the episode with the Jolly Green Giant. That experience had been so horrifying that I was having a difficult time erasing it from my mind. I looked through the open door leading to the powder room. The room was empty, and nothing had been disturbed.

Unlike the scenario that confronted me in my bedroom yesterday morning, I had no feeling of dread or apprehension. There was a pleasant warmth that seemed to permeate the walls of the laundry, filling the entire room. I felt a strange peace settle over me, which I had not experienced since I was a child. I stood there for just a brief period, savoring the moment. All sense of time left me. All I was aware of was a voice of some kind, masculine and strong, and yet gentle and compassionate at the same time. That wonderful, compelling voice echoed and reechoed throughout my entire being.

Mara, I've come to offer you salvation, if you are willing to accept it. I died for you because I love you.

That was all. There was nothing more. It was my special moment in time. Jesus had paid me a visit. He offered me that wonderful gift Sherry spoke of on Monday night. This was my moment of decision. Would I accept him or reject him? The opportunity may never come again.

I put the case of beer on the floor and dropped to my knees. Before I realized what was happening, I found myself lying in a prone position—my cheeks on the cool concrete floor and tears running down my face, like the small trickle of an endless stream into the drain—in the center of the room.

"Jesus, it was I. I killed you. It wasn't the Jews or even the Romans. It was I. You gave up your life so that I could live, not just in this life but for all eternity. Please forgive me. I'm a horrible sinner, but my friend Sherry told me that it really doesn't matter how horrible or how numerous my sins may be. What matters is that I am are sorry for those sins and that I promise to turn from the lifestyle that caused them.

You have the power to forgive those sins. She told me that I wouldn't be able live this new life I am about to enter by myself, but that you would help me get victory in my life if I just trust you and invite you in. I want to do that right now, Jesus," I sobbed through a myriad of tears.

I wept like I had never wept before. It seemed like someone had opened a floodgate inside me, and a lifetime of tears stored up inside was suddenly being released. It felt so good to be able to cry. All my life, I had been told that big girls don't cry. I needed to take it on the chin. I shouldn't be so full of self-pity. A lot of people had it worse than I did. And on and on and on. All these voices I listened to over my lifetime meant nothing to me right at this moment. I was crying, and it felt good.

Just then, I felt a strong, masculine hand take my hand and lift me to my feet. I looked at the place where I felt that hand grasping my own. I wanted to see the scar that the nail had made in that wrist, but I saw nothing.

The same familiar voice spoke once again, however, and told me to go and to sin no more. I knew I had received a great visitation from the One who saved me from my sins. I left my laundry room a different person than I had been when I entered it a few minutes before. I felt light and buoyant, free from the heavy load I had been carrying around for many years. I couldn't put it into words, not yet. I just knew that a wonderful change took place in my life and in my heart just now, and that I would never be the same again.

My first inclination was to call Sherry. I sat on my fireplace hearth, my heart still pounding in my chest from this experience. I dialed her number and waited. I heard a gentle, melodic voice on the other end.

"Sherry, is this you?" I asked. Her daughter, Chris, sounded just like her.

"Yes, this is Sherry."

"This is Mara, Sherry."

"Yes," she said, with a certain expectancy in her voice.

"Sherry, I just got saved. Jesus saved me."

For a second, there was complete silence on the other end. Then I knew she had placed her hand over the receiver because I could hear muffled voices praising the Lord and laughing excitedly.

Sherry came back to me after a brief time. "Oh, Mara, that is wonderful news. We've been waiting to hear from you."

"What do you mean, Sherry? Who's been waiting to hear from me?"

"I have our Bible study group at my home today. This is our regular Wednesday prayer meeting and Bible study. We were just praying for your salvation when the phone rang. I was going to let it ring, but then the Lord spoke to me and told me to answer it. He wanted the group to know that while we all were praying, he was answering that prayer."

"You know what, Sherry? I'm going to be the best Christian that ever lived."

Once again, I heard the muffled voices of women in the background laughing uproariously. I wanted to ask Sherry what was so funny, but I didn't want to speak out of turn. Evidently, they knew something that I didn't know.

"All right, now Mara. Jesus saved you, but that is just the beginning. You are a brand-new, baby Christian now, and He doesn't want you to stay a baby forever. It's just like us mammas. We have our babies, and they are beautiful and wonderful and everything else that babies are. But we don't want them to remain babies too long. We want them to grow up because that is the natural order of life.

"As a matter of fact, if they do remain babies, continue to dirty their diapers, drink milk from a bottle, and do other things that babies do, we mammas begin to get a little worried. We're waiting for them to make progress, learn new skills like walking and talking and eating grown-up food. If these things don't begin to happen, we get real worried after a little while.

"The same thing applies in the Christian's life. We begin our life in Christ by being *born again*. That's the spiritual birth that Jesus talks about in the gospel of John. Then, in the normal progression of spiritual life, we begin to grow. How do we do that, you ask? Mainly by daily reading and studying of the Bible and by learning to pray and worship God, and also by having fellowship with other believers.

"Then one of the best ways to grow is by sharing our faith in Christ with others who do not know Him. We can learn a whole lot from older Christians too. They have a lot of experiences they can share with the newer Christians because they've been walking with Christ for a while and have gained some spiritual wisdom.

"Mara, I could talk to you all day about how to grow in Christ, but the way to learn fast is to attend a Bible-believing church and see it demonstrated for yourself. Our regular midweek service is tonight. Would you like to join us and find out for yourself?"

"I would love to, Sherry. I'll have to ask my husband if he would object to getting the kids ready for bed tonight. If he's willing to do that, I will go with you."

We agreed that I would call her if I needed a ride, and she and Carly and some of her other friends would pick me up at six-forty and take me to their church to "get my feet wet." She prayed with me before we ended our phone conversation, thanking Jesus for saving me and asking God to lead and guide me in the way that he wanted me to go. I really never heard anyone pray like that. It was a beautiful prayer, and I could tell that it came from the heart. I wasn't sure, but I didn't think she read that from any written material she was holding in her hand. It appeared to be spontaneous.

I hope that I'll be able to pray like that someday, I said to myself.

After our phone conversation, I remembered that I had told Loretta that I would get Roni at three-thirty. I was ten minutes late.

CHAPTER 18

A NEW LIFE

Loretta met me at the door and invited me in for coffee. I declined her offer but told her I would like to take a rain check for another day, perhaps a day next week. It would have to be earlier in the day because I liked to be home when my two older children got home from school.

"As a matter of fact," I said, glancing at my watch, "I had better get Roni bundled up and into the car. The kids will be getting off their bus any minute now. It's such a bitterly cold day I think we'll take a ride down to the bus stop and pick them up."

"Your Roni is such a little lady, Mara. She and Jenny had a wonderful day together," Loretta commented, getting Roni's things out of the closet.

"I'm glad that she didn't give you any trouble," I added as I saw the girls coming up the steps from the game room.

"Hi, Mummy," Roni yelled, jumping into my arms as she reached the living room. "Jenny and I had fun today. When can I come back and pway with her again? We had so much fun pwaying with her baby dolls. They all have so many clothes that we just dwessed them and undwessed them all day."

"Umm, sounds like fun, girls. Hello, Jenny. I think we'll invite Jenny to our house next time you two get together. What do you think about that?"

"That would be good, Mummy. Can Jenny bwing her baby-doll clothes so we can see if they fit my babies?"

"Sounds like my daughter has confiscation on her mind, Loretta. I guess I'll have to get out some old material from my leftover scraps and make some new clothes for Roni's 'babies,'" I said, pulling the zippers up on her boots. "I'll call you next week sometime, and we can arrange to get the girls together again at our house, if that's all right with you."

"I'm not sure how well that will work, Mara, but we can try it. Jenny is very shy, and being the only child, I've been her exclusive playmate up to this time. I must say, though, she just loves your Roni, and they get along so well together. This has been a *first* for Jenny being with a child her age for this length of time."

"Whatever works for Jenny will be fine with us," I concluded, steering Roni toward the door. "Thanks again, and I'll be in touch."

Roni and I made it to the bus stop ahead of the bus. Evidently, the extreme cold weather made it difficult getting some of the buses started. They were all behind schedule. There were several moms and a couple of dads waiting in parked cars for their children. We all had the same idea. It was too cold outside to let the kids walk home today. Roni had me all to herself for a few minutes while we waited in our warm, cozy car for her sister and brother's bus to arrive.

Roni chattered happily about her day with Jenny and Loretta while I continued to bask in the pleasant warmth of the overwhelming experience I just had with Jesus a short time ago in my laundry room. I couldn't wait to share my good news with the family.

I'll do it at dinner tonight when I have everyone's attention, I decided, excited to get their reactions.

Rachael and Randy were elated when they saw my car and hurried toward it, relieved that they didn't have to face that long, frigid walk home.

"I'm a little late getting dinner started today, kids. So I'll give you your snack, and then I want you to begin your homework as soon as we get home. As soon as I get things started in the kitchen, I'll spend some time with each of you if you need help with your homework. I may be going out for a while this evening," I announced.

"Where are you going, Mommy? Tomorrow night is your night out. How come you're going out tonight?" Rachael asked, her lower lip protruding in disappointment at hearing this news. "I don't like it when Daddy puts us to bed. He never allows us to have a snack, and he doesn't read to us like you do. He always has a program on TV that he has to watch," she complained.

"You know Mrs. Drummond, our cookie chairman from Girl Scouts, Rachael? She has invited me to go to her church with her and Mrs. Bingham tonight. I told her if your dad was willing to get you kids ready for bed, I'd like to go with them," I explained.

"I really like those two ladies, Mommy, but why do they have to go to church on Wednesday nights? We don't go to church on Wednesdays. We go on Sundays," she insisted.

"I know that, honey, but they go to a different kind of church. Wednesday is called midweek service at Baptist churches."

"What is a Baptist church?" Randy asked, suddenly interested in our conversation.

"I don't know Randy," I responded. "That's what I want to find out. That's why I want to go there tonight."

Coming into the game room, I saw the groceries and some other packages I had acquired earlier in the day. They were sitting at the bottom of the steps where I had left them.

"Well, it looks like my bags didn't grow legs and walk themselves to the kitchen," I said. "Come on, kids. Give your mom a hand here. Randy, if you and Roni each grab a couple of small packages, and Rachael and I take the grocery bags, I won't have to make another trip."

"You're so siwwy, Mummy. Bags can't gwow wegs, can they? I never saw bags walking awound with wegs. That would be vewy funny if bags walked awound by themselves," Roni said, attempting to grasp the real meaning behind my last statement.

At this point, I considered the four-year-old mind and its literal approach to the English language. I decided that I had better drop some of the expressions I used to express myself. Roni was beginning to separate fact from fantasy, so why confuse the issue?

With dinner started, groceries put away, and Rachael and Randy involved with their homework, I was in the process of telling Mom about Roni's day with Jenny when I heard the garage door go up. Rand was pulling his car into the garage.

"Must be the weather," I remarked to my mother. "I bet they had a shortage of customers, being as cold as it is, possibly some cancellations, and he decided to close early."

My mind began to jump ahead to what I had potentially planned for the evening. *This could definitely be in my favor,* I thought. *If I can get dinner over with and the kitchen cleaned up a little earlier than usual, I could call Sherry and have her stop by at six-forty to pick me up.*

I felt strongly impressed to send up a little prayer. *Dear Jesus,* I prayed to myself, *please put Rand in a good mood so I can go to church with Sherry and Carly tonight, okay?*

That wasn't much of a prayer, I reflected, *but it is something that I really want to do tonight. So I'll just have to wait and see what happens. If I keep practicing, I may get good at this someday, like Sherry is.*

As it turned out, Rand was in an excellent mood. The bonus checks for last year's profit-sharing account had been handed out this morning. His check was much more than he had expected.

"I think I'll look into the possibility of buying one of those Boston Whalers I saw at the Watercraft show last month," Rand announced. "That would be a great boat to take on fishing weekends with my buddies this spring. We can use it for our family vacation later this summer too," he added.

"That's good news, Rand," I replied, with what I hoped would be sufficient enthusiasm to satisfy his need for acclamation. "You work hard so you certainly deserve to be rewarded for your efforts."

"You are absolutely correct, my dear wife. But a Boston Whaler is just the beginning. I'll own that company one of these days lock, stock, and barrel. What's for dinner, and how soon?"

"Swiss steak smothered in mushrooms, mushroom gravy, mashed potatoes, and green-bean casserole. We'll be ready in about twenty minutes," I said, checking the potatoes for doneness.

He came over to the stove and peeked at the steak and gravy simmering in a large iron skillet, cutting himself a sample as he often did. "Um, this is good, one of my favorites," he said, putting his arm around my waist at the same time.

He spun me around so that I would be looking directly at him and would not be distracted by preparing dinner. "You know, mamma bear, you would probably be a pretty good investment if you weren't drunk so much of the time. Let's hope that everything works out with this doctor I have you set up with on Friday," he added. "From what I've been told, he's one of the best in the business."

He looked into my eyes for just an instant, and immediately he backed away from me with a puzzled expression on his face. "I knew there was something different about you tonight, sweetheart. You haven't been drinking," he said, somewhat astonished. "What happened? Did the well run dry?"

"No, that's not it, Rand. But I do have some good news for you and the kids. We'll talk about it over dinner, okay?"

"I can hardly wait, my pet," he continued, his eyes still fixed intently on my face. "Evidently this is my lucky day. Everything seems to be going smoothly for a change. I hope your news is as good as you seem to believe it is."

"You can be the judge of that, Rand. Right now, will you please get out of the kitchen and allow me to finish dinner? The kids are doing their homework, and Roni is watching *Mister Rogers* in the living room. I'll call you all as soon as I'm ready to put the food on the table."

Moments later, the family had gathered around the table, hungry as bears the day after a winter of hibernation spent in their cave. Roni, as always, announced dinner and led her nana to her place at the table. This had become a ritual in our home since Aunt Mo-Mo's death. Roni was very proud of her new and very important task, and she was even prouder of the fact that she was the only member of the family who was able to convince Nana that eating dinner was an important function of the day, if one chose to survive for any length of time.

As I observed my family enjoying the food I prepared for them, I thought about some of the other extended members of our family who never began a meal without asking the Lord's blessing on their food. Granny was a strong advocate of this and insisted upon it at her own table. I had gotten away from it as I approached my teens. My turbulent life during those early years had been far removed from any positive thoughts of God. Praying over food before a meal was not even a consideration.

After marrying Rand and beginning our family, I thought it would be a good idea to reintroduce some of these religious rituals so that the children could benefit from them. By the time I actually got around to doing this, the older kids were already losing interest in anything spiritual. After a brief time, I gave it up as a lost cause. Other than attending mass on Sunday and CCD classes, which I had insisted upon for the kids, there was very little mention of God in our household.

Now, as I sat waiting for the right moment to share my good news with the family, I put grace before meals on my list of—things to do.

"Okay, kids—and, Liz, this includes you too. Mom has some good news she wants to share with us tonight, so listen up," Rand announced, breaking a brief moment of silence as everyone was about finished with dinner. "You have the floor, my dear. Carry on."

I shared all that occurred during the afternoon and that I had surrendered my life to Jesus as a result. I tried to tell my story exactly as I remembered it happening and to make it as simple as possible so that Roni would be able to grasp, at least in her child-like way, that something wonderful occurred in her mummy's life. For a brief instant, there was complete silence around the table.

Rachael was the first to comment. "Oh, Mother, don't be ridiculous. Things like that don't really happen to people," she said.

The voice was that of an adult male, rasping and ominous. It was not Rachael's voice or anything even resembling Rachael's voice. I had been watching her as she spoke. Her mouth was forming the words she appeared to be speaking, but the voice was not hers. I was shocked beyond belief. I looked around the table to get the reactions of the rest of the family members. There was none. They had not heard what I heard.

"Daddy, may I please be excused from the table now? I'm finished eating my dinner, and I ate all my beans," Rachael said, her voice once again returning to the familiar voice of my oldest child. "I have a lot of homework tonight. Mrs. Cooke is giving us an English test tomorrow."

"Go ahead, Rae. That's important. You need to get all your homework finished. I have a little surprise for all you kids when all homework has been completed, but not until then," he added in his usual dictatorial manner.

I was still gripped by the shock I had just experienced, but I attempted to keep my cool. I was anxious to get more reactions, especially from the two younger children. I wanted to be able to determine by their responses where Jesus might fit into our family life.

"What did you think about Mommy's story, Randy?" I continued, undaunted.

"I don't know, Mommy. I don't think about Jesus very much. We are learning all about him in CCD class. I'd rather learn how to put engines together. Daddy told me he would show me how to do that when I got old enough."

"Well, Roni, that leaves you, sweetheart. What did you think about when you heard Mummy's story?"

"I think that it was vewy scawy, Mummy. If someone took my hand and I couldn't see who it was, I would be vewy scawed. Jesus doesn't want to scawe us, does he, Mummy?"

"No, of course, he doesn't want to scare us, honey. He loves us," I assured her, but I could hear the disillusionment in my voice.

The two younger children then asked to be excused from the table and took off to the game room, where they could play undisturbed until it was time to get ready for bed.

"Well, Mara, you appear to be disappointed, but what did you expect? This story of yours is no more than one more imaginary fable out of *Grimms' Fairy Tales*," was Rand's summation of our conversation.

"To be quite honest with you, my dear," he added, "I am of the same opinion as the children, on a more sophisticated level, of course. You can believe whatever you want to believe, but how about leaving the family out of it? We've discussed religion before, and you know my feeling about the entire subject. I think it's a waste of time, complete nonsense. I only gave my consent for those CCD classes you insisted upon because we made a deal. I agreed to allow the children to attend the class if you would agree to take Rae and Randy out of the parochial school you had them enrolled in last semester. So we came to a meeting of the minds on religious education at that time, and I think we should let it remain there, agreed?"

"All right, Rand. If that's your final word on the subject, we'll leave it there. I did hear you say that you had no problem with me believing what I wanted to believe, though, isn't that correct?"

Without waiting for a response, I went on, realizing that an opportunity was opening for me. "If what you said is true, then my attending Sherry's church with her this evening shouldn't present a problem for you, is that correct?"

"No, I have no objection to that, just so long as you don't stay out all night like you did earlier in the week, and no stopping at your favorite bar on the way home from church either, Mara. I don't know what this sudden abstinence was today, but I just don't trust you out on the streets at night. You behave yourself, all right?" he admonished, slapping me on the behind as he went into the living room to watch the evening news.

I'm just another one of his kids, I thought to myself, *always being chastised for my bad behavior.*

"As a matter of fact," he added from the living room as an afterthought, "one of my big customers gave me a new board game his company is putting on the market this summer. He wants me to try it out with our kids and give him some feedback. It's supposed to be for all age-groups from four to adult—a game for the whole family to enjoy together, he says. That's how he's promoting it. I thought I'd give it a try with the kids after they finish with their homework tonight. I'll see that they're in bed by eight-thirty, but you see to it that you are home before ten o'clock, understood?"

I was nothing less than speechless. I felt like I was talking to a stranger. This stranger looked like Rand and sounded like Rand, but he certainly didn't behave like Rand. I murmured a brief thank-you prayer under my breath and called Sherry.

Never having been inside a Protestant church, I had no idea what to expect. Not only was I pleasantly surprised, I was elated.

Sherry and Carly had two other friends in Sherry's car with them when they picked me up. There was an atmosphere of joy and love that permeated that automobile such as I had never experienced.

Each of these women made me feel loved and accepted as though I had known them all my life.

When we arrived at the church, this same atmosphere was present within the walls of the small redbrick building. Evidently, the service had not yet begun. There were several men and two women sitting on the platform on high-backed upholstered chairs, which were placed side by side against the outside wall of the building. Back in the far-left corner of the platform was a small area completely enclosed in glass. Inside this partitioned area, there was a drummer with all his equipment. Two guitarists, a bass player, and a man behind a spinet piano occupied the area directly in front of the partitioned section of the stage.

Just as we took our seats, an attractive young woman came out on the platform, and the pianist began to play a familiar gospel song. She walked over to the piano and picked up the chord he was playing without missing a beat. Her voice was like that of an angel. I wondered where the church found her. She was very talented and could have named her price just about anywhere. I later found out that she was one of the pastor's three daughters and one of their regular soloists.

As impressed as I was with what was happening on the platform, glancing around the crowded sanctuary, I noticed that there were men and women in the center aisle. Some of them had large colorful banners, which they were waving in time with the beat of the music. Others were playing tambourines as they kept perfect time with the drummer who had now begun to play along with the guitarists. Everyone was swaying in time with the beat of the music. There were two young men up in front of the altar railing doing some kind of an intricate dance, one on either side of the podium.

I was in complete awe of all that was going on around me. I looked at Sherry, who was standing on my right and participating in this activity enthusiastically. I sensed some kind of an electrifying force sweeping over the congregation, and I was becoming a part of it. I was very comfortable in this exciting atmosphere, and I felt that I could stay here all night.

After several minutes, one of the younger men sitting on the platform came to the podium and gave all the announcements for coming events and speakers. Then another one of the men, this one considerably older, took the younger man's place and, with a list in his hand, began to call out the names of each member who needed special prayer, the emphasis being placed on those who were sick or hospitalized.

Someone who just lost a loved one was being prayed for, that God would grant peace and comfort in this time of great need. Although the man at the podium would begin to pray for each request, someone in the congregation would continue with the prayer, adding additional information about this individual. Evidently, the one praying was someone close to the one being prayed for. This was so personal that it touched me deeply. After the list had been exhausted, the man leading the prayer introduced the pastor of the church as the speaker for this evening's service.

A stately tall gentleman in his sixties, I guessed, walked to the podium with his Bible in hand. He had an abundance of snow-white hair and a deep baritone voice that was pleasant to hear. He greeted the congregation and first-time visitors and immediately got to the business at hand. The message that he had chosen for tonight was taken from the gospel of John, chapter three.

He spoke of Jesus's conversation with the Pharisee named Nicodemus, who visited Jesus by night. He elaborated on this portion of the scripture. Why had Nicodemus come to visit Jesus after dark? Could it be that he was ashamed to be seen with this young rabbi who was creating such a stir wherever he went? Much of what this Jesus had to say was very controversial and offensive to many of the scribes and Pharisees, but he was gaining popularity with the common people. Was Nicodemus in fear of losing his lofty position as a spiritual leader of the Jewish people should he be seen in the company of this Jesus?

"We can only speculate on Nicodemus's reason for stealth in this situation. The Bible does not speak in any detail regarding his motivation," the pastor said. "There is one thing we can be certain of regarding these midnight visits, and it is this: during their conversations, Jesus was able to answer satisfactorily the question that had compelled Nicodemus to seek him out.

"Nicodemus did not understand the concept of the *new birth*. Jesus had to show him that it was different from natural birth. It was a spiritual birth directly from God, and there was a certain requirement that had to be met in order to receiver this new birth. That requirement was that the one seeking after this experience must believe that He was the Son of God and would be lifted up on the cross to take away sin.

"Just as Moses had lifted up the bronze serpent in the desert to save the people from deadly snakebites if they would look upon that serpent, so too, anyone who believed that Jesus was truly God's Son sent to earth to be crucified for the sins of mankind would be saved for all eternity. Jesus also pointed out to Nicodemus that it was absolutely essential to be *born again* in order to first see and then to enter into the kingdom of God."

He closed his message by inviting to the alter those in the congregation who had never experienced this new birth, who had never trusted Jesus to save them so they could be assured that, one day, they too could become citizens of God's kingdom.

I understood his story of Jesus and Nicodemus. I knew in my heart that this is exactly what I had done yesterday afternoon in the solitude of my laundry room. I was "born again." I acknowledged that I was a sinner and needed the Savior because there was nothing I could do to save myself. I had to trust Jesus, God's Son, to save me.

On our way home in Sherry's car, I thanked her for inviting me to her church. I told her I knew what had happened to me yesterday, but I couldn't put it into words. Her pastor had confirmed for me in his message what I could not adequately describe myself.

"Sherry, Carly, and ladies," I announced, "I think your church is wonderful. I would really like to attend it on a regular basis. Maybe someday I can become a member."

I was sitting in the backseat between the two ladies whom I had just met tonight. Sherry and Carly looked at each other when I made this comment.

"Mara. I'm sure that Pastor Gentry would love to have you in our congregation, but in case you didn't notice, we are predominantly a black church," Carly reminded me.

"So what? That certainly doesn't matter to me, and I'm sure it doesn't matter to God. After all, those of us who have accepted Jesus into our hearts are all God's children, aren't we? Does he make a distinction because of the color of our skin, Carly?" I asked.

"No, he doesn't, but people do. We know that there should be no discrimination among races, but there is, honey. Face it. There's more discrimination on Sunday morning than any other day of the week. It's not right, but it is a reality. We're praying that this will change soon, but things of this nature take time. Ask Martin Luther King. He'll tell you all about it."

Evidently, Sherry had detected the disappointment in my voice, and she joined the conversation at this point. "Listen, Mara, I clean for a lady in Overton. God allowed me to share the gospel with her last year, and she gave her heart to Jesus, just like you did yesterday. She and her family attend a small Assembly of God Church in Belleview Park. The name of the church is Zion Assembly.

"This is very close to where you live. It's in the next township and probably wouldn't take you more than fifteen or twenty minutes to get there. As a matter of fact, the church we just came from is only about a mile from there. This lady's name is Phoebe

Mansfield, and her husband's name is Keith. They have five children who all attend Sunday school at Zion. They love the church and have become members there. The children like it too because there are several activities geared especially for children."

"Would you allow me to give her your phone number?" she continued. "I know she would be happy to have you join her and her family some Sunday soon to check out Zion Assembly."

"Okay," I responded halfheartedly. I liked the Baptist Church I had just visited and wanted to go back there. "I guess I could try it. You haven't led me astray yet, Sherry. By the way, what kind of a person is Mrs. Mansfield?" I asked her.

Sherry responded without hesitation. "She's your kind of person, Mara. You'll like her, I'm sure."

I glanced into her rearview mirror. She was smiling broadly with that beautiful sparkle in her eye I had come to love. This assured me that everything would be all right.

At that moment, Sherry pulled into my driveway. I glanced at my watch as the lady on my left prepared to get out of the car to allow me to get out behind her. It was nine twenty-five. I had beat my deadline. Rand would be surprised once again. It had been a memorable evening, one I would never forget.

CHAPTER 19
BOOT CAMP BEGINS

What a fantastic week this has been, I reflected as I placed several pieces of bacon in the large iron skillet, compliment of Granny. Rand was in the shower, and the kids were slowly but surely dragging themselves out of bed for yet another frigid trip to the bus stop after breakfast. I had a strong desire to stay in bed a little while longer this morning to mentally review all that occurred since Monday evening, but that didn't happen.

Rand woke me early to let me know that he received a call from the big boss. A special meeting had been scheduled for this morning as soon as the office opened, and he had to be there before the salespeople began to trickle in.

I made a few mental adjustments to my usual morning routine and jumped out of bed to get my day started a little earlier than usual.

Maybe I'll drive Rachael and Randy to school one more day. That way, I can give them a little more time at home this morning while I get Rand fed and out of here.

Mom, who had come out to the kitchen for an early cup of coffee and a breakfast roll, was watching me do my balancing act. "This has been an unusually cold winter, Mara. It's so hard on the children having to walk such a long distance to get their bus," she commented sympathetically, seeming to have read my thoughts.

"I guess so, Mom, but I remember walking up Center Street every morning with the wind whipping around my feet and the snow blowing so hard I couldn't see where I was going. But guess what? I made it, didn't I?"

"You kids were tougher in your generation than they are today," she added.

"And whose fault is that?"

"It's not anyone's fault, Mara. Things are just different in today's world. It seems like now there are two cars in every garage, sometimes three. If the kids miss a bus or need a ride for some other reason, there's always transportation available to take them where they need to go."

"We only had one car in the entire family," she continued reminiscing somewhat. "And it usually wasn't available because everybody wanted to use it at the same time. Do you remember that little gray Chevrolet that your granddad won in a raffle at the Fireman's Carnival, Mara?"

"How could I forget that Chevy?" I responded. "I couldn't understand why he never learned to drive. It gave me good practice as a new driver, though, so I—"

I was stopped halfway through my sentence. Rand had come into the kitchen and was ready for his breakfast. He hated to run late, and today of all days, he needed to be on time for work. He was in the process of accelerating the action for everyone involved in order to keep himself on schedule.

"Is my breakfast ready, woman? I have to be out of here in twenty minutes, so let's get the show on the road, okay?"

"Everything's ready, Rand. Let me flip these pancakes over while I warm the maple syrup, and your breakfast will be on the table in less than thirty seconds. Now you can't beat that for service, can you?"

Reluctantly, he admitted I was on the ball this morning. "As a matter of fact," he commented, "you've been very efficient all week. Maybe that new friend of yours, Sherry, is making a good impression on you."

I noticed that he failed to mention the fact that it had been over thirty-six hours that I had been completely sober. Since he watched my every move when he was home, I knew he hadn't missed this.

While he was finishing his breakfast and gulping down his second cup of coffee, he reminded me of our ten-thirty appointment in the morning. "Your Aunt Marcie will be here at nine o'clock, so that will give us plenty of time to get to the hospital. His office is across the street in the Medical Arts Building. If you have to drive the children to school in the morning on account of the weather, make sure you get gas in your tank. Better fill it up tonight while you're out with your friends. You need that extra weight in the rear end to keep from sliding."

"Our roads around here have been slippery this past week," he continued. "I think the township is running out of salt. Make certain you are ready to leave here at nine o'clock sharp tomorrow morning, got that?"

"Aye, aye, captain. Your wish is my desire. All orders will be carried out as commanded," I said facetiously, clicking my heels together and saluting.

"Don't be funny, Mara," he chided me. "This is serious business. Our future may hinge on everything that occurs in that office tomorrow, and don't forget it."

My dear blind husband, I thought, *you don't realize it yet, but God has worked a miracle in our home and in my life this week. I already saw the psychiatrist, and His name is Jesus. He accomplished in seconds what could take your shrink years to accomplish, if at all. I really don't need to keep that appointment, but since I agreed to it, I will keep my commitment.*

Aloud, I assured him that I would be ready and mentally prepared for tomorrow's appointment. Before he left the kitchen for work, he came over to the sink where I had started the breakfast dishes. I received my predictable peck on the cheek for being a good girl and following orders.

A few minutes later we heard the garage door go down and knew that Rand was on his way to work. I was always relieved when he was finally out of the house, and I knew my mother shared my sentiments. She had very little to say, I noticed, when my husband was at home. She would open up somewhat when he was at work or away from the house, however.

Rand had a way of making everyone snap to attention, the children and me, as well as my mother. She resented this in his makeup, among other things; and when he would begin to display signs of this overbearing attitude, she would retreat to her room. I attributed this undesirable trait in him to his time spent in the military. I only wished he would have left it there when he received his discharge papers.

"Mara, I forgot to tell you that your grandmother called you yesterday while you were out," Mom informed me, her voice somewhat apologetic for having forgotten to give me the message.

I didn't get to see my grandparents very often these days, but when either my grandmother or my grandfather called, I wanted to be told about it as soon as possible. I was concerned about these two dear old people in my life. They were both over ninety now, and Gram had sustained a near-fatal heart attack last summer. We were all still trying to figure out how she managed to survive it, but we were very grateful that she had.

"Listen, Mom," I responded. "Don't be so hard on yourself just because you forget to do something. It's not the end of the world. I'll stop in and see them this morning as soon as I drop the kids off at school. Maybe Aunt Harriet isn't going to make it in this weekend. Gram might need me to pick up some groceries for her."

"It didn't appear to be an emergency, did it?" I added as an afterthought.

"No, nothing like that, Mara. She wants the phone number of the man who does rototilling for folks in the area who don't have their own equipment. She said that you had it and would give it to her."

"Uh-huh, now it's my turn to admit that I forgot to do something. I'll take Jeff's number with me this morning when I stop in and see the folks. Sounds like she's going to have a garden again this year. God bless her! What would Granny do without her garden?"

"I'm going to take time out of my busy schedule this spring," I added. "While Rachael and Randy are at school, Roni and I will go down to their house a couple days out of the week until all the planting is finished. You can join us if you'd like to. It would do you good to get out in the fresh air and sunshine once in a while. You'd get a little color back in your face and some much-needed vitamin D."

Yes, I thought, *that's going to be a lot of work for Granny to do alone. Besides that, I know that the old folks get lonely for company during the week now that Grandpa isn't active with his real estate business anymore. Roni isn't much for helping in the garden, but the folks sure do get a kick out of having her around. Granny says she tickles their funny bone.*

This would benefit all of us, I reflected, making a mental note that this must take priority on my things-to-do list for the coming spring and early summer.

Glancing at the kitchen clock, I realized that the children needed to be in school within the next half hour.

"Let's go, kids," I yelled from the kitchen. "Put it in high gear. I'm going to take you to school again today. It is freezing outside. But don't think you have all morning to fiddle around because you're going in the car. You have exactly twenty-five minutes. You don't want to get to school late and have to sit on the dunce's stool, do you? I have your breakfasts ready and your lunch boxes packed. Now you guys do your part."

After dropping the youngsters off at school, I spent an hour with the folks and cleaned up the kitchen while Granny and I discussed plans for her garden. This always made for good conversation because both of us had an inherent love for the great outdoors and for all things that grow, with the exception of weeds, of course. After all, it was she who introduced me to the wonder of nature at a very early age, and I took to it like a baby duckling out for her first swim with Mama.

It will be fun getting dirt under my fingernails again, I thought wistfully.

I remembered my very first victory garden. I wanted my own even though Gram said that I could work beside her in the big garden. But no, I had to have my own. Gram finally agreed to it, and she handed me a shovel and a rake. We didn't have rototillers back in those days. Only the farmers who made their livelihood by farming or those people who owned equipment as a means of making money had the good fortune to own this expensive machinery.

Twelve hours after taking on this mammoth job, I found myself soaking in a hot tub of Epsom-salt water and scrubbing what amounted to a bushel of dirt off my body. I came close to falling asleep in the tub. I was so exhausted that I missed dinner, famished but too tired to stay awake another minute.

The last voice I heard from my bed was Gram telling everybody at the dinner table that Mara would think twice before she tackled another garden from scratch. "She thought all the hard work would be done for her by her guardian angel, I guess. Well, land's sake, she sure found out that it takes more than throwing a couple seeds in the ground and watching the weeds pop out of nowhere to make a garden grow flowers and vegetables."

But I did it again the next spring and for several springs after that—Gram and I working side by side in our gardens. Recalling those years with fond memories made me anxious for spring to come quickly so we could reclaim some of those happy moments we spent together so many years ago.

I called Jeff for her and made an appointment to have her garden tilled in late March or after the last hard snowfall, whichever came first. I could see her eyes come alive with excitement as I hung up the phone. After many years, she still found that the prospect of starting a new garden was something to get excited about.

Checking the time, I realized that the morning was pretty well spent. I wanted to sit with Grampa for a few minutes before I left for home. I hugged Gram and told her I'd see her again next week with a promise to bring Roni with me. Aunt Harriet would be coming in from Blairsville, where she and Uncle Clyde were now living. Although it was a distance of about fifty miles between the two homes, my eldest aunt—though once again employed full-time—spent every weekend with my grandparents, shopping, preparing meals, and cleaning the house for them before she left for home after lunch on Sunday. She was very devoted to her parents.

Driving home, I had my mind on Grandpa. He seemed to be failing appreciably since his most recent stroke. It had left him partially paralyzed on his left side. He had been quite active up until that time, conducting his business on a daily basis. The stroke put an end to all that, leaving him unable to walk without assistance.

For the most part, his days were spent in his easy chair, with very little left to do but stare aimlessly at the television screen. It had become difficult to reach him with conversation. The dullness in his eyes told the whole story. Life no longer held much meaning for him. There was nothing more to look forward to. The next event he obviously had to face would be death. Even Roni, who had captivated him since her toddler days, was not able to pique his interest this winter.

I despised thinking about things like this. Our family had been blessed with good health and longevity of life. With the exceptions of Aunt Tammie and Aunt Millie, who had passed just recently, our entire family was intact.

Now that I had a personal relationship with the Giver of Life, it was easy for me to recognize that it was God's goodness and mercy that enabled this to be. Undeniably, we had our share of difficulties over the years, but we hung together and eventually weathered the storms of life each of us was required to face.

Forcing myself to put this negativity out of my mind, I pulled into the garage. Roni, who had stayed in bed this morning, came running to greet me as I walked into the game room. "Hi, Mummy. Why didn't you cawl me? Nana told me you went to see Gram and Gramps. I wanted to go too," she said, shooting me an accusing glance.

"Sweetheart, it was just too cold for you to be out this early today. I even had to take your sister and brother to school again. The buses were late, and it was much too cold for children to stand at the corner waiting for a bus that might not come. Besides, I peeked at you, and you looked so warm and comfy that I thought I'd let you sleep in this morning. Come on upstairs with me, and I'll get you some breakfast."

"Nana got me bwekfast, Mummy. She made me Mickey Mouse and Donald Duck pancakes for bwekfast. I like it when you and Nana make me those kind of pancakes, Mummy. They taste bettew."

"Really," I said as we entered the kitchen. "Why do you suppose that they taste better, Roni?"

"I don't know why they do, but they just do," she responded, ending the discussion.

"Well, Mom, you certainly are bright-eyed and bushy-tailed this morning," I commented enthusiastically. "I understand that you did the Mickey Mouse sculpture on the pancakes you made for Roni."

"That's right," she responded cheerfully. "I heard you tell Rand last evening that you had a lot of ironing to catch up with. If that's on your schedule for today, I think Roni and I will play Chutes and Ladders for a while, at least until lunchtime. That will help you make a little headway on it."

"Well, gee, thanks, Mom," I responded, somewhat surprised. "That certainly will help the cause. I'll take a break after lunch and spend some time with my little pancake lover before Rachael and Randy get home from school this afternoon. This appointment that I have to keep in the morning will take a big bite out of my schedule, but if I can get a few things accomplished today, it will help considerably."

I was aware that my mother was nobody's fool. In spite of her mental condition, she had a keen awareness of what was going on in our household. She never interfered, nor did she ask questions of a personal nature, but her discernment was such that she had figured out that Rand and I had a lot of problems in our marriage. In spite of the fact that we did our best to cover them up when she or the children were within hearing distance, it was becoming obvious that the situation was getting worse. There had been enough said in open conversation to allow her to form her own conclusions.

She also figured out why I always had so much ironing to do. She knew there wasn't enough ironing for our family alone to keep me busy in the laundry for two or three hours every day of the week. She was aware of my drinking problem but never made a comment about it. Evidently, she had put two and two together and had come up with the answer to this additional activity in my daily workload. I needed money to support my habit. It was as simple as that.

She knew all about alcoholism. My dad had been borderline when they separated for the final time, and Uncle Henry had run the gamut of vices during his teen and early adult years. Henry had become a violent alcoholic as he reached adulthood and landed in jail on more than a few occasions. My grandparents had been awakened many nights by a knock on the door or an urgent phone call from the police. Henry had been a source of much anguish to both of them as well as to his siblings.

I left Nana and Roni at the dining-room table with a stack of Roni's games. It appeared that she had more in mind than a game of Chutes and Ladders. When Roni found a willing playmate, she took full advantage of the situation.

It made me feel so good to see that my mother's condition had improved over the last week or so. With Aunt Mo-Mo's passing and Mom's subsequent depression, I was becoming somewhat concerned that my aunt's death would cause yet another setback in her condition. Evidently, the new medication was working well for her, and now I realized to whom it was I should express my gratitude.

As I entered the laundry to begin one of my jobs for the day, I realized I would be able to eliminate all three of these ironings I was presently doing every week for other women.

This will give me more time to spend with the kids this summer, I thought, and it would allow more time available for Gram's garden as well.

I was beginning to realize how horribly bound I had been by the demon of alcohol. Being free from this bondage would open doors of opportunity that would be constructive and worthwhile.

Thinking ahead to later this evening when I would be meeting my drinking buddies for our regular Thursday evening get-together at Sammy's, I wondered how they would take this news. I didn't realize it at the time, but I was in for a rude awakening.

CHAPTER 20

A TOTAL MIND CHANGE

As I entered Sammy's, I saw Aunt Marcy and Uncle Jack seated back in the corner booth with a couple whom I did not recognize. They beckoned me to join them. At the same time, one of our regular people, Hutch Manning, told me he had seen me come in and had ordered a drink for me. Ted had already put it on the bar in front of the empty barstool where I placed my jacket.

Hutch picked up his drink and moved closer to where I would be sitting.

"Hi, Hutch. Thanks for the drink," I said, grabbing his hand and shaking it. "Where's Nancy tonight?"

"She'll be along in a bit, Mar. She's working overtime. Emergency was busier than usual today, and they needed an extra OR nurse to fill in for a few hours."

"My aunt and uncle want me to meet the couple that are with them tonight. I have to talk to Marcy anyhow about tomorrow morning and make sure she has her time right. Rand and I have to leave the house for a ten-thirty appointment up north. She has a tendency to run a little late sometimes, so I think I'd better remind her one more time that she needs to be at our house by nine o'clock."

"I'll be back in a minute or so, Hutch," I added, moving in the direction of the booth where Jack and Marcy were sitting.

"Okay, Mar, but here's your boilermaker," he said, taking my shot glass of whiskey and mug of beer from the bar and handing them to me. "We don't want you to lag behind tonight. No sense in the rest of us being tipsy while you still have your feet on the floor," he responded, a slow, familiar grin moving across his handsome features.

"I don't think you'll have to worry about that, Hutch. I'm already tipsy," I said, returning the beer and whiskey to the bar. "Besides, we're early tonight. There are only a few of us here so far. I'll be right back."

I pulled a chair away from one of the tables and sat down at the booth where my aunt and uncle sat with their new friends. "Hi, y'all," I said, focusing my attention on the new couple. "I don't believe we've met. I'm Mara, Jack and Marcie's niece and a regular here on Thursday nights."

"Hi, Mara. I'm Joe Marletti, and this is my wife, Teri. We're new in the area, and your aunt and uncle were nice enough to invite us to join your group tonight. They found out that we both like to drink beer and play poker, so that made our day when they invited us to come to Sammy's with them tonight."

"We just moved into the house two doors down from your aunt and uncle last week," he continued, "so we really don't know anyone in the neighborhood yet. We understand this is the bar with the most action, especially on weeknights."

"Well, I don't know about that, Joe. We do have a good time when we get together every week," I responded. "There's a nice group of people who come here. No troublemakers, so that makes it a safe place to be on a Thursday night."

I turned my attention to Teri, who had not had the opportunity to open her mouth as yet. Evidently, her husband, Joe, was the communicator in the family. Teri appeared to be rather reserved and perhaps a little shy.

"So where do you folks come from? And what brings you to our fair city?" I asked Teri, attempting to draw her into the conversation.

Before Teri had a chance to answer, Joe was at it again, monopolizing the conversation as before. I had already made up my mind. I really wasn't impressed with this man.

Jack broke into the conversation at that point, pointing to the bar where Hutch was sitting. "I think Hutch is trying to get your attention, Mara. He's pointing to the drink he got for you. I think he wants you to get back there and drink your beer before it goes flat."

"Okay, folks. I'll be back in a little while, and we can take up where we left off," I responded. "In case I forget to mention it anymore tonight, Marcie, I just want to remind you about tomorrow morning. You will be over at our house by nine o'clock, won't you? You know how Rand is."

"Oh, don't worry, Mara, I know how your husband is all right," she said, a touch of annoyance in her voice. "I'll be there if we don't have a foot of snow by then. You did hear the forecast on the six-o'clock news, didn't you?"

"No, as a matter of fact, I didn't hear the news tonight. I was busy with the kids," I said. "How much snow are we supposed to get?"

"It's supposed to be a dandy, anywhere from twelve to sixteen inches," she replied.

"Hmm, well, that would upset the applecart, wouldn't it?" I responded, a feeling of optimism coming over me.

"You can't fool me, little niece. I can tell by the look on your face that you would welcome a snowstorm about now," she said, winking at me with an all-knowing smirk on her face, which spoke volumes. She and I shared a common secret.

Rand had confided in Marcie and Jack about the appointment he made for me with the shrink from North Allegheny Medical

Center. They also knew I was not looking forward to this meeting but agreed that something had to be done about my out-of-control condition. Both my aunt and uncle were appalled by this. We only saw each other on Thursday nights here at Sammy's and twice a month when we played cards in the same poker club.

On rare occasions, the family would get together on Sundays after church, but that was all. They had no idea that I drank daily and often to the point of no return. Naturally, Aunt Marcie and I were blood relatives, and for this reason, she minimized the gravity of my condition. After all, she and Jack knew how to put away the booze too, so they certainly weren't going to criticize me for something of which they too were guilty.

"Okay, Marcie, that will remain our little secret, won't it?" I whispered in her ear as I got up to return to the bar and Hutch, who was waiting patiently for me. By this time, several of our other friends had arrived, and some were preparing for our game of slot bowling, which we played every week.

"Look out for Hutch, sweetheart. I think he has designs on you this evening," Jack warned me, half joking, but with a serious tone to his voice as well. "You know how Mr. Romeo comes on to pretty ladies when his wife isn't with him. So be careful, Mara."

"Don't worry, Unc, I can handle the ladies' man. But thanks for your concern. I have enough problems right now," I added. "I certainly wouldn't want to take on any new ones, would I?"

I made my way back to my barstool, greeting members of our group on the way. By this time, the bar was filling up, and the evening's festivities were well under way. Hutch worked his way to a stool next to mine and pulled mine away from the bar so I could seat myself comfortably.

"Sweetheart, you are going to need a fresh draft. This one has been sitting for fifteen minutes. It's bound to be flat by now," Hutch said. "Hey, Ted," he yelled to Ted, picking up the mug of beer and motioning to the bartender to bring another one in its place. "Give this little lady a fresh draft, please. She let the first one get stale, and we can't let that happen, can we?"

"You know what, Hutch," I interrupted. "Don't worry about it. I'm really not in the mood for drinking tonight anyway."

"You're not in the mood for drinking, Mara?" he repeated, a look of incredulity on his face. "What's the matter? Are you coming down with something?"

Before I had a chance to answer, he pulled his cigarette case from his jacket pocket and carefully took a freshly rolled marijuana cigarette from it. He placed it on the bar and began to move it toward me. "Try one of these, Mar," he said. "It will help whatever it is that is bothering you."

"Hutch, you know I don't do marijuana. Put it back in your case, please," I said, somewhat irritated that he would even attempt to offer me one.

As I looked again at the small cigarette he placed on the bar, it began to move toward me unaided by human assistance. It writhed and curled like a tiny white snake but continued to move in the direction of my hand, which I placed on the bar while talking to Hutch. I sat gazing at this object in absolute horror. I was literally frozen to the barstool on which I sat. Remembering my recent confrontation with the Jolly Green Giant, under my breath, I uttered the name of Jesus. Immediately, whatever it was that held me spellbound was broken. I jumped down from the barstool, put my jacket on, and headed for the door.

"Sorry, Hutch, I have to leave," I called to him over my shoulder. "I shouldn't have come here tonight. But thanks for the cold draft. You drink it and tell my Aunt Marcie I'll see her in the morning, okay?"

Before he was able to recover from my unusual behavior, I was out of there and heading for my car. I knew without question that I would never enter Sammy's Bar & Grill again. That chapter of my life had closed, and I couldn't have been more relieved.

Approaching my car, I noticed it had begun to snow. At least an inch of the fresh white stuff covered the parking lot since I had arrived here a short time ago. I could feel that familiar Presence permeating my entire being once again.

Father, I prayed, *I have the faith to believe that you took away my desire for alcohol. It's been a few days now, and I have not had that intense craving that has plagued me for several years. I know you delivered me from this addiction. Since it was you who have done this, then why should I have to keep the appointment Rand made for me with the psychiatrist tomorrow? Father, if you don't think I need to go there, then will you please let it snow all night so that the roads will be impassable in the morning and the appointment will have to be cancelled? I would be so grateful if you would do this for me.*

I looked back at the entrance to Sammy's to see if Hutch was following me to my car. Relieved that there was no one behind me, I jumped in and turned on the heater and wipers. For just a few seconds, I sat back and thanked my Heavenly Father once again for all that he had done for me this past week. As I pulled out of the parking lot, I took one last look at the life I was leaving behind. With his help, I would never return to this place, which had been the source of much sin in my life.

My Thursday evening babysitter, Jeannette, was amazed to see me walking up the steps to the dining room. It was nine o'clock, and I was home already and stone sober.

"Hi, Jeannette. Surprised to see me so early?" I said, removing my boots and jacket on the stairwell.

"Oh, Mrs. Reuben," she replied, "I am so glad you came home early. The latest forecast calls for twelve to fourteen inches by morning. I am petrified to drive in this kind of weather. Thank you so much for thinking of me."

I withheld comment, knowing that Jeannette was not the reason I came home early. I was beginning to see the wisdom in what God had done tonight. Not only would Jeannette be stranded at our home, but I would have had a difficult, if not impossible, time on my way home if I had left the bar at the usual time. It also appeared that God was in the process of answering my prayer. If the weather forecast was accurate, the roads would indeed be impassable in the morning, and Rand would be forced to cancel our appointment.

"Jeannette, I'm going to pay you the usual amount. It's not your fault that the weather is horrible tonight," I said, handing her our agreed-upon amount for four hours of babysitting.

"You get your things on and get out of here before the roads really get bad. Right now, the roads are passable, if you take it slow. You will have enough traction to get you home because there's been very little traffic tonight to pack the snow down and cause it to become slippery."

"Okay, Mrs. Reuben, and thank you so much. The kids were great tonight, even Randy. I made them hot chocolate, and we played board games for an hour. They all went to bed without any problem. I feel guilty taking this much."

"Hush, girl. Now, you get out of here. I'll call you during the week because there's going to be a change in my schedule. I won't be needing you anymore on Thursdays, but if you're available on Wednesday evenings, that will be my new weeknight out. You can let me know. And, Jeannette, call me when you get home, okay? I'll be saying a little prayer that you don't have any trouble on your way home."

"Oh, ah, thanks for that," she replied. The amazement in her voice was a clear indication that she was certainly not expecting me, of all people, to say a prayer for her safety.

As I closed the door, I did utter a brief prayer for my babysitter's safety as I promised.

I went up to the bedrooms to check on the cherubs. Satisfied that they were all sleeping soundly and snuggled under their blankets, I returned to the kitchen to make myself a pot of tea. I didn't know if Mom heard me come in, but I thought I'd make some extra in case she wanted to join me.

After a few minutes went by, I surmised that she was in bed for the evening. I took my cup of tea into the living room and turned on the weather channel. Yes, it appeared that everyone I had spoken with this evening had the forecast correct. An accumulation of twelve to sixteen inches was expected by daybreak. The forecaster was excitedly reporting some statistics that were rather alarming.

Records from the past twenty years were being broken tonight. As I stared at the television screen, it was becoming more evident with each passing moment that Rand and I wouldn't be making that trip to North Allegheny Medical Center in the morning. I breathed a huge sigh of relief and uttered a sincere thank-you to the great snowmaker in the sky.

At that moment, the phone rang, and I moved quickly into the kitchen to answer it so that the sound of it ringing wouldn't awaken anyone. The voice on the other end was that of my Aunt Marcie. She sounded totally freaked out.

"Mara, what in the world happened to you tonight? Hutch came over to our booth and told us that you had to leave in a hurry. Are you not feeling well?"

"I'm just fine, Marcie. In fact, I've never been better," I responded enthusiastically. "This is a subject that I'd rather not discuss over the phone, but I don't want your curiosity to get the best of you, so I'll give you a brief explanation. On Wednesday afternoon, I had an encounter with Jesus, and he took away my desire for alcohol. What do you think about that?"

After a brief silence, I received a response from my aunt that I had not expected. "You'll get over it, Mara. I know that you aren't looking forward to seeing that psychiatrist in the morning, but don't let some silly notion keep you from getting help, if that's what you need. In my opinion, I think Rand is overreacting to your situation. Besides," she added, "have you looked outside? It's coming down in snowballs. None of us is going anywhere in the morning."

I was too disappointed in my aunt's reaction to my good news to continue the phone conversation. I ended it abruptly by telling her that I would have Rand call her in the morning if he wanted to cancel our appointment.

What in the world is wrong with these people? I wondered as I hung up the phone. *First, my own daughter Rachael and then one of my dearest aunts. They should be elated at hearing my news, but instead, they're in total disbelief. Don't they know that Jesus is capable of performing miracles today as he was when he walked on this earth?*

The phone rang again. This time, it was Hutch on the other end. "Mara, are you all right?" he asked, genuine concern in his voice.

"Yes, I'm okay, Hutch," I responded. This time, I was a little less exuberant and not so quick to tell him my story. My aunt had taken the wind out of my sails. I really didn't want to be disappointed by yet another negative opinion.

"Look, honey, I really don't have any business prodding you for an explanation about what happened earlier at Sammy's. I'm home and, incidentally, the roads are becoming atrocious. I have to go get Nancy in a few minutes. She's stranded at the hospital.

"I just want you to know that I am genuinely concerned about you," he continued. "First of all, I need to apologize for offering you a hit. I knew you didn't appreciate that. But to tell you the truth, Mara, I've been watching you closely these past two or three months. Tell me if I'm wrong, and I hope that I am, but I'm going to ask you anyhow. Are you struggling with alcoholism?"

"What makes you think I'm addicted to alcohol, Hutch?" I asked cautiously, choosing my words carefully.

"It's because I have that problem, Mara. I've come to the point where I'm willing to admit it. I've been attending AA meetings for the last six weeks. Becoming intimately involved with people who are regulars, I've come to the conclusion that if I'm going to be honest with myself, I have to admit that I'm just like them.

"The moderator says that until we get to that point, there's no hope of recovery. I've been in denial for so long. I needed a real jolt to shake me loose from this mind-set. Well, I got that jolt. Nancy finally put her foot down and put it down hard. She gave me an ultimatum. Either I kick this habit within six months, or she is leaving me. It's my choice—it's either her or the booze."

I heard his voice crack at this point. I knew he was holding back the tears, trying to play the role he adopted for himself—that of a handsome, debonair man about town with a devil-may-care attitude. Hutch had a reputation for being heavy on the charm, quick-witted, and even quicker coming on to women. I realized at this moment that he was playing a role. It was evident that he loved his wife and didn't want to lose her because of his addiction to alcohol.

As I listened to his story, I made a quick mental assessment. I would share with him the experience I had with Christ yesterday afternoon. If he could accept this as a valid solution to his problem, maybe he would respond to Jesus's invitation and accept his gift of salvation as I had done.

I was about to begin to tell him what happened to me when I heard the garage door open. "Hutch, Rand just came home. I'm going to have to cut this conversation short. He would not understand, nor would he believe that we're talking about alcoholism. You understand, don't you?" I asked.

"Yes, of course, I do, Mar. I don't want to get you in any trouble with your husband. But I do have something on my mind that I wanted to discuss with you earlier this evening at Sammy's. I believe that I may have the solution to my problem and what I believe may be your problem as well. When can we talk?"

"Can I call you on Friday evening after I get the children into bed?" I asked, not quite certain that I wanted to get involved in any way with this man, even if it could prove to be beneficial to him. "Rand's never home on Friday evenings, so that would give us adequate time to discuss whatever is on your mind," I continued.

"That will be fine, Mar," he responded. "Nancy will be home, and she may pick up the phone when you call, but that's okay. I expressed my suspicion about you to Nancy. It was she who suggested that the three of us attend this place that I want to tell you about."

"Okay. Good-bye. I'll call you on Friday night. I must go now."

As I hung up the phone, Rand came into the game room, yelling for me to bring him a change of clothes. Evidently, the clothes he was wearing had gotten wet, the storm being as ferocious as it was, and he needed to get into something dry.

I grabbed his jeans, a fresh sweatshirt, some underwear, and socks and hurried down to the game room to see what was going on. I was appalled to see him half sitting and half lying on one of the couches. He had managed to get his topcoat off, as well as his boots. The pant leg to one of his new suits was ripped from the knee down, exposing a bloody mess underneath. There was a gash on his temple, which dripped blood down his cheek onto his suit coat and the white shirt underneath.

"Oh, good Lord, what happened to you, Rand?" I blurted out as I pulled the wet and bloody clothing from his shivering body.

After expressing his pain and frustration, he emitted a few of his favorite expletives as a preface to relating a story that could only have occurred during a snowstorm such as the one we were experiencing tonight.

He stopped at Wally's, one of his after-work haunts, for a couple of beers on his way over to Sammy's. He knew I would be there and thought he would warn me of the snowstorm that was on its way. He was surprised to see I had left the bar early. He had gotten into a conversation with Jack and Marcie and the new neighbors who had come with them, and then he and Jack decided to shoot a game of pool.

It wasn't until sometime later that a patron leaving the bar for the night returned, having seen what was happening outside. He expressed his concern to those inside. The snow was falling rapidly, so much so that, since he had come into Sammy's earlier in the evening, there had to be at least three additional inches on the ground. Not only that, he said, but the visibility was zero. We were having a whiteout. He recommended that everyone get home while they could.

Rand continued with his story as I cleaned the blood from his face and leg and applied peroxide to the lacerations, relieved that neither of them was deep enough to require stitches.

He decided to heed the warning made by the patron who had returned to the bar to give his assessment of the weather. Rand left the bar and made his way with difficulty to the place where he parked his car. As he opened his car door, much of the snow covering the roof began to slide into the car and the driver's seat. Caught off guard, he released the door—and because he was parked on a slight grade and because of the extra weight the snow had caused—the door careened toward him, the sharp corner hitting him on the side of his face.

Momentarily stunned by this, he grabbed the door and slammed it closed, catching part of his overcoat and the pant leg of his suit in it. To reopen the door, it was necessary to rip the clothing free from the jammed door. He had no idea how his leg had been in the way, but the evidence was right there in plain sight.

By this time, I had bandaged both injuries and helped him get into some warm, dry clothing. Checking his new London Fog topcoat, which he had thrown on the floor in an effort to get some of his wet clothing off, I saw it was damaged just as the pants to his new suit were ruined beyond repair.

"Well, I guess you win this round, mamma bear," he announced, somewhat disgruntled. "We won't be going anywhere in the morning. I'll call the doctor's office tomorrow and reschedule the appointment."

"I just took another look outside while I was disposing of your clothes," I said. "I would venture to say that there won't be a soul in that medical complex anytime soon. It hasn't let up at all in the past three hours. Looks like we're in for the worst storm of the winter."

Changing the subject as I helped him up the stairs, I reminded him that it could have been a lot worse. "I believe that the Lord sent one of his angels to protect you from more serious injury, Rand. We need to be thankful for that," I said with firm conviction.

He did not respond to my comment, but there was a look on his face that I could not identify. I had never seen that expression before.

CHAPTER 21

A HOME AWAY FROM HOME

As we pulled into the large parking lot of Zion Assembly of God Church, I turned to Phoebe in amazement. This is the same church that captured my attention a couple of weeks ago. It was the church that I passed on my way home from the bank the day I made the cookie-sale deposit for our Girl Scout troop.

Phoebe opted to sit with me in the backseat of their station wagon, surrendering her usual place beside her husband, Keith, to their son Keith Jr. Realizing that our time spent together this morning on the way to church would be limited, she wanted to make good use of that time so she and I could get acquainted.

Their only daughter, Candice, was on my left; and the three younger boys—Ronnie, Travis, and Shad—sat in the middle seat of the station wagon.

Phoebe had called me this past Monday to invite me to attend church with her and her family this weekend. She would have called sooner, she said, had it not been for the snowstorm of the previous week. When the storm finally spent itself, we found ourselves blanketed in twenty-two inches of this strikingly aesthetic winter wonderland, which resembled mounds of stiffly beaten egg whites.

As lovely as it was, it caused much hardship and devastation. Roads all over the county had been impassable for several days. Electric power lines were down due to the weight of the heavy snowfall, leaving hundreds of homes in the area without heat and light. Schools and churches, as well as most businesses, were not able to conduct business as usual.

"This is so ironic," I commented to my new friend. "This tiny church, surrounded by the massive parking lot, caught my attention while I drove by here a couple weeks ago, Phoebe. I couldn't understand why such an insignificant piece of real estate would capture my attention to the degree it did. Now I think I understand."

"It would seem that God was giving me a preview of coming attractions," I continued. "How could I have possibly known that I would be attending this church within a few short weeks?"

"Remind me to tell you why the parking lot is so out of proportion to the church, Mara," Phoebe replied. "This little church has a big future according to a prophecy made over it even before the location had been chosen. It's an exciting story, but one that I won't be able to finish right now. Keith just found a parking spot close to the front entrance so I guess we're ready to get out."

I couldn't identify the feeling that gripped me as I made my way through the path that had been previously shoveled for those attending church this morning. As I entered Zion Assembly with the Michaels family, I experienced a combination of awe and expectancy intermingled with some apprehension and perhaps even a little fear. This was only the second time I had ventured into a Protestant church. Stepping into the foyer, I felt the same familiar spirit I had experienced at that little Baptist church where Sherry and Carly had taken me that Wednesday evening a few weeks ago.

The pastor, Reverend Carlton, was standing at the entrance, cheerfully greeting everyone who entered. Keith introduced me to this quiet, unassuming minister, reminding him that I was the lady Phoebe told him about a couple of weeks ago.

The Pastor took my hand and gripped it firmly as he looked at me expectantly. "So, young lady, what is this news you bring to us this morning?" he asked, his piercing blue eyes never leaving mine.

A feeling of total peace overwhelmed me as I shared with him that I received Jesus as my Lord and Savior just a couple of weeks before.

He smiled at me and responded, "Did you know that all the angels in heaven were rejoicing over your salvation that day, Mara? As we here at Zion will also be doing the moment I introduce you to the congregation during the service this morning."

"Oh, Pastor," I responded, somewhat alarmed, "do you have to do that? I really don't like having attention drawn to myself. This is my first time in this church, and I don't know anyone here."

"How about if I draw attention to Jesus and not to you? Would that make you feel a little more comfortable?" he asked. "Besides that, the congregation will be delighted to hear what happened to you. You wouldn't want to keep such phenomenal news to yourself, would you?"

He continued, "You may not realize it just yet, Mara, but the day you surrendered your life to Christ was the most important day of your life. You need to share the good news with your brothers and sisters in the Lord. But even more importantly, you are to share your good news with those who do not know him."

His gentle persuasiveness convinced me that I should allow him to make the announcement to the congregation.

"Okay, Pastor, you know what's best, I'm sure. Do whatever you feel you need to do."

"That's the girl," he responded. "This congregation won't be strangers to you very long. They are a friendly bunch of people. Ask Keith and Phoebe if my assessment isn't correct."

I walked into the sanctuary with the Michaels family. Keith found a pew about midway that had sufficient space to accommodate the 8 of us, and we took our places with Phoebe sitting beside me.

"I will try to answer any questions you may have about the service, Mara. Remember, my family and I are relatively new Christians too. I believe you will like it here if you decide this will be your future church home. The bottom line is this," she added, "God is now in charge of your life if you want him to be, and he will lead you where he wants you to be for his purposes, as well as for your benefit. It is totally different from what you've been accustomed to. Given a little time to make the transition, I know you're going to love it wherever our Father leads you." Phoebe gave my hand a gentle squeeze.

A casual glance around the sanctuary revealed a nearly packed house, even though we still had fifteen minutes before the service began. The sanctuary, to my pleasant surprise, was quite lovely. The exterior of the building was white clapboard with simple lines and few embellishments. Other than the stained glass windows on either side of the building, it was a very ordinary-looking church with a small bell tower at the main entrance.

On the other hand, the sanctuary was beautiful. The pews were padded and matched the lovely wine-colored carpeting throughout. The ceiling was very high, and the pillars at both sides of the room extended all the way to the ceiling, curving as they followed its contour. They touched each other at the very top. Between the pillars were the stained glass windows depicting several Bible scenes of Jesus during various phases of his public ministry.

The platform, similar to the one at the Baptist church, was raised four steps above the main section of the sanctuary. There was a long bench against the right wall where the pastor and whoever was involved in the service could be seated, each awaiting his turn to minister. The choir loft on the back wall had several staggered benches facing the congregation.

Above the top bench, closest to the wall, was an open area, which I found out from Phoebe was the baptistery. Over this area hung a plain large wooden cross on which was draped a purple cloth. I noticed that, like the cross at the Baptist church, the likeness of the crucified Christ was missing. I thought that this was very strange and made a mental note to question Phoebe about this omission.

This entire area was designed to be the focal point and was illuminated by floodlights coming from somewhere behind the pillars. The podium was on the left side of the platform, strategically placed where the entire choir loft could be seen. Missing was the small room enclosed in glass for the percussion instruments. In its place was a magnificent pipe organ directly behind the podium, and in front of the deacon's bench was a shiny black grand piano. Once again, as in the other church, there was a railing running along the full length of the platform. The first step was in front of the railing so that one could kneel there to pray if he felt the need.

I was held spellbound by the beauty of this place. There was a deep sense of peace, and yet a feeling of electrically charged expectancy was present as well. As I turned to Phoebe with a few questions I had ready for her, Keith left the pew where we were sitting and went forward to the front of the church where the pastor was waiting for him. Together they walked up the few steps of the platform where they both took a seat on the deacon's bench.

Evidently, Keith was scheduled to take part in the service. I was able to get a full view of his face from my vantage point. When the family picked me up for church, I thought he looked vaguely familiar. Somewhere hidden within the deep crevices of my mind, I suspected I knew him from somewhere in my past, perhaps when we were children or young adults.

At that point, Phoebe turned to me with a quizzical expression on her face. "A penny for your thoughts, Mara," she said laughingly. "You seem to be overwhelmed."

"I guess you could say that, Phoebe," I responded. "First of all, I really didn't expect to see such beauty. The exterior of the church is so commonplace I guess I was totally unprepared for what I would find on the inside."

"Yes," she replied in agreement. "It is lovely, isn't it? This building is new. Can you smell the newness? It was only completed fifteen months ago, and the original members moved into it about a year ago. I believe the dedication ceremony was held about this time last year. Keith, the kids, and I began to attend here shortly after that, and it certainly didn't take us very long to realize that we had found a permanent home."

"It was Sherry who told you about this church, wasn't it?" I asked.

"Yes, it was, Mara, and Keith and I will be eternally grateful to her for that. It is all and more than what we ever dreamed it would be." She added.

We love Pastor Carlton. Just wait until you hear him preach. It goes much further than that, though. He is a devoted man of God and a true shepherd."

"I am looking forward to hearing him preach, Phoebe."

As I glanced at my watch, anxious for the service to begin, out of the corner of my eye I could see a very unusual-looking woman take her place behind the grand piano. As she got her music in order, I couldn't help but notice her well-endowed figure and the exotic beehive hairstyle she wore.

Phoebe responded immediately to my unasked question, "That's the pastor's wife, Marion. She has a beautiful soprano voice, and wait until you hear her play the pipe organ. She's a very talented lady. You won't hear her on the organ today, though. She and Keith are going to do a piano medley. Their voices blend well together since he is a tenor," she added.

So Keith is a soloist, I thought to myself. "Where did you two meet, Phoebe?" I asked.

"Actually, it wasn't far from here, Mara. There's a popular dance hall in Castleton that both of us attended as teenagers. It was called the Globe back then. It's still in operation but under new ownership, and it has another name."

"Really?" I asked. I was beginning to put the pieces of this puzzle together. That vital last piece was still missing, but I was getting closer.

"Was Keith from Castleton? Did he have several brothers?" I asked.

"The answer to both questions is yes, Mara. Did you know my husband?" she asked.

I had her total attention at this point. "I believe I did, Phoebe," I responded. "Back when I was beginning elementary school, my mom and my aunt both agreed I should have a parochial school education. The closest Catholic school from where we lived was in Castleton, a distance of about five miles. They knew I would be required to take a trolley to get to St. Agatha's, and it would be necessary for me to travel alone, in spite of the fact that this would be my first experience with the outside world.

"Mom decided she would hire one of our trusted neighbors to accompany me each day until I felt familiar enough with the routine to travel back and forth on my own. Both she and my aunt were employed during the week, so it was impossible for either of them to commit to this task."

Phoebe was on the edge of the pew by now and was waiting with expectancy for me to finish the story.

"This is what I vividly remember, Phoebe," I resumed. "All the grade school students were required to arrive an hour before the first class began each morning to attend the mass at church which was located across the street from the school."

"We first graders were assigned the front seats," I continued, "so the nuns could keep a watchful eye on us. I remember looking up to the choir loft, which was located in the balcony, to see who was singing the mass. The very first time I did this, I saw six boys from approximately seven to fourteen years of age. They were arranged according to size, the tallest to the shortest. They appeared to me like a flight of human steps all dressed in their dark-blue choir robes.

"Sometime later I found out that these boys were all brothers and that they lived a very short distance from St. Agatha's in Castleton. I never met Keith at school, but periodically I would see him playing with the other boys on the playground. I saw him and his brothers every morning, however, because they did the responses for the mass on a regular basis.

"Many years later, I ran into him again. It was during my high school years. I was in my third year and attending a Catholic all-girl academy in Castleton. As I recall, our class was preparing for the junior prom. One of my close friends was dating your husband at that time and attended the prom with him. Yes, that's it. That is how I knew him. As I recall, I never got to know Keith well. I was dating someone else, and he was dating my friend Kay. Our paths did cross on occasion though."

Phoebe was astonished. "It certainly is a small world, isn't it, Mara?" she said.

"Yes, it is," I agreed vehemently.

At that moment, a distinguished-looking middle-aged gentleman approached the podium with a number of announcements to make. Having completed his list, he introduced a gospel song recently made popular by the Gaither Trio. He announced that the pastor's wife, Marion, and Keith Michaels would do their rendition of this song, along with two other selections to complete the medley. Marion would do the piano accompaniment.

I was totally in awe of their performance. They both possessed the talent of highly paid professionals, and indeed, their voices blended beautifully. As they were completing their final selection, the choir, moving in a single file, quietly took their places in the choir loft and waited for their cue to begin their selection for this morning's service.

Once again, I was overwhelmed by their professionalism. There was so much talent in this congregation that it made my head swim. But it was more than that—it was something intangible that I just couldn't put my finger on, something magical, ethereal. I was so totally caught up in enchantment of the moment I didn't even notice that Pastor Carlton had come to the podium.

Meanwhile, the choir director asked the congregation to stand and participate in the worship by joining in the singing. The lyrics were displayed on a large overhead screen to the right of the baptistery. I was able to participate to some extent in the congregational worship as a few of the selections were familiar to me.

When this part of the service was completed, the pastor asked anyone attending the church for the first time to introduce themselves to the congregation. Then we were directed to turn in our seats and greet four or five people before we sat down. This was the easy part for me as I did not know anyone in the congregation with the exception of the Michaels family, or so I thought.

The people surrounding our pew welcomed me enthusiastically, asking my name and what part of town I had come from. Once again, I was totally caught off guard by the genuine friendliness of these people. Everything experienced in this church was new and exciting. I felt as though I had died and gone to heaven, or at least to a heavenly place where everything was beautiful and perfect in every way.

After a brief time of fellowship, Pastor Carlton asked everyone to be seated. He had a very special message to bring to the congregation this morning, he said, one that the Lord had placed on his heart to share a few weeks earlier. The time had not been right just then; but this morning, he felt, was the appropriate time. The subject of his message was David, the first king of Judah, and why he was a man after God's own heart.

I knew little about David except for the fact that he defeated Goliath with a slingshot, a stone, and excellent aim. He was only a shepherd boy, perhaps fifteen or sixteen years old; yet in spite of that, he confronted Goliath, a giant of a man who was outfitted in full battle array, and defeated this giant with the Lord's help. After he became king of Judah and Israel, he sinned against God by having an illicit affair with Bathsheba, another man's wife.

I pulled out my small pocket notebook so I could take notes on this sermon. I had a deep desire to learn what was in the Bible, and my instinct told me I could learn much from this gentle, loving man of God. I sensed that he knew God intimately, and I wanted so much to have the same kind of relationship with this wonderful Creator and his precious Son who had died in my place and whom I had so recently invited into my life.

It took me all of one moment after he began his message to realize that this man was totally different in the pulpit than the man Keith had introduced me to a short time ago. That gentle, soft-spoken pastor had become a human dynamo in an instant. Something transformed him as he began to deliver his message.

He had gone to the pulpit with several notes in his Bible, but as he began to speak, something got hold of him. His notes, carefully placed in his Bible, were now falling to the floor. He made no move to retrieve them. He had become completely oblivious of the fact that he needed to consult them but continued to preach with a passion I had never before witnessed. About five minutes into his sermon, I knew in my heart that this was the church where God wanted me to be. I looked down at my empty notebook, so completely absorbed in what this man of God had to say that I forgot to take notes.

CHAPTER 22

BOOT CAMP CONTINUED

The fragrance of spring blossoms filled the air, and the warm, soft sunlight of early April kissed the earth with the promise of the quick return of good weather to the western Pennsylvania area. We were leaving behind us memories of bitterly cold days and a snowfall in early March, which broke all previous records for this area since 1950, exceeding a depth of twenty-three inches.

It went without saying we welcomed the coming of spring with greater anticipation than usual this year. The arctic blast of 1970 was now behind us.

Looking back on the previous year, 1969 had been a bittersweet year for our family. Aunt Mo-Mo, one of my mother's younger sisters and a great favorite of all the family, had been diagnosed with stage 4 stomach cancer in October and took her final breath of life a few hours before the beginning of the New Year. That same night, just hours earlier, we welcomed into our growing family a brand-new baby girl, Sandy, Aunt Marcie's second granddaughter and my cousin Janice's second daughter. My grandmother's sage prediction had once again come true.

"I've never seen it to fail," she would say. "When God takes a loved one home, he will be sure to replace the one he took."

The great event of my own life came on a February afternoon when I received Jesus Christ as my Savior by faith in his shed blood and subsequently entered into the family of God with the assurance that I would spend eternity with him.

This was not recognized by my family members as anything of particular importance, certainly nothing to equal the birth of a new baby or the passing of a beloved family member. But to me, it was the greatest gift that God could ever impart to a member of his creation. Not only did I have the assurance my sins had been forgiven and I was saved from the unquenchable flames of hell, but my life had changed in other ways as well.

I was free from that heavy burden I had carried around with me for most of my adult life which I could now identify as sin. He took away my addiction to alcohol and the steady flow of obscenities that, in a fit of anger, would roll from my lips like warm butter off the edge of a silver knife. Of course, being the hypocrite I was, I attempted to be certain that none of the children were within hearing distance before I unleashed my tirade of obscenities.

Hopefully I was becoming a better wife, although I realized that this was a work in progress. Rand took advantage of my newfound faith by spending more and more time away from home and from the children and me. But somehow, God's grace proved sufficient in spite of a less-than-satisfactory family life. As a matter of fact, because of Rand's frequent absence from our home, I found I had more time for the study of God's Word while the older children were at school.

I purchased a children's Bible for Roni and spent time with her each day, reading to her from this beautifully illustrated book. She enjoyed the pictures of familiar Old Testament stories and was curious to know every detail about each event and each person involved. The time spent together proved to be beneficial and so worthwhile for both of us. Often, Mom would sit with us and listen intently as I attempted to answer Roni's multitude of questions.

Vicky had surrendered her life to Christ in mid-April, and we were now having Bible study at my home every Tuesday morning. Vicky's mom, Barb, and other ladies from both of our neighborhoods attended these meetings on a regular basis. Mrs. Jackson, the lady who prayed with Vicky's mom to receive Christ, became our teacher. She had been a Christian for many years and had an excellent knowledge of the Bible. We were a captive audience, united in the desire to learn as much about Jesus as we could through the study of his Word.

Most of us were brand-new to the faith, products of the Charismatic Renewal that was presently sweeping across the nation. It was born right here in our own city of Pittsburgh in 1968, and the fires of revival spread from coast-to-coast over the past few years. Some of us had just recently attended the Charismatic conference hosted by our own Duquesne University in the inner city. Thousands of people from every part of the country flocked to the Pittsburgh area to attend these meetings. We were privileged to hear some of the greatest Christian speakers of our time.

In the past, I could often be found at Sammy's or some other bar in the area, slowly but with determination working on a buzz that would temporarily block out all the frustrations and miseries that life had dealt me. Things were different now, thanks to Jesus Christ. Sunday mornings and Wednesday evenings, I could be found at Zion Assemblies of God with my children. Vicky and her kids were getting involved at Zion as well.

Although Zion was a recently formed fledging church, we had a wonderful program for the kids and teenagers. The amazing growth in attendance over the past year could be attributed mainly to this. The previous decade had stripped our children of prayer and Bible study in the schools, so now it was the enormous job of the local church to fill the gap and work diligently to restore all that the enemy had stolen from our youth. I felt in my spirit that I would have a part in children's ministry when the pastor felt I was ready for ministry.

Although my family members didn't comment very often about this sudden change in me, I could sense the alienation that was becoming very obvious in some of them, especially the drinkers, Jack and Marcie in particular. Gram and Mom were elated, of course. They didn't question the reason for the sudden change in me, but they were grateful for the result.

Aunt Harriet thought it might be a good idea if I would talk to a priest and perhaps consider the possibility of joining a convent when the children were older. Always the die-hard Catholic, she just didn't get it, although I did my best to explain what happened to me. I also suggested that perhaps she might consider inviting Jesus into her heart as well. She was appalled with this suggestion, stating emphatically that she was baptized a Catholic as an infant and would remain one until she died. She knew who Jesus Christ was and to be introduced to him personally was not what she considered necessary.

This first Sunday of April, I had taken yet another step in faith. When I found out that infant baptism was not biblical, I decided I would be immersed just as Jesus had been in the Jordan River by John the Baptist just before he began his public ministry. He had done this as an example of what every Christian should do in order to openly testify of the inner change that had occurred in his or her life.

I was one of fourteen candidates who had been instructed in the necessity of receiving this sacrament. This was an act of obedience to God. Being baptized in water certainly didn't save us, but it was the public confession of our faith in Christ. The church was growing by leaps and bounds, and the pastor had his hands full just about every Sunday, baptizing new Christians. As busy as his workload was becoming, he loved every moment of it, praising God for the great increase we were seeing.

Returning home from the service, I dropped the kids off at our house first and then went immediately to share the events of the morning with Vicky. She had been observing me closely since I had told her about my conversion. When she married Ernie, she had abandoned her Lutheran denomination to become a Catholic. Her hope was that both she and Ernie would be of one mind as to the religious upbringing of their five children. This eventually became one more disappointment for her. It was only weeks after their wedding that Ernie left the Catholic faith, never setting foot inside a Catholic church again, except to attend weddings and funerals.

Although Vicky became skeptical about religion in general, she had to admit that a definite change had taken place in my life. In addition to that, her mom, who lived about fifteen minutes from us, had also experienced this "new birth" about the same time I did. She was now attending a weekly Bible study at her next-door neighbor's home. It was this lady who had prayed with her mother and led her to Christ.

Vicky was in a state of confusion. Although I invited her to attend Zion with me, she indicated that she had better wait awhile to see if my conversion was real. She had been disappointed in the past and didn't want to see this situation repeated. She felt she knew me well, she said, and observed that I had a tendency to "go off the deep end" sometime. Now that I was living a sober life, she wanted to see if this was real or if perhaps I was having another "brain spasm," as she put it.

I found her in her kitchen preparing dinner for the family. When she saw me walk into her kitchen, the expression on her face was priceless.

"Now, what in the world have ya'll done, Mara? Lordy, did ya'll fall in the creek on yur way home from that church ya'll are going to?"

I had forgotten about my hair. It was still wet from the dunking.

"Oh, Vicky, I'm sorry to burst in on you like this. It's just that I'm so excited to tell you about this morning that I guess I forgot my manners. I should have called you first," I said apologetically.

"No, that part is okay, Mara. I show up on y'all's doorstep all the time without an invitation. That's not it, honey. It's y'all's hair that startled me. How come it's all wet?" she questioned, that same incredulous expression on her face.

"I got baptized during the service this morning, Vicky," I responded.

"You did what?" she asked. "Mara, ya'll got baptized when you were a baby. Why did ya'll do that again?"

"I should have told you about this on Tuesday evening when we were at the scout meeting, but I wasn't sure I was ready to go through with it yet, so I didn't say anything," I explained.

I knew from the look on her face that she wasn't going to let go of this until she got the whole story.

"Can you interrupt your dinner preparation for a few minutes?" I asked. Pulling out a kitchen chair, I sat down at the table and gestured for her to do the same.

"Ya'll bet yur life, I can," she responded enthusiastically. "I sure don't know what's going on with you and my mother, but I want to find out."

We sat for a full hour as I went through every detail of the morning's events. I wasn't too good at explaining the scriptures that supported the command to be baptized in water. I only realized that, deep within my being, I knew this was something God wanted me to do, and I had to respond in obedience.

Vicky listened intently, asking an occasional question. "Well," she concluded, "I think the only way to know for sure if this is for me is to go to y'all's church with you and find out for myself. We're having company for dinner tonight, but maybe Wednesday or next Sunday morning would be a good time. Would ya'll have room for me? I don't plan to take the kids until I know what's going on over there, so there will only be one more in your car."

"Sure, Vicky," I responded. "Anytime is fine. Let me know, and I'll pick you up."

In my excitement to share my experience with Vicky, I had forgotten it was lunchtime, and I knew the kids must be starving by now. I was relieved to find Rachael had decided to play little mother today. She made peanut butter and jelly sandwiches for the four of them. Their nana had joined them in the kitchen and poured each one a glass of milk. She was getting all the details of the morning's events.

This had been only the second time that the children accompanied me to Zion. They were a little shy the previous week and didn't have a whole lot to say. Today was an entirely different story.

Rachael and Randy had been taken to the Sunday school department and directed to the appropriate rooms for their age-group. Roni was bubbling over with excitement, as was her usual response to any new experience she enjoyed.

"I weally like it there," she confided to her nana. "We had so much fun. The teacher gave us cwayons, and we cowered pictures of Jesus and the bad soldiers who nailed him to a cwoss and then we cut them out and pasted them on a big whiteboard. We all took turns telling the stowy of what happened—and guess what, Nana?"

She continued without stopping to take a breath, "I am the oldest one in my cwass, so I will only be there for a wittle while, and then I get to go with the bigger kids. I'm weally excited, but I like the wittle kids that I'm with now, so I will pwobabwy miss them, and I will miss my teacher too," she concluded, her voice expressing a bit of regret.

"Well, it would appear that you and the children have made a good move, Mara," my mother commented. "They seem to be having a good time."

"It would seem so, Mom," I agreed. "But I'm going to take my time having them make the transition. This is a big move in all our lives."

"Oh, by the way, Mara," she said, changing the subject, "call Hutch Manning. He's wondering why you haven't called him. He said that he and his wife are attending another church in the area and that he had invited you to go with them some Sunday."

"Okay, Mom. I'll get back to him later this afternoon. I've got to get a bite to eat and blow-dry my hair first," I responded.

"Yes, I was wondering why your hair is wet," she said.

"I was baptized this morning during our service," I responded.

"I had you baptized when you were three weeks old," she reminded me. "Didn't that one take?"

"No, it didn't, Mom," I answered.

That ended the conversation on the subject, at least for the present time. Later in the day, I responded to Hutch's phone call.

"Hello, Mar. How's my favorite drinking buddy?" asked the familiar, easygoing baritone voice on the other end of the line.

"Hutch," I replied, "I'm doing fine, but I'm sure not anybody's favorite drinking buddy these days, I'm happy to say. How are you and Nancy?"

"We're doing okay," he responded, "but we sure miss not seeing you at Sammy's anymore." He added regretfully, "It leaves a big void in our Thursday evenings."

"I wanted to get back to you to let you know that I won't be taking you up on your invitation to attend your church anytime soon. I found one of my own, as a matter of fact, one that I'm really happy with," I responded enthusiastically. "Guess what, Hutch. The Lord took away my addiction," I added. "I haven't had a drink in six weeks, and it feels good."

"Well, that's great," came his reply with considerably less enthusiasm. "What's the name of your church?"

"Hutch, it's that new Assemblies of God Church about a mile from where you live. It's in Hillsdale on the main road to Castleton. You've probably passed it hundreds of times on your way to and from work. The place is really taking off. They've added over forty new members since I started to go there last month. As a matter of fact, I was baptized this morning, and I'm thinking of becoming a member when they extend the invitation to join the church this summer."

"That must be Zion you're talking about," he said, not particularly surprised with my news. "That place is getting a reputation for being one of the fastest-growing churches in the area these days."

"You and Nancy should make it a point to give it a try one of these days," I said. "You guys might fall in love with the pastor and the congregation like I did."

"Maybe we will do that, Mar. Right now, I'm still trying to make up my mind about this Kingdom Hall that I was telling you about. The people are great, but they don't seem to have that magic touch you've found. I'm still sipping the grog, and Nancy is still determined as ever to get me out of her life if I don't stop. I've got a few months left to decide what to do, so I would appreciate your prayers," he confided in me, more sincere and determined than I had ever known him to be.

"Kingdom Hall, did you say, Hutch? I've been told that the Kingdom Hall is a cult church. From what I understand, the people who attend there are Jehovah's Witnesses. You know those people by reputation, I'm sure. They come two by two knocking on doors on Sunday mornings. They specifically target people who don't go to church, that's why they choose Sundays to make their visits."

"Better be careful and check them out thoroughly, Hutch," I added. "I understand that once they get their hooks into you, they don't let go too easily."

"Okay, Mara. So now after six weeks, you've become an expert on which church to attend? Is that what you're saying?" he questioned, somewhat sarcastically.

"No, that's not what I'm saying at all, Hutch. You and Nancy and I have been friends for a long time. You know that I have your best interest at heart, don't you? I'm not trying to patronize you, only to warn you," I shot back at him.

"They don't even believe that Jesus is the Son of God. They think that He's some kind of a prophet or something. You and I are out of the Catholic faith, and we both know that he is the Son of God and that he died to save us from our sins. That's a fundamental teaching that we both grew up believing. There's a lot of false doctrine going around these days. I don't want to see you getting caught up in any of it, that's all."

"I'm sorry that I jumped all over you, Mar," he said after a brief hesitation. "That was unthinkable. I know you have our best interest at heart, and I will promise you this. Nance and I will visit your church one of these Sunday mornings, and maybe that pastor of yours can talk some sense into my head," he responded, bringing the conversation to a conclusion.

"Okay, Hutch, I'm going to pray that God keeps you on track and that you'll follow his leading. Just remember one thing, and then I'll let you go. Don't pick the church first and then try to find Jesus there. He might not be in that church. Give your life to Jesus first, and then you can be sure that he will lead you to a church where he can be found. You're a good friend, and I want nothing but the best for you and Nancy and your marriage."

After I hung up the phone, I thought of so many things I wanted to say to Hutch but didn't quite know how to go about it. I had much to learn about the Christian faith. I didn't even ask him if he wanted to accept Christ as his Savior. If he had said yes, what would I have done? I didn't know how to explain salvation at this point, let alone lead him to the Lord.

Then God or the Holy Spirit or whoever was in charge of this situation reminded me of my own experience, still so fresh and new to my life. Sherry wanted to pray with me that evening at her home, but I turned down her request. That didn't keep Jesus from saving me a few days later. He can break through any roadblock the enemy tries to put between the sinner and himself if the sinner is seeking him with sincerity.

Instead of being defeated by my failure to pray with Hutch and perhaps win him to Christ, I thanked God for the opportunity to have spoken to him about my own life and how it was being changed day by day.

The two younger kids were in the game room with Rachael and one of her friends. They were attempting to teach the younger children how to play a new game that I had gotten for the family. This would allow me time to change clothes and do my hair before I started dinner. I already made a series of changes necessary to move our dinnertime back an hour so the kids and I could attend Sunday evening service at seven o'clock.

There would be no opportunity to follow through on this tonight, I realized. Rand called just as I got home from Vicky's and informed me that he and his three fishing buddies were getting ready to leave the lake and that he would be home before six o'clock, in time for dinner.

While I was fixing my hair, Rachael appeared at the doorway.

"What's wrong, honey?" I asked, noting that she seemed to be experiencing some physical discomfort.

"Mommy, I don't feel good. My head started to hurt during church this morning. Mrs. Michaels went to the altar with me during the altar call. She asked me if I wanted to receive Christ as my Savior a few minutes before that, and I said that I did. But when Pastor Carlton prayed with me, all I could think about was the pain in my head."

I took a closer look at her. "Where does it hurt, Rachael?" I asked, somewhat concerned. "You didn't get hit on the head at school during gym last week, did you?"

Rachael was the healthiest of our three children. Of course, all of them had their bout with measles and chicken pox, but Rae didn't come down with the colds and sore throats that the two younger children frequently succumbed to. She appeared to have a strong immune system.

"No, Mommy, my head didn't get hurt at school or anywhere else. It just started to hurt at church this morning," she explained.

"I'm going to give you a couple of baby aspirins, honey. You can lie down for a little while, and maybe that will make your headache go away," I said as I took two small orange pills from the bottle I had taken from the medicine cabinet.

"Did your friend Judy go home? What are the kids doing downstairs?" I asked, attempting to direct the conversation away from Rachael's headache.

"Yeah, Mom. I told Judy that I didn't feel good, so she went home. Randy and Roni are still playing the game we taught them. They're all right," she assured me.

I hugged my oldest child as I folded down the blanket on her bed and prayed a short prayer asking Jesus to take away her headache.

"Now, you jump in here, little girl, and get cozy under your blanket. You may just need a little nap today. Remember, Mrs. O'Conner allowed you to stay at their house later than usual last evening so you and Patty could finish working on your cooking badge. I'm sure you'll feel better after the aspirins do their work and you get some much-needed sleep," I assured her.

Dinner was ready to put on the table when Rand returned from his fishing expedition. Randy ran downstairs to the garage to meet his dad when he heard the garage door go up. Although Rand attempted a few times to include our son in his fishing trips, Randy had very little interest in the sport. He hadn't developed the virtue of patience as yet, and this is much needed when sitting in a boat waiting for a big fish to swim by and grab your bait.

Randy did enjoy seeing what treasures his dad had taken out of the cold waters of Lake Erie as a result of his unique skill.

Generally, these early-spring trips garnered a better catch than at other times of the year. The croppy bass were coming to the surface in the lakes at about the same time the trout were running upstream, and Rand managed to get his limit of both each year.

"Hey, Mommy," Randy yelled, taking two steps at a time on his way to the kitchen. "Wait till you see all the fish Daddy caught this time. He's got a great, big one down there with the other ones. He said that one of his friends measured it, and it was twenty-one inches long. It's a great big fish, that's for sure," he continued, excited to relate some of the highlights of the trip before his dad had the opportunity to do so.

Rand followed Randy upstairs, a satisfied grin on his face. "Yes, we had a productive weekend," he announced, washing his hands in the sink. "I'll finish the cleanup after dinner. The fish are already filleted, so all I have to do is repack them and put them in the freezer."

Nana, Roni, and Rachael were already seated around the table. Rachael evidently was tired as she had slept for two hours after I put her down. Happily she announced that the headache was gone.

Once again, things had settled down to a normal routine. It was at times like this that I wanted to thank God for his goodness and for his many blessings by giving thanks before our meal. Rand was against praying aloud for any reason. It was his contention that if a person felt the need to pray, it should be done silently. He did not want to be included in something that was of no interest to him. One needed to keep his religious convictions to himself.

During dinner, Rand enthusiastically did a play-by-play description of the events of his fishing weekend with his buddies. Of course, once again, he had taken the most fish, and none of the other men could even come close to his twenty-one-inch walleyed pike.

"You know," he said proudly, "I thought about taking that one to the taxidermist to have it mounted. But since you and I will be going to Canada this summer, Mar, I thought I would wait for that 'big one' that's waiting for me at Deer Lake. They get a lot bigger up in that lake. More fish than fishermen, I guess," he mused. "Gives them a chance to grow up."

Rand's reference to the fishing trip that we were planning later in the summer caused me to recall the conversation I recently had with my Aunt Dar. They made the trip to the Pittsburgh area frequently, usually once a month when the weather would allow. Now that my grandparents were well up in years, Aunt Dar felt the need to visit as often as possible.

Uncle Lenny was taking care of my grandfather's accounting for his real estate business. Grampa's most recent stroke had incapacitated him to the extent that he could no longer handle the work that still needed to be completed to dissolve the business. It was tax time, and as a result of that, Lenny felt he had to be in Pittsburgh as often as possible in order to meet the deadline for filing.

He could usually be found behind my grandfather's huge roll top desk in Grampa's office, diligently tabulating columns and columns of figures. He would come up for air when the dinner bell sounded, spend a few minutes socializing with Rand, and then go back to work.

Aunt Dar, on the other hand, spent most of her time running between visits with Gram and playing with our two younger kids. Randy and Roni loved Aunt Dar, and they were always delighted when they knew that she, Carol, and their Uncle Lenny would be coming into town. Carol, the only child born to my aunt and uncle after fourteen years of marriage, was, of course, the apple of their eye. Rachael was three years younger than Carol, but they had been best buddies since we had begun to spend weekends in Ohio visiting them.

Their most recent visit occurred the week following my conversion. Aunt Dar had always been the most spiritual of the six sisters born to my grandparents. Aunt Harriet was the religious sister, but Dar was more spiritually inclined. Her focus was on God—not the organized church—and why he took such a great interest in his creation since we were all a bunch of ungrateful eggheads.

She and Len hadn't regularly attended an organized church for many years, nor did they attempt to raise Carol with any particular beliefs. They sent her to a parochial school mainly for the good general education she was receiving, not necessarily for her to become involved in the Catholic faith. That would be Carol's decision to make when she was old enough and mature enough to do so, Uncle Lenny had felt.

I related to Dar, who listened intently, every detail of that unforgettable day of Jesus's visit.

"That's a very interesting story," she commented when I had finished. "You know how I feel about God, Mara. I guess I don't really know him because I have a lot of unanswered questions. I know there is something missing in my life. Perhaps it's as you say. Perhaps I can know him as you say that you know him now. Perhaps if I surrender my life to his Son and ask forgiveness for my sins, I will be able to have a relationship with him as well. I don't know about all this. I've given it a lot of thought over the years, but I haven't come up with any concrete conclusions yet."

"But that's not to say that I'm minimizing your experience," she added quickly. "You say you haven't had a drink since this happened? Well, that tells me that something of consequence did occur that day—and, Mara, it had to be supernatural. If you had only known how desperately the family tried for so many years to get your Uncle Henry off the booze without success, you would understand why I know that it is supernatural when something like this happens to a person. What about Rand? What was his reaction to all this?" she questioned.

"Rand made an appointment for me to see some shrink he heard about. We were to be at his office the morning of the big snowstorm.

The roads were completely impassable. He rescheduled, but when he realized, after two or three weeks, that I hadn't had a drink for a while, he cancelled that appointment as well," I explained.

"Nothing more has been brought up about the subject since then," I added. "You can be sure that I wouldn't open that can of worms. I never wanted to see that doctor in the first place. As you are well aware, because you and Lenny arranged to have my mother placed under the care of one of the best psychiatrists in Pittsburgh, he didn't do her a bit of good. If anything, the electric shock therapy he ordered for her on several occasions had an adverse effect, if anything. I know you both meant well, but I'm certain that you'll agree that the outcome of those treatments proved to be a dismal failure."

"Did you tell him that the Lord had done that for you?" she asked, avoiding my comments.

"Yes, I did, Dar."

"And what was his response to that?" she questioned.

"My dear Aunt Darlene, I don't use that language anymore. That's another sin that Jesus has taken out of my life. Without quoting him verbatim, he thought it was just so much rubbish," I added.

"I know you have a great deal of respect for Len, Mara. But let me tell you something about your esteemed uncle. He feels very much like Rand does about God. He just can't be bothered with anything that involves our spiritual nature. In fact, he doesn't even believe human beings have a spiritual nature. He feels there's nothing like plain, good old-fashioned common sense to handle all the problems in life.

"Depending on God to help us out of rough situations is like depending on a wheelchair. To Len, that is a sign of weakness. In fact, in my experience as a psychiatric nurse, I found this to be true of a lot of men, and a few women as well. They don't want to admit that they need anyone to come to their rescue. They'll handle it themselves, thank you."

"I certainly can't speak for any other men, but I know I have one tough cookie on my hands, Dar," I replied, somewhat discouraged.

"Okay, since we're on the subject of your husband, Len and I have come up with an idea that might be beneficial to all of you, especially the children," she said with a touch of excitement in her voice.

"I'm all ears, my dear aunt. What's on your mind?" I asked, not knowing what to expect at this point.

"We were discussing your situation the other evening, and we think that we have come up with a possible solution, or at least the beginning of a solution," she began. "We both came to the realization that you and Rand have never had a vacation away from your mom and the kids since you've been married. You guys need a honeymoon, a time away by yourselves to discover each other, maybe learn to appreciate each other and what you have together. How do you feel about that?" she asked.

"Whoa, Dar, that's a lot to throw at someone all at one time. My first thought is that I would probably feel like I was having a rendezvous with a perfect stranger. In over a decade of marriage, it's been all work, having and taking care of babies, dealing with a mentally challenged mother, making money, and meeting deadlines. I think I would feel very awkward being alone with my husband under these circumstances. I know that sounds strange, but that's how I feel," I responded.

"That's exactly what I'm talking about, Mara. Your marriage has never had a chance to get off the ground. Len and I are offering you the opportunity to try it out and see what you think."

"Here's the plan," she continued. "Len has six weeks' vacation coming. He's got to use it before the end of the year or lose it. He's willing to stay at home with me for two or three weeks in August, and we'll bring your mom and the kids to our place. This is what we do in August anyway. The only difference is that Rand and Len have gone to Canada on fishing trips in previous years while you and your family stayed here with me. This time, it would be you and Rand going away together while the rest of the family stays here.

"Len will be close by to handle any unforeseen problems if he's needed. Carol is fourteen now, so she and Rachael can help keep the two younger children in line. They all love the pool, and I would be sure that they were supervised at all times. You know me, Mara, safety first. You could leave on vacation with your husband with the full assurance that your mom and the children are in good hands."

I remember standing there looking intently at my aunt, attempting to process what I had just heard.

"Why in the world would you two be willing to do this for us, Dar?" I asked, stunned beyond words. "This is a huge responsibility. It would create a lot of additional work for you—more cooking, more cleaning, and more childcare than you are accustomed to. You know that my mother is of little assistance, don't you?"

"Of course, I know that, Mara. No one in the family is more familiar with your mother's condition than I am," she responded. "To answer your question—and let me be completely honest with you, Mar—if you don't get some help and get it soon, your marriage is finished. Len and I have been watching your lives for years now, and it's obvious that things are deteriorating. Do you want the same kind of life for your children that you had growing up as the result of a broken home?"

"No, of course, I don't," I replied without hesitation. "In the short time that I have known the Lord, I've been praying that he would intervene in both our lives and heal this marriage. I really believe that God answers prayers, Dar, and I'm believing that he will work things out for us."

"Could it be that this is the way that God has chosen to begin working in your lives?" she continued. "Maybe you're missing Him if you're looking in another direction. Might this be an answer to your prayers coming from an unexpected source?"

I hadn't considered this possibility, but I knew Dar had hit upon something important.

"You're right, Dar. This could be the answer," I agreed. "I'm willing to try it if Rand is in agreement."

"He is," she shot back with lightning speed. "Len has already spoken to him, and Rand is willing to give it a try. He's going to give Len sufficient money to cover food for all of us while you two are in Canada. We want nothing more from you with the exception of a good report when you return from your 'fishing honeymoon' in Quebec."

We hugged each other as we ended the conversation. It was settled. Rand and I would take Mom and the children to Dar and Lenny's home the first weekend of August and drop them off on our way to Canada. We would shop for all the food and load it in the boat before we left for Ohio. This would alleviate the need for any food shopping for at least the first week of our absence.

As my thoughts once again returned to the present, I focused my attention on my husband. He had acquired a captive audience in our three children. As he related every detail of how each of the fish had been caught, especially the walleyed pike, there were exclamations of delight uttered by both Randy and Roni. They never grew tired of hearing Rand's fish stories. Rachael had become somewhat subdued over the past few years, however. This was becoming a little old to her, but she wouldn't excuse herself from the table in fear of missing something.

Rand always appeared to be so much more animated, more interested in life in general, when he was talking about things he loved to do. Fishing had always been one of his great loves.

Maybe this won't be as bad as I thought it would be, I mused. *He's always in such a great mood when he's talking about his favorite pastime. It's even better when he's engaged in it.*

Well, Lord, if this is what you have in mind for us, I prayed to myself, *as Dar believes that it is, I'm going to continue to pray about this vacation as a possible turning point in our marriage. Maybe this will be the beginning of something new and wonderful in the Reuben home.*

Little did I know that, within a very short time, all these plans for a fishing trip to Canada and the possibility of the restoration of a failing marriage would be dashed to pieces by an event so disturbing, so horrendous, that any possibility of being able to pursue these plans was out of the question.

CHAPTER 23

A WILDERNESS EXPERIENCE

The ringing of the kitchen phone penetrated the silence of our home. It was unusually quiet this morning. Earlier I had taken Rachael and Randy to school. Roni was invited to spend the morning with one of her little friends, so I decided to treat my two older kids to an extra fifteen minutes of leisure time at home while I helped Roni get dressed and gather her playthings that she wanted to take with her.

Having returned home from dropping them off at their various destinations, I thought about the few things I needed to do in preparation for our regular Tuesday morning Bible study. We had started with only Vicky, her mom, her mom's friend, and a few of my neighbors and had grown to around eighteen women each week. I was elated at the increase as there were unsaved ladies attending the study.

For reasons of their own, they wanted to study the Word of God. They also enjoyed the teachings and testimonies of the guests I had invited. We welcomed them with open arms, praying that the Holy Spirit would pay us a special visit each Tuesday with his convicting power that brought salvation. Two weeks ago, a lady from the other end of my street accepted Christ during the study.

She was now attending each week in an effort to understand more fully the things of the Lord.

This morning, I had invited Sherry Drummond to join the group as guest speaker. Sherry was in the process of preparing for ordination. Her children were now in their teen years and capable of looking after themselves for brief periods of time. Raising all five of them in the fear and admonition of the Lord, she had little fear of alcohol, drugs, or bad companions infiltrating their home in her absence. Nevertheless, she scheduled her time away from home for when her children were in school or when Carly or one of her other friends were available to oversee their activities during her brief and infrequent absences.

Her family would always be at the top of her priority list, and it was evident. She had raised, almost single-handedly, five of the nicest, well-mannered young people I had ever had the pleasure of knowing. Her oldest son, Freddie, a senior in high school, had felt the calling of God in his young life and this past winter to enter the ministry. He was praying for sufficient money to come in to cover his expenses for this coming fall at a local Baptist divinity school.

The family funds were such that there was rarely any money available to cover anything other than the necessities of life. Sherry did cleaning for Phoebe Michaels and two other women on a regular basis. God had miraculously multiplied this modest income just as Christ had taken the five loaves and two fishes and multiplied them to feed five thousand men, as well as the women and children. Sherry lived a life of faith, waiting on the Lord to supply all her needs and the needs of her family.

I was most anxious to hear what the Lord had laid on her heart to teach during our meeting this morning. When she taught the Word, her messages were always relevant and without compromise. I truly loved this woman. She was one of God's special handmaidens.

My thoughts went back to a few months before when she had spent so many precious hours with me, giving me scripture after scripture in order to explain why it had been necessary for God to send His only Son to the cross. She had gotten through to me that night because it was only a few days later that I surrendered my life to Christ.

I was still smiling to myself as I picked up the receiver. On the other end of the phone, there was an unfamiliar female voice who introduced herself as Mrs. Myers, the elementary school nurse. In a few brief sentences, she turned my world upside down.

"Mrs. Reuben," she began, a tinge of regret in her voice, "I certainly hate to be the one to break this news to you, but I really believe it will benefit you and your husband, as well as your daughter Rachael. The quicker you take action regarding this situation, the better it will be for all concerned."

"I was called into her sixth grade English class by her teacher some time ago to observe your daughter," she explained. "Rachael was not aware I had been called to monitor her behavior. I returned to the same class for subsequent observations over the next several weeks. Finally, just to be absolutely certain that my suspicion was accurate, I called Rachael into my office this morning. I checked her eyes and other visible signs indicative of this illness.

"I had her walk a straight line for me and had her perform a few other simple exercises to determine proper balance. She told me that she was getting headaches and that they had become more severe in the past few weeks. It is my judgment that your daughter has epilepsy. She exhibits every sign of this disease in its infancy. I would strongly recommend that you contact the neurological department of Children's Hospital as soon as possible and get her an appointment with a neurologist.

"They will schedule a series of tests, an EEG, various x-rays, and possibly use some of the newer technological equipment that is now available to aid them in their evaluation of her condition. I must warn you that there is no cure for this disease. Should she begin to convulse—and she will if my assessment is correct—her seizures can be often arrested to a great extent by medication. That's the best news I have to offer you, Mrs. Reuben. I'm sorry. Please call me if there is anything I can do for you."

I replaced the hand piece of the phone and stood staring at it, hoping against hope that it would ring again with the voice on the other end saying there had been a mistake, that I should ignore that first phone call. It was meant for someone else. But the phone was silent. The same phrases continued to run through my brain—*your daughter has epilepsy, no cure, epilepsy, no cure, epilepsy, no cure.* My hands began to shake, and my body began to break out in a cold, clammy sweat.

O God, I prayed. *I thought that when I received your Son into my life, things would begin to improve. I heard from someone at church that our children would be protected from accidents and serious illnesses. If that is so, what is the problem? Rachael is an innocent child. She never harmed anyone. In fact, she is a very loving, obedient child. Why did this happen to her?*

I looked at the kitchen clock. The ladies would be coming for the Bible study in a few minutes. I had to get the large coffeemaker from the top shelf of a cabinet, but my legs wouldn't move properly. I seemed to be in a state of semi paralysis. I was afraid to attempt to get up on a step stool for fear that I might fall. Reaching for the phone, I tried to call Vicky, but my hands were shaking so violently that I couldn't dial her number.

All right, Mara, I told myself. *You've got to get control. Better yet, you have to let God take control of this situation. He knows all about it. Just trust him.* I repeated this to myself over and over.

The doorbell rang just then. The ladies were beginning to arrive for Bible study. Somehow I managed to get from the kitchen to the living room on very unsteady legs in order to open the front door.

"Hi, Mara," Vicky greeted me in her typical exuberant fashion. She needed only to take one look at my face to know that something was amiss. "My goodness, honey, what is wrong with ya'll?" she asked, an expression of genuine concern on her face.

I fell into Vicky's arms and began to sob violently. After relating what I could remember of the telephone call that had come from the school nurse, Vicky led me to the couch. She quietly sat down beside me and took a clean tissue from her purse, wiping the tears from my eyes. Then she put her arm around me and, patting me gently on the back, spoke words of encouragement, assuring me that everything would be all right.

"Okay, Mara," she said softly, "the ladies will begin to arrive anytime now. I'm glad I decided to come over a few minutes early. I thought I might be able to help ya'll with the preparations before they got here."

"Tell me what needs to be done, and I'll do it, honey," she added as she continued to speak to me in that gentle, unflinching manner she always possessed during emergency situations. It had a soothing effect on my nervous system, and I began to feel peace returning to my entire being.

"I tried to call you, Vicky. I was trembling so badly that I couldn't even dial your number. I believe that God sent you over here a few minutes before the others arrive to get me settled down. He knows just what we need, doesn't he?" I asked rhetorically, not really expecting an answer.

"Yes, he certainly does," she replied in agreement. "I see the coffee hasn't been made. I'll take care of that, Mara. I know where ya'll keep everything, so just leave this to me," she added as she headed for the kitchen.

The ladies began to arrive, and I was able to welcome them in a relatively normal manner, thanks to Vicky. No one suspected that I had just received earth-shattering news, which had literally rocked my world.

Sherry arrived before most of the other women, accompanied by Carly. She asked that I introduce her and give a brief summary of the ministries in which she was involved in order to establish her credibility as a Christian active in the Lord's work.

When all the ladies arrived and got settled, I introduced Sherry, giving everyone a brief summary of her many accomplishments. She opened in prayer and then gave a moving and relevant teaching on child-rearing, following the guidelines outlined in the Bible. The ladies were enchanted with her ability to communicate this subject so thoroughly. Many of them, like myself, were presently raising a family and found her message to be very informative. Sherry loved the Lord passionately, and this love manifested itself in the way that she lived her life and through every word she spoke. She was a beautiful Christian woman, inside and out.

Following Sherry's teaching, Mrs. Jackson continued with her study on the book of John. Many of us were new Christians, and we needed to become grounded in the fundamentals of salvation. Mrs. Jackson had wisely chosen a book of the Bible perfectly suited to our needs. When she completed her teaching for the morning, she asked for prayer requests. At this point, I began to develop a lump in my throat, which prevented me from speaking. I sat silently in my chair attempting to hold back the tears.

Evidently, Vicky had been observing my struggle, so she took it upon herself to become my spokesman in this instance. "Mara has a very special prayer request this morning, ladies," she announced. "She received a very disturbing phone call from her daughter's school nurse before our meeting began. From all indications, Rachael has epilepsy. She recommended that Mara and Rand seek medical care for her immediately."

The initial reaction to this announcement was stunned silence throughout the group of women. This was a terrible malady, often accompanied by serious repercussions, and it hit close to home. In fact, it hit this home and the oldest daughter of their hostess.

Mrs. Jackson spontaneously broke out in prayer for Rachael's complete and rapid healing. Many others joined in to express their heartfelt concern for Rae and asked God to keep his hand of mercy on each member of the Reuben family. Others prayed healing scriptures, reminding God of his promise of physical healing because of the stripes that Jesus had suffered at the cruel hands of the Roman soldiers.

I was the last person in the living room to pray aloud. It was my first experience doing this, and as I had observed other Christians at church pray extemporaneously, I suspected it would require a huge step of faith on my part to accomplish this. Because of the burden on my heart for my beloved Rachael, when I opened my mouth to pray for her healing, all my concerns seemed to fade into the background. I merely told God how concerned I was for my daughter's health and asked him to heal her in the name of Jesus, his Son, who paid dearly for the healing of his people. I acknowledged the fact that all things were possible for him. He is a great, big God, and if he could speak the world into existence, it would be an easy matter for him to heal my little girl.

Talking to God had been as easy and as natural as talking to one of my children, my mother, or one of my friends. I didn't have to use big, impressive words when I prayed. God wasn't impressed with my vocabulary, but He was concerned with the sincerity of my heart.

The Bible study group broke up after coffee and a brief time of fellowship. Most of the women present were close to my age. Generally speaking, we were all married and raising a family. The older ladies in the group like Mrs. Jackson and Vicky's mom, Barb, had retired husbands at home. Both men had health issues that necessitated their wives being with them a good part of the day.

For these reasons, it was only on rare occasions that anyone lingered once the study ended. We all said our good-byes and expressed the hope that we would meet again the following week for prayer and the study of God's Word. Many of the ladies embraced me at the door with words of encouragement regarding my situation. They all promised to keep Rachael in prayer through the coming week.

When the last lady had gone, I closed the door and returned to the living room to discover that Vicky, Sherry, and Carly were still seated and engaged in serious conversation.

Sherry got up and came to me, taking my hand. "Mara," she said, those dark, piercing eyes searching mine, "would it be all right if Carly and I stayed an extra half hour or so? I would like to speak with you about a few things. If you have made plans to be anywhere this morning, please tell me and we can do this another time."

"No, I have no plans other than pick up Roni at a neighbor's house. If you give me just a moment, I'll call Loretta to make sure it's all right with her if I leave Roni at her home for an extra hour. Sherry, you and Carly are always welcome in my home. You know that. I'm in need of some encouragement, and I can think of no one who can provide it like you three ladies can.

"Vicky has already given me a great deal of support. She came over before the Bible study began and settled me down. I was a basket case after I got that phone call. Some Christian, eh?" I commented, judging myself for the weakness I displayed.

Vicky had already gotten her jacket from the hall closet and was getting ready to leave as I ended my phone call with Loretta. "I guess I should go now and let ya'll get on with yur business," she said, putting on her jacket and retrieving her purse from the closet.

"You have a small child at home, don't you, Vicky?" Sherry asked. "I guess that you're anxious to get home."

"No, not really" was the reply. "Mom went to our house after she left here. She thought that Mara might need me to stay with her for a while this morning, and she volunteered to babysit until I got home."

"I'd appreciate it if you would stay, Vicky. You and Mara are good friends, and I want those of us who know her well to be here to pray with her before Carly and I leave," Sherry said. "Would you be willing to do that?"

"Of course, I would," Vicky replied. "I thought that maybe ya'll had things to say to her that I shouldn't be a'list'nin' to."

"I do have things to say to her, but you need to hear them too," Sherry explained. "You're a brand-new Christian. I understand that you received Christ just a couple of weeks ago, Vicky, so you can benefit from what God has laid on my heart to share with Mara."

It was obvious that Vicky did not want to be excluded from any conversation that Sherry would initiate. She had a sincere admiration and a growing love for this dear saint of God who had been so instrumental in my salvation. She quickly returned her jacket to the closet and offered to make a fresh pot of coffee. Both Sherry and Carly declined the offer, each moving to the dining room and sitting at the table.

"I took the liberty of coming in here, Mara," Sherry explained. "Sitting across from one another in close proximity to one another provides a much more intimate atmosphere for discussing the things I want to touch upon."

"That's fine with me, Sherry. Please feel free to do whatever you feel to do," I said, taking a chair directly across from her where I could give her my total attention.

"First of all," Sherry began, "you shared with me last week that you had been baptized in water at your church in early April. Is that correct?" she asked, her eyes ablaze with compassion. "The Holy Spirit laid a burden on me while your Bible teacher was opening the study in prayer. I believe that if I follow his leading, I can help you get through this trial you have so suddenly found facing you."

"It would be wonderful if you could do that for me, Sherry. This new life is so different from what I've been accustomed to.

I don't know how to reach out in faith to God for answers to this dilemma—and yes," I added, "I was baptized in water on April 4."

"All right," she said, going on, "get some paper and a pen. You too, Vicky. I want both of you to write down some scripture references. We're going to have a mini-Bible study about a couple of very important principles in the Word of God.

"I'm not going to take the time right now, but I want both of you to read the account of Jesus's baptism and his following wilderness experience when the Holy Spirit led him into the desert to be tested. These accounts can be found in the book of Matthew, chapters three and four. Read them when you have a little extra time and ask the Holy Spirit to give you a full understanding of what happened here."

"In the meantime," she continued, "I will explain to the best of my ability what was happening in this portion of Matthew. Jesus was being baptized by John, not because he needed to be but as an example to all believers who would someday be his followers. The Bible says that he did this to 'fulfill all righteousness.' This marked the beginning of his public ministry.

"It was at this time that God the Father acknowledged him as his son in whom he was well pleased, and that the Holy Spirit, in the form of a dove, descended upon him. The entire Trinity was present during this event. Also keep this in mind, and this is so important, girls—this occurred at a public place, the Jordan River, where multitudes of people gathered regularly to listen to John preach. John's disciples, curious onlookers, as well as the scribes and Pharisees who would become the enemies of our Lord witnessed this event.

"This is very similar to what happens during our present baptismal services. We go down in the water of baptism, and when we come up out of the water, we acknowledge to everyone present that we have left our old life of sin behind and have become new creatures in Christ. This is a public act, just as Jesus's baptism was a public act. Coming out of the water, the one being baptized is asked by the pastor to give a brief testimony as to what had occurred. The response should be one acknowledging that Christ has become Lord and Savior of that person's life.

"This should be a spontaneous response. The one doing the baptizing should never attempt to put words into the mouth of the one being baptized. This is his testimony and his alone. The book of Romans, chapter ten verse nine, puts it this way: if we confess with our mouth the Lord Jesus Christ and believe in our heart that God has raised him from the dead, then we will be saved. Write that reference down, girls. It is vitally important that you have a clear understanding why it is necessary to be baptized in water when at all possible."

At this point, Sherry took a brief break in order to allow this to sink in. There was a lot that had to be absorbed.

"Mara, you should have a fairly clear understanding of water baptism since you have been baptized very recently. I believe that most churches give a brief teaching on the reason for participating in this sacrament before the service begins, isn't that right?"

I assented with a nod.

"Vicky, did I explain this to your satisfaction?" Sherry asked. "You will probably be going down in the water yourself one of these days, so you might as well learn what it's all about while we're on the subject."

"Oh, thank ya'll so much, Sherry. Ya'll made it crystal clear. The day that Mara was baptized, she made an effort to explain this to me, and I sort of got it. But now I understand it completely," she exclaimed, a look of relief moving across the features of her pretty face.

Sherry glanced quickly at her watch. She indicated that she had quite a bit to convey to Mara as yet. The Holy Spirit had laid it upon her heart to minister comfort and an understanding of what was happening in her life and especially of why this was happening.

Sherry looked at Carly, who had been quietly listening to Sherry's comments. "You have an appointment today, Carly," Sherry said. "I don't want to make you late."

"I'm fine, Sherry," Carly responded. "I still have an hour before I have to start getting ready. I'm good for forty-five minutes yet if you think that will be enough time."

"Yes, that will work, Carly. I really do want to get through all that the Holy Spirit gave me for Mara this morning while we were praying for Rachael's healing or possibly deliverance, whichever the case may be."

What's deliverance? I thought to myself. *I haven't heard that word yet. I sure hope that's in her explanation of the things that I should know.*

Sherry caught the blank look on my face and assured me that everything I needed to be aware of would be discussed and thoroughly understood by the time she and Carly left my home in forty-five minutes.

"Okay," Sherry continued, "the next thing I want to talk about is the fact that immediately following Jesus's baptism, the Holy Spirit led him into the wilderness to be tempted by the devil. You may ask the question, 'Why was this necessary?' I'm going to answer that question, but once again, I want both of you to carefully and prayerfully read chapter four down to verse twelve.

"When the devil came to Jesus, he appealed to the three things that human nature is prey to—the flesh, the world, and the devil. First of all, Jesus was hungry. Who wouldn't be? He had fasted from food for forty days and forty nights. Satan knew Jesus was in a weakened condition. If he had any possibility of making Jesus fall, now was the time. He told Jesus that *if* He was the Son of God, then he would have the ability to turn the stones lying all around them into bread. Jesus rejected Satan's trap to satisfy his flesh with bread and instead responded with scripture. He said to Satan, 'It is written, man shall not live on bread alone but by every word that proceeds out of the mouth of God.'

"Satan did not give up that easily. After that, he suggested that Jesus throw himself off the pinnacle of the temple by saying that *if* he was truly the Son of God, God would dispatch his angels to rescue him from the fall. Jesus countered once again by using scripture against Satan's demand: 'You shall not put the Lord your God to the test,' he said. Had this demand been met by our Lord, this would have allowed Satan to become the victor over him. Once again, by using scripture, Jesus defeated the scheme of the enemy.

"Finally, still attempting to break Jesus's will, which would have reduced him to a mere mortal man, Satan took Jesus to a high mountain and showed him all the kingdoms of the world, offering to turn these kingdoms over to Jesus if he would fall down and worship him. By this time, Jesus had heard enough. He said to his tempter, once again using scripture as his weapon against the onslaught, 'Get behind me Satan, for it is written, you shall worship the Lord your God, and him only will you serve.'

"Do you see the pattern here, Mara? As Jesus was preparing for His brief public ministry, he did something that was not required of him in order to be the example to others. Then he allowed the Holy Spirit to lead him into the wilderness where he spent time in prayer and fasting. At the point of his greatest need, Satan appeared to him and tempted him to forsake his divine nature and embrace his human nature. He refused to bend to Satan's demands and literally turned the tables on him by quoting scripture in order to defeat each of his temptations.

"What do you get from this, Mara? Do you see any similarities between this portion of scripture and what you are faced with right now?"

"Yes, I certainly do, Sherry," I said. "I could sense light illuminating my spirit as the Holy Spirit began to minister to me. First of all, by being baptized in water, Jesus displayed his readiness for ministry, and by this very public act, he let everyone know just who he was and why He had come. There was still one thing that he had to undergo, and that was severe testing.

"Three times Satan attempted to trip him up, and three times he used the Word of God to counteract these temptations. Throughout the ordeal, he trusted his father to deal with the enemy, who was attempting to usurp his authority and his kingdom."

"All right, that's good so far, Mara," Sherry replied. "But be more specific. How does Jesus's actions apply to your situation?"

"Well, I see a parallel here, and don't get me wrong, Sherry. There is no way that I would ever attempt to compare myself to my Savior, God forbid! But a parallel does exist. I was baptized in water as Jesus was baptized in water. After he was baptized, the Holy Spirit immediately led him into the wilderness to be tested. This pattern was the same for me. A few weeks ago, I was baptized; and a short time later—this morning, as a matter of fact—when I received the bad news from the school nurse, my wilderness experience began. This was the beginning of testing for me."

"That's it, Mara," Sherry replied, that warm, engaging smile brightening her face. "Now, let's complete the picture. What did Jesus do when he was being tested?"

My response came quickly this time. I didn't have to think it through. The answer was right in front of me. "He used the Word of God to counter Satan's attacks," I said, assured I had answered her question correctly.

"All right, but how does one do that? Jesus didn't have the Bible with Him during his wilderness experience so that He could quote scripture. The Bible had not yet been written," Sherry replied.

I had to think about this. The answer wasn't instantaneous this time. After a brief pause, I felt confident enough to respond to her question. "I would have to say that Jesus was quoting Old Testament scripture as we know it. There was no Bible, as you point out, Sherry, but there were scrolls that were preserved. Eventually, what was written on those scrolls was compiled into what we have today, the Old and New Testament Bible."

"You're doing all right so far, Mara. I have one last question for you in order to complete this picture. If you're attacked by the enemy, how would you immediately counter his attack?"

"The only logical answer that I can give for this is that I would have to have some scripture memorized so that when the attack comes, I could have the appropriate verse of the Bible on the tip of my tongue and ready to speak out in order to counter the enemy's attack. Is that correct?" I asked, not quite sure this was the answer Sherry was looking for.

"That is correct," she replied. "You appear to be in tune with God, Mara. Continue to seek him and stay in the Word. Begin to memorize the Word. It will be your double-edged sword as you do battle with the enemy, and don't doubt me. You will do battle with the enemy."

Sherry looked at Vicky, who had been eagerly absorbing every word that came from Sherry's lips. "Were you able to get an understanding of anything I said today, Vicky?" Sherry asked her. "You are new in the Lord, and it takes time to process all this. But as you study and seek the Lord in prayer, the Holy Spirit will make this real to you, and you will find that he is with you always."

"I'm not sure I can remember too much of what ya'll said, but I took some notes, and I'll review them, Sherry. I'm grateful for the extra time ya'll took with Mara and me today. I know that ya'll have a busy schedule."

"Ladies, I have a lot more than I would like to share with you, but the time is gone for today," Sherry said, somewhat regretfully. "I must get Carly home so she can get ready for her appointment."

Sherry turned to me. "Mara, if you can arrange to stay for a brief time after our Friday evening prayer meeting, I would like to share with you what the Spirit has imparted to me regarding Rachael's situation. I wanted to get to that this morning because you are going to need the wisdom of the Holy Spirit to deal with this situation. Unfortunately, our time has run out for today."

As Vicky and I walked with them to the front door, we embraced each other warmly, promising to keep both of them and their families in prayer during the week.

Carly gave me a an extra special hug and assured me that she, Sherry, and the rest of their Wednesday and Friday prayer groups would be made aware of Rachael's diagnosis. "There will be much intercession made in behalf of you and your family, Mara, be assured of that. We love you, and know that when God's purpose has been accomplished, Rachael will be healed."

CHAPTER 24

WIELDING THE DOUBLE-EDGED SWORD

I was suddenly awakened by some kind of an uproar coming from the girls' bedroom.

Oh, dear God, I prayed. *It's Rachael. I just know it's my baby having a seizure. The school nurse warned me this would happen.*

I looked at Rand, who was sleeping soundly beside me. I certainly didn't want to handle this alone. I needed emotional support at a time like this. I shook him roughly, knowing how difficult it was to wake him from a deep sleep.

"What's wrong with you, Mara? Are you having a bad dream?" he muttered, half asleep.

"No, Rand, it's Rachael. She's having a seizure, just like Mrs. Myers said she would. Come with me to the girls' room. Maybe we can stop it somehow."

"You take care of it, Mar. I'm no good confronted by situations like this. I wouldn't be able to do anything for her anyhow. My understanding is that you have to let the seizure run its course. She'll eventually stabilize. Just go over there and make sure she doesn't bump her head on something or fall out of bed," he said, turning his face to the wall.

I jumped out of bed and headed for the girls' bedroom across the hall. I could hear my heart pounding in my chest. Once again, I could feel my skin becoming clammy as it invariably did when I was faced with a crisis situation.

As I opened their door, I witnessed a spectacle that terrified me. Rachael's blanket had been pulled from the bed by her convulsing body. I called her name, but there was no response. She was unconscious. I glanced quickly at the twin bed beside hers. Roni had not heard the commotion, thank God. She was sleeping peacefully.

I attempted to put my arms around Rachael in an effort to lessen the severity of the seizure. It was to no avail. I just sat beside her on the bed, tears streaming down my face, hoping that it would soon end. I took my husband's advice and made certain that she didn't hit her head by placing her pillow between her head and the headboard.

There was nothing more that I could do for her. I felt so completely helpless. Sherry's admonishment echoed and reechoed through my entire being: "When confronted by the enemy, you must use the Word of God, the two-edged sword, to send him running. He's a fierce adversary, but he can be defeated. Always remember that, Mara. God will win every battle in the long run."

I had not as yet memorized any scripture. All I could think of to say was the name of Jesus, which I continued to repeat over and over. After what seemed like an eternity, the seizure began to subside. In a short time, her body became quiet and slowly returned to normal.

Rachel attempted to move to an upright position, but she was totally disorientated. She looked around the room with a wild look in her eyes. She had no conception of what had happened. Then she noticed me sitting on the bed beside her, but she attempted to remove my arm from her shoulder. There was no recognition. She did not know who I was.

This caused terror to rise in my heart. This was even worse than the seizure itself. *Is this the way she is going to remain?* I thought. *Will she become a vegetable, a child who does not even recognize her mother?*

In the trauma of the moment, I had once again lost contact with God. But now, observing her in this condition, I began to pray in earnest, *O God, bring my little girl back to me. Let her be as she was before this horrible thing happened to her. Don't let her become a vegetable. She is such a loving, happy child, God. Please make her normal again. And thank you, Father, that Roni didn't witness this horrible sight. She loves her sister so much. She would have been hysterical if she had seen what I saw.*

Just as I finished whispering that prayer, I heard a very weak voice calling my name.

"Mommy, Mommy, what happened to me? I woke up because my hand became so numb I couldn't feel it. It scared me so bad that I sat up in bed, and then that's all I remember until now. My head hurts, Mommy. Could I have two of those little orange pills like you gave me before when I had a headache?" Rachel asked.

I put my arms around her and held her close to me. She was back to normal again, thank God. I uttered a prayer of thanksgiving to my Father for restoring my daughter to her normal self. Evidently, the seizure hadn't caused any permanent damage, at least nothing that was evident as yet.

"Yes, honey, you stay in bed. I'll get you two baby aspirins and a glass of water from the bathroom."

I was gone only the time it took me to get the aspirin and water. She was fighting to stay awake, but she appeared to have returned to a normal state.

Rachael was exhausted after her ordeal and wanted desperately to go back to sleep. I feared she may have another seizure during the remainder of the night. I decided to crawl in beside her. This way, I would know immediately if there was to be a recurrence of this seizure. She was scared to death it would happen again, and so was I.

I nestled up close and put my arms around her. After a few minutes, she fell asleep in my arms and slept soundly the remainder of the night. I lay awake for some time, reliving this horror. It had been a nightmare, all right, but it was a nightmare that does not end when you wake up.

The following eighteen months were a living hell. Each Wednesday would find Rachael and me making the trip across town to Pittsburgh's Children's Hospital. By this time, Rachael had been examined and reexamined by a myriad of neurologists, undergone scores of various kinds of tests, and had been interviewed by a number of psychiatrists and psychologists who were on staff at the hospital. I was assigned to my own psychologist, who spoke with me about many subjects while Rachael was in another part of the hospital being tested on various kinds of equipment to determine one thing or another.

I discovered that my psychologist was in need of a psychologist himself, so I introduced him to the Great Physician one Wednesday afternoon, and he received Christ as his savior. We continued to meet for our weekly chats, and we covered a variety of doctrines. It was like the blind leading the blind. But it turned out that it was an hour well spent each week for both of us. We grew spiritually as a result of studying the Word of God through the week in an effort to share with each other what we had learned. It was the only bright spot of my experience at the hospital.

It would be unfair of me to suggest that any of these people were not doing their jobs well because they were. Nonetheless, in their final analyses, they could find nothing physically wrong with my daughter. Rachael had received every test the facility had to offer, but nothing of consequence had been discovered.

After several unsuccessful attempts, they were able to arrest her frequent seizures through the use of two drugs that were prescribed together. Prior to that, she was having seizures throughout the night, sometimes as many as three or four over an eight-hour period, and always when she was asleep. I had to look on the bright side, and I thanked God that no seizures occurred during her waking hours.

During the day, she was able to carry out her routine normally. She missed very little school, spent time as usual on scouting and other social activities with her friends, and could always be found in church with her siblings and me on Sunday mornings and Wednesday evenings. I had much to be thankful for.

There were many people praying for her during this time. Visiting evangelists laid hands on her, anointing her with oil. All-night vigils were called in her behalf, but it seemed the timing was not yet right for her healing. In my heart, I knew one day the Holy Spirit would intervene, and finally she would be free of this malady that plagued her. Jesus paid the price for all our diseases, and my Rachael's malady certainly was not excluded from that number.

As time progressed, I noticed that Rachael's personality had begun to change. Instead of the sweet, loving child she had always been, she was becoming rebellious and somewhat disobedient. She was no longer the patient older sister to Roni but would become bossy and irritable with her for no particular reason. Roni began to avoid her sister more and more often. This was a living nightmare for which there was no end, it seemed.

I spent a lot of time on my knees during this time, seeking God for answers. From the very beginning of this ordeal, I understood that this was my wilderness experience. I knew I was being tested. No matter what happened, I realized that I had to keep my eyes on God. I had to keep my faith in him regardless of what we were going through. I had to learn the Word of God and know how to use it effectively against the enemy. God was in control, and one day I knew we would have the victory.

Other than attending church twice a week and taking the children with me, I did not leave the house in the evenings during the first year and a half of Rachael's illness. Placing a babysitter in the position of experiencing a grand mal seizure would have been an unwise and a cruel thing for me to do to a young girl. Once the doctors found the combination of drugs that arrested her seizures, I felt somewhat less anxious about being away for short periods of time, always being careful to leave a number where I could be reached.

Sherry visited me occasionally during this time of confinement as I found it necessary to drop out of her Bible study on Friday evenings. If she visited during the evening hours, she would pray with Rachael and anoint her with oil. We would agree together in prayer for her complete healing. After three or four of these visits, Rachael began to resist Sherry's efforts to pray for her.

I found this to be disturbing and totally foreign to Rachael's compliant nature. She had always loved being with both Sherry and Carly during the times they would help out with various Girl Scout activities. Sherry, however, knew what was behind Rachael's behavior and assured me we would discuss this in the near future during one of her morning visits when Rachael was at school.

I did not have to wait long to find out what was on Sherry's mind. Her previous visit had found Rachael becoming increasingly more resistant to her prayer.

After dropping Rachael and Randy off at the bus stop, I took Roni to Vicky's home next door. Vicky agreed to take care of Roni until after lunch. She and LuAnne, Vicky's youngest child, played together well; and Vicky had faithfully come to my rescue when I needed her, especially during this difficult time I faced with Rachael. She knew Sherry was coming to discuss something of grave importance regarding Rachael's illness, and she wanted to be available to help when she could.

I was making a fresh pot of coffee when the doorbell sounded, indicating Sherry's arrival.

"Good morning, Mara," she greeted me cheerfully. Her soft but vibrant voice and the radiant smile on her lovely face were enough to lift my spirit.

"Good morning, dear friend," I responded, taking her jacket and hanging it in the coat closet. "Come out to the kitchen, Sherry. I have fresh coffee brewing and a Danish if you're interested. Roni's with Vicky and Lu Anne this morning, and my mother is in her room. She's already had her breakfast, so I don't think she'll make another appearance. She knows you are here and wants to let us alone to discuss whatever is on your mind."

"Okay, then we will get right to the point," she responded as I placed a cup of hot coffee and a Danish in front of her. "You told me that the doctors could find nothing physically wrong with Rachael after they finished a conclusive examination, is that correct?" she asked.

"That's right, Sherry. There were several specialists who worked with her. She had every test available in Children's Hospital to determine the cause of epilepsy in a patient and they found nothing."

"All right. Would you mind if I asked you a few very personal questions?" she continued.

"No, not at all Sherry. I want to get to the root of this, and if anything I say would be enlightening to you, I would be more than willing to answer your questions as honestly as I know how."

"Good," she replied. "I felt certain that you would want to cooperate to the fullest to help find the cause of Rachael's illness. First of all, do you recall if there was ever any trauma she was exposed to even as a baby or a small child? I know that your marriage is rocky, at best. You told me this yourself, Mara, and we have been praying for God to intercede in this area. Has there ever been a serious confrontation between you and your husband that Rachael may have witnessed?" she repeated, this time being more specific.

I paused for just a few seconds, marveling that my good friend was able to touch on something none of the psychiatrists had even considered.

"Yes, Sherry, there was something very traumatic that occurred here about four years ago," I responded. "Rand and I were having a particularly rough time of it that year. I had been informed by one of the corporate bosses from his company at an annual Christmas party that Rand always had an eye for the ladies. Their company wanted their management people to be good family men. Rand obviously did not fit this criterion. He advised me that I had better get a firmer grip on the reins.

"Rand was a hard worker and highly motivated. He wanted to reach the top of the corporate ladder. Management could see that he had the potential to do so, but he had one obvious flaw that could damage his career. Women were his downfall, he had said. He didn't elaborate, but that was all I needed to hear. My wise, elderly grandmother had been telling me the same thing for years, but I refused to believe her. She had no concrete evidence to support her suspicion. This was merely a supposition on her part.

"Uncle Lenny confided in me that Rand had told him one evening—during one of the many fishing trips he and Rand had taken together, when they both had too much to drink—that variety was the spice of life. He was quite satisfied to be married to me, but he didn't feel the need to have an exclusive sexual relationship with one woman. The world was his oyster, he had told my uncle, and there were many pearls to be found.

"Lenny originally planned to keep this information to himself, but when he realized that our marriage was deteriorating, he warned Rand that his lifestyle was not conducive to a happy relationship. He shared this with me not to create trouble but to advise me to confront Rand in an effort to induce him to change his ways before it was too late."

"Well, Sherry," I continued, "to make a long story short, I deliberately got involved with a recently divorced man whom I met at Sammy's. My thinking was two could play the game, and I determined to play it to the hilt. One evening, I snuck away to this man's apartment at his invitation. Nothing of any consequence occurred between the two of us, thank God, but Rand watched things develop and tracked me to the man's apartment. He pounded on the door and carried on like a maniac until the maintenance man had to be called to order him to leave the premises.

"He did leave, Sherry, under threat of police arrest for disturbing the peace. But when I arrived home, he was there to meet me. I cannot describe what followed, but I thought that my children were going to lose their mother that night. It was some time before a policeman arrived at our door and arrested Rand. Rachael witnessed part of this before my mother intervened and took her to her bedroom and locked the door."

"This is pretty much what I suspected, Mara. Now let me tell you what can happen under these circumstances," Sherry replied, those dark, piercing eyes penetrating my very being. "Children are very vulnerable, and the enemy knows this. He always looks for ways to infiltrate them. When a child's loved ones, those who care for them and are the most important people in their little lives, are physically threatened, this is when the spirits make their move.

"As I recall, you told me that the day you received Christ and were sharing your experience at the dinner table, Rachael's response was to discourage you. Actually, your entire family didn't think much of your news, but when Rachael commented, her voice was unfamiliar. It was a deep, rasping male voice—I believe you told me—that no one heard but you.

"Mara, evidently, the demon had already found a home in your daughter's body. This was the demon manifesting to discourage you. Oftentimes, when a child has experienced trauma such as your child did at such an early age, the spirit will lie dormant, hiding in its host for the proper time to manifest. You indicated the adverse changes that took place in Rachael immediately after the seizures began. The demon was making himself known."

I couldn't respond to this. I was totally dumbfounded. I had never heard of anything like this. Certainly my church had never mentioned demon possession. When they prayed for Rachael, they prayed for her "healing," not for deliverance from demon possession.

When I finally recovered the use of my voice, I looked at this unusual woman sitting across from me at my kitchen table. It had only been a little more than a year that I had known her. But I knew that she was sincere, and I knew that she loved God and wouldn't mislead me in any way.

"How do you know all this?" I asked her, my head still reeling from what I heard.

"I'm involved in the deliverance ministry, Mara," she responded. "This is what our Wednesday afternoon prayer meeting is all about. We minister to women who are in need of what we have to give them."

"Would you be willing to minister to my daughter?" I asked, hoping that her answer would be yes.

"Mara, I would love to be able to help Rachael, but there is a problem with working with young children," she explained. "They are frightened to death to realize what has happened to them. As a result of the spirit of fear that has entered them along with—in Rachael's case—a spirit of infirmity, it is almost impossible to work with them at such a young age.

"Fear overwhelms them, and they become resistant to this type of ministry. There's an account of a boy in the book of Matthew who was an epileptic. The Bible tells us he often fell into fire and into water. Jesus cast the demon out this boy. We don't know his age, but I have checked all the accounts of people who were delivered from demon possession, and this is the only recorded account that deals with a boy that I could find.

"The Bible also tells us that nothing is impossible with our God, Mara, and we know that the Word of God cannot be disputed. What I am saying is that I feel that it would be wise on your part to delay this type of ministry until your daughter is old enough to have a clear understanding of what is involved. You told me a few months ago that the doctors have finally come up with a combination of drugs that have been able to control Rachael's seizures. She hasn't had any breakthroughs lately, has she?" she asked.

"No, thank God. It's been seven weeks now without a seizure. We're continuing to pray for a complete healing, though, or as you express in Rachael's situation, a complete deliverance," I replied.

"Trust God with this one, Mara. I know you're anxious to have your little girl return to total normalcy. But wait on the Lord on this one, okay? He will establish the right time and the right people to minister deliverance to her."

Then Sherry added, leaning forward in her chair, "I'm here this morning for another reason aside from the one we have been discussing, Mara."

"What would that be?" I inquired, somewhat surprised. Sherry had a full schedule, and I was well aware of that. I was so grateful to her for spending as much of her valuable time with me and my family as she did. I assumed the conversation had ended, and she would be getting ready to leave.

"That would be you, my dear," she replied, a hint of a smile forming on her beautifully shaped lips. Not waiting for a reply, she continued, "Mara, I've been watching your life over the last few months since you surrendered your life to Christ. You made it a point to be baptized in water as soon as possible after your conversion experience, and that is good. Now I'm wondering if you have been seeking the Holy Spirit's fullness."

"Do you mean the baptism of the Holy Spirit, Sherry?" I asked. She nodded in answer to my question.

"Yes, I have, Sherry. Now that I'm aware of this 'second blessing,' as some refer to it, I want to receive the infilling of the Spirit. I've gone to the altar on several occasions, but nothing has happened. We're getting a lot of good teaching from Pastor Carlton on how to receive the baptism with the initial evidence of speaking in other tongues. I guess I'm either not desperate enough or not surrendered enough. All I know is that I want everything that God has to give me. He tells us in his Word that if we seek, we will find, and that is what I am doing."

"You're doing the right thing, Mara," she replied. Once again, there was that hint of a smile on her lovely face. "It's just like the experience of salvation. Continue to seek, open your heart to receive, and the Mighty Baptizer will fill you."

"The reason that I'm pursuing this line of questioning has to do with a few things that you have shared with me since you have become a Christian," she added. "You mentioned seeing strange animals, like wolves, slinking along the concrete wall of my neighbor's home. I believe this occurred a couple of times when you were attending our Friday evening Bible study."

"Yes, that was rather unusual, to say the least," I responded. "They really didn't look like any animal I had ever seen before. Probably *wolf like* is the closest description I could come up with. The strange thing about them was that they were slinking along the top of the wall, walking back and forth, as though they were on guard duty or possibly looking for something. It was weird."

"Uh-huh," she said, "and what about that green man that attempted to throw his chain around your neck the morning after I witnessed to you at my home? That's a rhetorical question. You already gave me a pretty thorough rundown on that incident, so there's no need to repeat it. Then I believe that you told me about dark, hooded ethereal beings, shadowlike in appearance, at the foot of your bed for several nights in a row. You had awakened Rand out of his sleep, but he saw nothing. He told you that you were dreaming, as usual, and insisted you go back to sleep."

"Right on all accounts, Sherry. I was puzzled why you never commented. Surely there must be an explanation for all this. It's not a figment of my imagination. I know these bazaar things never happened to me before I got saved. Even in some of my worst drunken stupors, I never saw pink elephants like a lot of drunks say they see."

"Mara, I will attempt to explain all this to you now. I wanted to let that rest for a little while until you got some of the Word of God into your spirit. Now you will have a clearer understanding of what has occurred."

"You evidently have gotten glimpses into the supernatural world," she explained. "This is a frequent occurrence, so don't think that you're losing your mind or anything like that. God allows this with certain people for reasons of His own. If it will make you feel any better, I have seen those same wolf like creatures.

"The first time that this occurred, a few of my Bible study members and I went down to that house to find out what those things were. There was nothing there. We did it twice after that with the same result. We could find no trace of these creatures. We investigated further. The house was now vacant. It had been unoccupied for some time.

"I spoke to the elderly woman who lived next door. She insisted that the house was haunted. She put her home up for sale, but because of the rumors surrounding the people who had lived next door, her house would not sell. She got discouraged and took it off the market a few months before, thinking that if she waited it out, sooner or later, the talk would die down.

"I asked her if she ever had to call the dogcatcher to get rid of those nasty-looking dogs that were walking along the top of the concrete-block wall behind the vacant house. 'This is the first time

I ever heard of any dogs on the property,' she had told me. 'I certainly never saw any animals over there, and I'm here almost all the time. You know, since you seem to have such an interest in that place, maybe I should share something with you,' she added.

"'Now, this is just a rumor. I can't confirm it, but this is what I heard. I heard there was a family of four who lived in there. They had two children, both teenagers. Rumor has it the father molested his daughter repeatedly. She was forbidden to tell her mother or her older brother under the threat of death. But the way the story goes, the brother got wind of it one night and killed his dad.

"'Now, I'll tell you that I was not an eyewitness to this. I moved in here after my husband died last year. It appears they moved out of the neighborhood a few years ago, and since they weren't friendly with any of the neighbors, no one knows where they went. You folks seem interested in finding out what happened there. If you want to pursue it, there are ways to find out,' she told us.

"The women who were with me," Sherry said, concluding her story, "thought it best to put this entire matter behind them, as I certainly did. We had many more important things to do than to chase what may have been nothing more than a rumor. One day we would know. Until then, we decided to put it in God's hands.

"Mara, I'm telling you about these strange happenings because, in many cases, they are real. Fallen angels roam this world, seeking to inhabit living hosts. When a person who has been possessed with these things dies, the demon will look for a person or animal, like the wolf like creatures that we saw, in which to take up residence. There's a whole lot to this ministry because there are multitudes of people who—because of the sin in their lives, the lifestyles they pursue, or just because they are innocent children, like your Rachael—are prey for these spirits."

"Why are you telling me all this, Sherry?" I asked. "I don't want any part of this ministry. It's creepy. As a matter of fact, I asked

God to take these things out of my life when those hooded creatures began to take up residence at the foot of our bed."

"I just want to make you aware of something, Mara. You are
now seeking more of God as you press in to receive the baptism
of the Holy Spirit. Are you aware that there are spiritual gifs given
when you get the baptism?" she asked.

"Yes, the pastor gave me some books to read on the gifts of the
Spirit. From all indications, we don't get to pick the ones we want,
is that correct?"

"That is correct," she said. This time, she broke out in a hearty
laugh. "We do not get the gifts that we want. We get the gifts that
our Heavenly Father finds us most suited to. I wouldn't be surprised if this is one of the gifts he has ready for you. From all the
unusual things you have been experiencing since you accepted
Christ, prepare yourself for that possibility. Let me remind you
of something. A little while ago, you said you are seeking God for
anything He is willing to give you. Did you mean that or not?"

"I'm putting you on the spot," she said, with that twinkle in her
eye that I loved to see. "You are a mere babe in the faith. You need
the milk of the Word right now. There will be time later for the meat.
Well, my sweet Mara, I see by my watch it is time for me to go. There's
just one more thing I have on my mind for you to think about and
take to the Lord. Then we'll end this little discussion in prayer.

"I believe we made some real progress today, but I do want
to add this: the gift of discernment comes in several forms. The
one who receives this gift doesn't necessarily have to move into
the spirit realm where his or her constant companions are green
giants, black- hooded creatures or wolf like animals that walk back
and forth on walls. This gift is the keen ability to discern between
spirits as well. The book of 1 John has some things to say about this
gift in chapter four. Study that when you get some extra time."

"Where would you use this gift?" I asked. "It seems to me that
all the sinners running around need to get saved and delivered.

One doesn't need discernment to see where they're heading if they don't get their act together. The people in the churches don't have any need for this gift. They're all saved."

At this statement, I heard a loud gasp come from my friend and teacher. "Lord, God Almighty!" she yelled aloud. "Would you please open this lady's spiritual eyes, and do it quickly, if you don't mind!"

"What was that for?" I asked innocently. "Isn't that the way it happens, Sherry? You get saved—maybe alone like I did—or someone witnesses to you, and you say the sinner's prayer with them. Or maybe someone coaxes you to attend a special service with them in your church. Then you go up for the altar call if you're under conviction and get saved right in church. That's probably the most convenient way." I continued, "That way, you already have a church to go to and don't have to wait on the Lord to find you one."

Sherry got up from her chair as I completed my explanation of Church Membership 101 according to the gospel of Mara. She walked to my side of the table, put her arm around me, and said very somberly, "Let's pray, Mara. You need it, and so do I. I also need to go."

After praying, we said our good-byes. I thanked her for all the time she spent with me, and I assured her I would check all the scriptures she had given to me to study. I left her at the door with the promise I would attempt to learn something worthwhile by the next time we met.

CHAPTER 25

CARDBOARD CHRISTIANS

It took me just about six weeks to get it. I was learning, and learning quickly that not everyone who professes to be a Christian belongs to Christ.

Maybe that is just a bit harsh. I don't want to be judgmental, I said to myself. *Could it be that these people are carnal Christians? One of the ladies who comes to our midweek service told me there are two kinds of Christians, spiritual Christians and carnal Christians.*

I immediately checked this out and found there is much to say about the word *carnal* in the book of Romans. Checking all scriptures that included the word *carnal,* I found out that, in all cases, carnality has to do with enmity against God. To be carnal is to be sold into sin, and to be carnally minded is death.

That woman, Mrs. Dickerson, must be either blind or brain damaged, I thought. *I sure don't see a Christian being any of these things. It doesn't appear that anyone carnal is going to make it to heaven. Funny thing, Mrs. Dickerson told me that, because she has been a Christian for so many years, God authorized her to give advice to new Christians coming into the church body. That's why she visits our church on Wednesday evenings. She's not a member at Zion.*

At Pastor Carlton's advice, I purchased a new Strong's Exhaustive Concordance, and I needed to get acquainted with it. Pastor called me into his office a few days shortly after the baptismal service took place. He wanted to lend me some additional books he felt I should read and perhaps a bit of advice to go with them.

"Would you like me to close your office door?" I asked.

"No, Mara, thank you just the same," he responded. "I always leave my office door open, especially when young, attractive ladies come to see me."

"What! Why in the world would you do that, Pastor?" I inquired.

"You are young in the Lord, my dear. But there is something you need to know right at the outset. The Bible-believing, spirit-filled church is one of the enemy's biggest targets, and the pastor's office is in the crosshairs of his aim."

"Wow," I exclaimed. "I thought everyone in the church— especially an evangelistic church like Zion—was saved, or they wouldn't be here."

"Oh, my dear, how I wish your assumption were true," he responded. "It would certainly relieve me of most of my burdens. Read one of Jesus's parables in Matthew 13:24, and I think you will get the picture soon enough."

"I've already read all the gospels, and I remember that parable quite well. I wanted to ask you about that, Pastor. How can a Christian tell the difference between a saved person and one who has been deceived into believing he or she is saved? I presume this is what is meant in that passage in which Jesus talks about the wheat and the tare growing together. The parable indicates that they look alike in their early stages."

"That is correct, Mara. One cannot tell the difference between the two when they are young plants. As they mature, both develop tassels. This is when the change occurs. The wheat will exhibit soft, pliable tassels. On the other hand, the tare has tassels that are hard and inflexible. There are four kinds of tares found in the Holy Land, Mara' the most common of which, in the wheat field, is the bearded darnel."

"The darnel is a poisonous grass," he continued, "almost indistinguishable from the wheat while the two are growing into blade. But when they come into ear, they can be separated without difficulty. I believe that is the reason why the slaves of the landowner in this parable, who perceived the two grains growing together, were commanded by the landowner not to disturb them but to allow them to remain together until harvest time when the reapers would be ordered to first gather the tares and bind them in bundles to burn them.

"After that, they would harvest the wheat and gather it into his barn. The reason he gave command for this action was that, had the two plants been separated before maturity as the landowner's servants wanted to do, the wheat would have been pulled up with the tares and discarded in the process."

Testing me to determine if I had learned anything of value from his explanation, he presented me with a challenging question. "Can you glean any spiritual application from this parable, Mara?" He leaned forward in his chair, his steel-blue eyes fixed intently on me as he waited for my reply.

"Yes, I believe I can Pastor," I replied, after thinking about this for a brief time. "The tares or unsaved people, who are found in the local body of believers, are dangerous. Like the darnel, they spew poison that can be very harmful to those who are genuine Christians by spreading false doctrine, gossiping, and creating division within the body. They often target very young blades of grain, or new Christians, and can go so far as to destroy their ability to grow into wholesome, mature wheat that can bear fruit."

"Aha," was the response that came from Pastor Carlton. "You've nailed it. That was the answer I was looking for," he said, his flawless English revealing only a faint hint of a British accent. "You see, my dear, this is what I was attempting to convey to you the last time we met. It is obvious that you are reading your Bible, and I commend you for that. I also think you took my advice and purchased a good concordance, is that so? You are really beginning to dig for the gold and precious gems that are very often hidden within the pages of this precious Word of God."

"Yes, to both questions, Pastor," I responded, very pleased with myself that I was on the right track.

"Continue to do exactly what you are doing, Mara, and develop the habit of daily prayer in your life, preferably in the early morning when you get up. The enemy of your soul would like to see you postpone your quiet time with the Lord. Often, when a well-meaning Christian makes a habit of doing this, the many activities of life begin to take priority, and prayer is put on the back burner."

I sensed the meeting was ending. I realized the pastor had much more to do than spend more time than required with any one person. I pushed back my chair and reached for my purse and jacket.

"Sit down for one moment more, if you will, Mara. I have some books from my library that I would like for you to read at your leisure, if you have any leisure time. How is Rachael? Any new developments in her situation?" he asked with genuine concern. "She is a lovely young girl, and in God's time, she will experience deliverance from this malady that plagues her life."

"She's doing fairly well, Pastor. The doctors have been able to control her seizures with a combination of drugs. The positive side of this story has been that the seizures have been all nocturnal up to this point, so they didn't affect her daytime activities. Her life is relatively normal. She can enjoy, to a certain extent, doing what she likes to do without fear.

"I'm thankful to God for this, and I'm also grateful for all the people from Zion and for you, Pastor Carlton, who have prayed for her deliverance. I know that prayer works. I have had many answers to prayer in the brief time I have been a Christian. Oh, and while we're on the subject, I thank God for a pastor like you, if you don't mind my saying. Your preaching is so anointed. I am learning so much from your messages."

"Why, thank you, Mara. I will never turn down a compliment," he responded, a little twinkle lighting up his piercing blue eyes. "If you don't mind, we need to have a word of prayer before you leave. We here at Zion are keeping your unsaved husband, Rand, and your two other children in prayer. You stay faithful to God, and he will bring them into the circle of safety."

After praying with the pastor, I left his office grateful that we had such a man of God to look after the sheep at Zion. He had the heart of a true shepherd, and he guarded his sheep carefully and lovingly.

Many years have passed. The journey has been long and often dangerous. Many times, I have looked back, remembering that informative conversation I had with Pastor Carlton years ago. It has served as a guidepost through the decades. I have been confronted with many difficult situations and even more difficult decisions, which had to be made as a result of the circumstances I faced.

Later in that summer of 1970, Vicky and her mother were baptized in water, indicating the change that had occurred in their lives and expressing a desire to follow Jesus Christ.

I was asked by one of the senior Sunday school teachers to take over the junior-aged class, which she had taught for so many years. Her health issues would not permit her to continue. This marked the beginning of having the privilege to teach the Word of God to all age-groups for almost a half century.

At the same time, Vicky took over the preschool-aged children's class and continued with her beloved three-year-olds for many years. Our rooms were across the hall from each other in the Sunday school department. We were both elated that God had seen fit to entrust these little ones to our care and to have the privilege to teach them the Word of God.

At the same time, the pastor asked both of us if we would be willing to help him with the bus ministry he was introducing as a new outreach ministry of the church. I immediately joined the group, realizing the potential for soul winning through this ministry. Vicky, always the cautious one, waited for some time before coming aboard. Though I disliked having to give up my Girl Scout troop, I felt I could better assist young people to make decisions for Christ if I were associated with a church function rather than a community program.

Although I continued to maintain complete freedom from alcohol, I still continued to fight the nicotine addiction. As a result of Rachael's strange illness, I did extensive research on this subject and decided to seek help through the deliverance ministry operating out of Zion. After several sessions with the team, I experienced complete freedom from nicotine, along with several other pieces of baggage I had carried into my salvation experience with me. Vicky had some baggage problems as well. I suggested the deliverance ministry to her based on my excellent results, but she bulked at the idea. She wanted no part of it.

A few years after joining the church, I was on my way to the pastor's office to ask his advice on something regarding the bus ministry. Phoebe Michaels was in the office transcribing a letter the pastor had dictated. Phoebe and I had become close friends from the first day she and her wonderful family introduced me to Zion Assembly. She felt the calling to help the full-time secretary with her many duties.

Zion was growing by leaps and bounds. It seemed like everyone involved in any type of ministry was constantly busy attempting to keep up with the inflow of work. As I walked into the office, I saw

Phoebe was working alone on this particular day, so I decided to take just a moment and say hello. She was crying at her desk, her head in her hands.

"What in the world is going on, Phoebe?" I asked. "It takes a lot to make you cry. Is everything okay at home?"

"Yes," she managed to get out between sobs. "Everything is all right at home. But everything is not all right at Zion."

I knew she wanted to share this burden with me, but she was sworn to secrecy. I certainly had to respect that, and I promised to pray about the situation, whatever it was, that had her so upset.

One day, a few weeks later, as I took my paperwork from bus-ministry visitation into the office, something like a lightbulb lit up in my brain. Coming up the stairs behind me was the head deacon from a nearby Assembly of God church. He was holding the hand of Pastor Carlton and his wife, Maureen's, three-year-old daughter, Holly. The pastor and Maureen were directly behind them. I greeted them all warmly.

As I took a closer look at this group of people, it became painfully obvious that Holly strongly resembled the man holding her hand. I sensed that this man was her real father. I immediately excused myself and went into the empty sanctuary where I could have time to regain my composure. After I put my paperwork away, I left by another exit so that I would not have to confront them again.

I called Phoebe as soon as I got home and told her that the Lord had just revealed the scandal to me.

"I'm relieved that you know, Mara" she replied. "It's better that you found out the way you did because it will be announced from the pulpit during the service in the morning that the Carltons will be leaving us in three weeks."

How could this happen? I thought to myself. I was overwhelmed with shock.

I stayed on at Zion for the next five years, working with the bus ministry and teaching my class. It was never the same. One day, the pastor who replaced Pastor Carlton informed me he was terminating the bus ministry because of the expense of keeping the buses fueled and running.

Many people, children, and their parents and relatives had come to faith in Christ as a result of the bus ministry. God richly blessed this ministry because it had become the vehicle by which many souls had been saved. Why couldn't he trust the Lord to bring in the finances to cover the expenses incurred by this ministry? The pastor and I had a heated discussion about this, but the pastor is the boss, and that was his final word on the subject. Shortly after that, I gave up my class and left Zion.

No matter where I went, it was always the same. One church that I visited had a very good-looking divorced man in charge of the singles' Bible study. I was still too naive to realize what took place there until one of the women who had been jilted by him warned me that I was next on his list. I had finally divorced Rand based on firm evidence that he was being unfaithful, but did this made me eligible to get involved with this man? No, thank you, Satan. You are not pulling me into this.

It was at this time I began to pray in earnest for the gift of discernment. I received the baptism of the Holy Spirit sometime before, and I felt the Spirit was leading me in this direction. I thought of the many times Sherry had sensed in her spirit that God had given me this gift when I was baptized in his Spirit, but because of the fear I had regarding its manifestations, I needed to stir up this gift which was already mine.

I remembered, once again, my conversations with Pastor Carlton. Over time, my sense of discernment was sharpening. It was becoming an everyday occurrence for me to find myself testing the spirits to see if they were from God. There was such a need for this gift of the Spirit. More and more false prophets and teachers were emerging. Christians, both old and new, were being deceived.

What part would I play in this ministry? Only the future held the answer.

AFTERWORD

Zion Assembly thrived spiritually under the supernatural work of the Holy Spirit and grew to become one of the largest Pentecostal churches in the Pittsburgh area.

Pastor Carlton and his family were transferred to a little-known town in a farming area near the West Virginia border, where he pastored a small congregation of farming folk for many years until his recent death.

Vicky O'Conner, with her children, continued her membership with Zion Assembly for several years after which time she transferred her membership to another Assembly of God church closer to where she had moved after divorcing her husband, Ernie. Ernie died recently of alcohol poisoning.

The writer left Zion Assembly of God in 1978, disillusioned by the closing of the thriving bus ministry through which many children and, in some cases, their parents and relatives had come to know the Lord as their personal Savior. She moved from church to church for several years, teaching the Word of God to teenagers and young adults.

After divorcing Rand in 1983, she relocated to Melbourne, Florida for a brief period of time. It was here at a local Christian church that she met the editor of *Charisma* magazine who encouraged her to pursue her dream of completing *Cardboard Christians*.

By this time, she had experienced a bizarre number of happenings that prompted the writing of this book.

The book was put on the back burner as God brought a wonderful Baptist man into her life in the late 90s. They were married in the year 2000 and subsequently were called to birth the only non-denominational church in the small lake town where they lived. Although this wonderful husband, a fantastic gift of God, Rev. James Faulkner, went to be with the Lord seven years later, the Open Door Fellowship is very much alive under the care of a new pastor who is on fire for the Lord and completing the work that had been started several years before.

Concluding on a happy note, Rachael received total healing from Epilepsy when she reached her mid-twenties. She is now married and has relocated to the West Coast where she and her husband are presently engaged in the operation of two successful businesses. She is the mother of two adult children and the author's only great-grandson. She remains in perfect health to this day.

Randy has remained unmarried and he lives in the Pittsburgh area where he owns and operates a successful business.

Little Roni is all grown up now, married to her college sweetheart, a handsome airline pilot, the mother of a lovely and talented teen-aged daughter and a successful business woman in her chosen business profession. They also reside in the south hills area of Pittsburgh.

The writer's mom received Christ as her personal Savior while living in Melbourne, Florida. She gave her life to Christ in 1984 while living in that state. The following year, after a brief illness, she succumbed to Lung Cancer and in September of 1985 was ushered into the presence of God. Over a period of time, several other family members also received Christ as their personal Savior by faith in his shed blood.

Sherry Drummond was escorted to heaven four years ago to meet the Lord she loved so fervently and served so faithfully throughout her life.

Last, but by no means not least, Rand is presently residing in Florida with his second wife. Recently, he was visited by all of his adult children to share in the celebration of his 85th birthday. To the writer's knowledge, Rand has not as yet surrendered his life to Christ. With the multitude of prayers that have been made on his behalf, the writer is confident that God has heard each one of them and that, one day in the near future, she will receive the good news of this marvelous transformation. It is her fervent desire that one day in the near future she will once again be reunited with her husband and three children in God's eternal kingdom.

Made in the USA
Columbia, SC
13 March 2018